Whale Hunt
in the Desert

Whale Hunt
in the Desert

The Secret Las Vegas
of Superhost Steve Cyr

by Deke Castleman

Huntington Press Publishing
Las Vegas, Nevada

Whale Hunt in the Desert

The Secret Las Vegas of Superhost Steve Cyr

Published by
Huntington Press
3687 South Procyon Avenue
Las Vegas, Nevada 89103
telephone: (702) 252-0655
facsimile: (702) 252-0675
email: books@huntingtonpress.com

ISBN: 0-929712-91-9

Cover photo: Mark Sennet
Cover design: Bethany Coffey Rihel
Interior design & production: Laurie Shaw

Whale Hunt in the Desert is dedicated to
Mim and Lou Castleman
and the memory of Susan Berman and Melissa Rubin

Acknowledgments

This book is the end result of nearly 15 years in the Las Vegas and gambling information business, encompassing dozens of sources (many of whom don't want to be identified). All who advanced the editorial cause of *Whale Hunt* will recognize their contributions within these pages, which will have to suffice as a thank you. The one contributor who probably doesn't want to, but must, be named is Dave Berns, the most connected business writer and skilled interviewer a word-processing hack such as myself could ever ask for.

A big thank you to the Boca Bookies—Susan Christopher, Debbie Johns, Sandi Kitzes, Janice Lempereur, Kerry Lobello, Janice Reich, Harriet Rosenberg, Bonnie Sigel, Lynn Soreide, Jeri Wexelbaum, and especially Amy Kenneth—for their comprehension and encouragement.

A way-big thank you to the fine friends of and stellar staff at Huntington Press, among them: Anna Halbert, confidence-builder; Max Rubin, who came up in the old school and introduced us to Cyr; Richard Munchkin, his incisive interview with Billy Walters in his excellent *Gambling Wizards* was invaluable; Dick Odessky, rest in peace; Ian Andersen, international whale in a class of one; Lora Shaner, brilliant and tough; Doug Meyer, the world's most erudite 24-year-old; Wendy Tucker, the little nuclear reactor; Laurie Shaw, who always goes above and beyond; Bethany Coffey-

Rihel, who's put up with a lot since 1991; and, of course, Anthony Curtis, who through force of will and superior gamesmanship not only holds the whole thing together, but makes it grow and prosper—and is a fine editor to boot.

The biggest thanks goes to Steve Cyr himself, for the proverbial without-whom-none-of-this-would've-been-possible.

Finally, the love goes to Adam and Jonathan Castleman and Kathy Harrer, who keep the old man propped up.

Author's Note

A few people, places, and pieces in the chronology and narrative have been combined, compressed, or otherwise gently manipulated in the interest of flow and continuity.

Contents

Prologue
The Greed and the Fear

Whales are big. At up to 100 feet long and 180 tons, the blue whale is the largest creature this planet has ever seen. Not all whales are monsters. Still, one of the smallest, the pygmy right whale, is 20 feet long and ten tons—longer than a giraffe and twice the weight of an elephant.

Whales are rare. The 45-foot-long humpback is one of the most common and it numbers only 35,000. Fewer than 5,000 blue whales are known to exist. The northern right whale population is estimated at 500.

Whales are intelligent. Roughly 50 killer whales in captivity in aquatic theme parks and aquariums around the world are trained to do elaborate tricks, including interact with young humans.

Whales are mythical. No lesser legend-spinners than the Bible, Melville, and Disney gave us Jonah's savior, Moby Dick, and Pinocchio's Monstro.

Finally, for their valuable meat destined for exotic markets, whales are hunted to the ends of the Earth.

❖ ❖ ❖

Somewhere along the line, the term whale was also inserted into the gambling lexicon to describe the biggest bettors in the casino universe. In the lingo, "whale" denotes the

world's richest men and women (but mostly men) who play
casino games at the highest allowable stakes.

No one knows for certain how many of these highest of
high rollers there are. The largest table-game bet currently
taken in Las Vegas is $250,000, but only seven or eight hu-
man blue whales can handle that kind of action. The second
stratum tops out at $150,000 per hand, a level manageable
by up to 50 players worldwide. A hundred more can "fade"
$100,000 a hand.

Theirs is a firmament of 35-person entourages, flown in
to Las Vegas on business jets, private aircraft, or chartered
jumbos. They're shuttled by fleets of stretch limousines—
stocked with Dom Perignon and Beluga caviar—to places
such as the Mansion at MGM Grand, among the world's most
exclusive accommodations. There, concierges, VIP hostesses,
casino hosts, casino executives, limo drivers, butlers, personal
chefs, and, yes, hookers cater to their every whim.

Whales can receive as much as $250,000 in free play sim-
ply for walking through a casino's door, with the promise of
up to a 20% discount on their gambling losses. If they don't
feel like partaking in private dinner parties prepared in person in their 15,000-square-foot penthouse villas by flambé,
salad, and pastry chefs, they can strut their stuff into five-
star restaurants and scribble their names on $20,000 dinner
and drink tabs.

For a quickie spending spree at the Forum Shops at Caesars or the Grand Canal Shoppes at the Venetian, they're
given $25,000 or $50,000—in gift certificates, so they don't
have to sully their hands with filthy lucre.

Cases of $600-a-bottle champagne. Boxes of $100 hand-
rolled cigars. Thank-you cards attached to Beemers and
Hummers and Vipers shipped direct to specified addresses
or kept on hand for their exclusive use in Las Vegas.

Fishing trips to Alaska. Whitewater rafting in Costa Rica.
Cruising the Greek Isles on private yachts. Annual courtesy
calls by casino-corporation presidents, chief executive offic-

ers, or chairmen of the board.

These are the perks routinely lavished on casino whales.

In return, the gambling leviathans are willing and able to risk from $50,000 to $250,000 a hand and can win or lose up to $20 million over the course of a gambling holiday.

How can this breed lay down mortgage-sized wagers play after play, hour after hour, day after day? The same way a working stiff can spend $20 a week on lottery tickets. A comparison between gambling bankrolls of $20 and $2 million might be incomprehensible to the worker (and, for that matter, to the whale), but it's all relative. The stakes make even the largest casino owners sweat, but to whales it's Monopoly money. A $150,000 bet to a man with $1 billion in liquid assets is the same as a $15 bet to a man with a $100,000 bankroll.

The man with the $100K isn't a whale; he's a mere high roller. But make no mistake—anyone who can fade $5,000 per hand or even as relatively "little" as $2,500 or $1,000 a pop is a coveted casino customer and there are thousands upon thousands of them in the U.S. alone. High rollers are mini-whales, but they're big fish all the same: corporate executives, investors and traders in the financial markets, superstar entertainers, actors, and athletes, owners of cash businesses, as well as bookmakers, loan sharks, drug dealers, and robber barons.

But from the pygmy to the blue, all casino whales have two things in common: a boundless bankroll and the gambling gene. The former imparts the capacity to risk $1,000 and up per hand. The latter consists of specialized chromosomes that govern the production of testosterone and adrenaline, oversee the acquisition and disposition of an excess of capital, and manage the pursuit of the unknown.

This is the gene that compels the gamblers among us to get in the action, expressing itself initially with love ("I'm winning the casino's money!"), then greed ("And I want to win more!"). Or first with fever ("I've lost my money to the casino!"), then fear ("And I've got to get it back!"). The gene and the bankroll join in a double helix that has neither beginning nor end: Risking the bankroll stimulates the gene, which motivates the risk.

The casino business is nothing if not the master manipulator of boundless bankrolls and gambling genes. And the specific casino employee who's the stroker of the love and stoker of the fever is the casino marketing executive, also known as the player-development representative and host.

Upwards of 500 hosts ply their trade in Las Vegas. And of them all, the host among hosts, the manipulator among manipulators, the champion harpooner in the modern-day whale hunt in the desert is a character named Steve Cyr.

Part One
Whale Hunters

"Canst thou draw out Leviathan with a hook?
Upon earth there is not his like ...
Will he speak soft words unto thee?"
—Book of Job

"Players are power, baby!"
—Steve Cyr

1

All in a Night's Work

Steve Cyr (pronounced seer) is standing at the back of the Joint, the Hard Rock casino's chic concert hall. He's rocking out to the wailing guitars and pounding drums of a makeshift band consisting of a blackjack high roller and three of his musician friends. It's been a dream of this player, Jeff Armstrong, to perform at the Joint, and Cyr sold the idea to the Hard Rock bosses. In return, Armstrong will spend a couple of hours at the tables betting $10,000 a hand. But for now, he's up on stage, opening for the Fabulous Thunderbirds.

Cyr's cell phone rings. He answers, listens, then speaks. "Okay, I'm on my way. I'll be there in five minutes. Hold tight." He pauses, then says, "Relax, Kirsti! Who's the man, baby? I'll handle it."

He hurries down toward the stage and gives a thumbs-up to Mr. A. (Unless the two are extremely friendly, a casino guy addresses his player by the first initial of his last name. Calling him by his first name is too familiar, while using his full last name could, inadvertently, compromise his privacy.) Cyr signals that he's got to run, but he'll be back in a while. Then he blows through the casino and out the front door, where his silver Trans Am sits at the curb, as if he's the only car owner who happened to drive to the 600-room Hard Rock that Saturday night. He dukes off a ten-spot to the parking attendant in the valet cubicle, who hands him his keys. He hops in the car and peels out for points north.

This little errand is a favor for Mr. B, the multimillionaire owner of a Midwest foundry and a frequent megaroller at the Las Vegas Hilton. Mr. B likes to stay in the Conrad Villa, one of three penthouse suites on the 30th floor of the 3,174-room resort.

Cyr screeches up to the Hilton's porte cochere, tosses his keys to the valet, rushes into the casino lobby, and storms the VIP Services office. "Mister B! Great to see you again! Hi, hi," he greets Mr. B's stunning girlfriend, and the girlfriend's stunning girlfriend, standing on either side of the gambler.

"Cyr—what the *hell* kind of bullshit are you pulling *this* time?" Mr. B launches into a tirade. "Not only do I not get my Villa, but there isn't a single *suite* in this whole fucking hotel? You're gonna put the *three* of us in a *room*? With *one* bed? I'm going to the Mirage!"

"Wait a minute, Mister B. C'mon now," Cyr cajoles, taking the short balding 60-year-old steel man by the elbow and maneuvering him out of earshot. The superhost's shrug, directed toward the statuesque early-thirtysomething women, says it all: *Hey, what can you do? Shit happens.*

Suddenly, Mr. B sputters, "You mean to tell me that there's not another room in the whole hotel? Not even *one* with two queen beds?"

Cyr mumbles something.

"The hell you say! Not another room in the whole friggin' *city*?"

Cyr hangs his head and shuffles his feet.

Mr. B is apoplectic. "No way! Not one night, not one minute! Fuck the hotel room, fuck the Hilton, fuck Las Vegas, and fuck you!"

After a suitable amount of fawning and wheedling and laying it on with a trowel, Cyr manages to calm Mr. B and talk him into just one night in the room, with the promise that he can have the Conrad Villa tomorrow and for the rest of his stay and for the rest of his life. Mr. B grabs the key from Kirsti, the gorgeous young VIP hostess, then marches out in a huff, barely pausing to collect the two women.

Cyr watches them go, then turns to Kirsti, whose wide eyes and quivering lips betray her panic over the thought of getting fired for screwing up Mr. B's reservation. He smiles and asks, "Think he'll get lucky?"

Kirsti's countenance goes blank, then slowly rearranges into a smirk as she realizes that the whole scene was a set-up straight out of a bad script for the standard opening of a low-budget porn video, the one where the one man maneuvers the two women into the one bed.

Steve Cyr has done his job.

❖ ❖ ❖

Cyr dictates the night's itinerary to Kirsti, who dutifully logs it in her appointment book. He then cruises the Hilton casino to check on his other players and finds one, Gus Johnson, at the cage (casino cashier). Gus is feeling fine tonight. He's first in line at the cage, waiting to cash out a mess of checks (casino chips) he's just won playing $15,000-a-hand blackjack. The stocky six-foot-two 39-year-old is dressed in blue jeans, T-shirt, etched leather boots, and a varsity jacket sporting the MGM Grand logo. He's in town for his regular weekend jaunt of gambling, partying, and chasing women. Emphasis on the chasing women.

A twentysomething supermodel-type is standing at the cage counter. She's six feet tall *without* the purple four-inch stilettos. Her miniskirt matches her shoes, with nothing but sheer stockings and perfect legs in between. Thick blond hair cascades down her long back. And she's alone.

This girl's excited—wiggling around, fluffing her hair, grabbing the bars of the cage after tossing two handfuls of checks on the counter. She even coos at the cashier as she watches him deftly stack her chips in neat piles of reds, greens, and blacks, tally them up, and announce, "Nine big ones."

The girl squeals, "And I started with just fifty small ones!"

For Gus, watching her squirm confirms the old gambling adage: "Money is the ultimate aphrodisiac." If this blond gets laid within an hour, she'll have all *kinds* of orgasms. Only thing is, she doesn't know it.

But Gus does. He licks his lips. He sidles up to her as the cashier counts out the bills. He stands close.

Surprised, she turns her head, leans away, and looks at him with barely concealed suspicion and distaste.

Gus doesn't miss a beat. He leans in and murmurs in her ear, "I'll trade you for it."

Suspicion morphs into confusion, scrunching up her face. "What did you say?"

"I said, I'll trade what you have for what I have."

Confusion first gives way to puzzlement, but gradually the girl relaxes and the corners of her mouth turn up just so. Now she knows he's coming on to her, just another horn dog sniffing around. Still not sure what he's selling, though, she asks, "What do you have?"

It's Gus' turn to crack a smile. His eyes gleam as he answers, "Well, that's what you're gambling on, isn't it? I know what you've got"—and he looks her down and up, for just a fraction of a second, though long enough—"nine hundred dollars. But you don't know what I've got." He shoves his hand into his jacket pocket and rattles his own mess of checks.

"Oh! Is *that* it?" The light bulb switches on and this girl positively sparkles. "You wanna trade chips!" You can almost hear the gears turning—"You wouldn't *believe* this guy"—as she plans how to spin the tale to the girls at the office on Monday, or maybe even to whoever gets lucky with her later. "You must think I'm crazy!" she exclaims. "This is almost a thousand dollars!" She grabs the bills and turns her back, then turns around again and repeats, "*A thousand dollars!*"

Gus watches her flounce off and disappear into the crowd, turning horn-dog heads every step of the way. He chuckles to himself. The soft-spoken hustler is the founder and chairman of a dot-com that on this particular weekend boasts a market cap of $500 million.

"You can't score if you don't take shots, right?" he says to Cyr, who's been watching the encounter from a few steps away. Gus reaches into his pocket, pulls out 12 brown chips, and tosses them onto the counter. "That's the difference between men and women," Gus intones. "Women fear loss. Men pursue the unknown."

"You would've done it, too," says Cyr, as the cashier stacks up the bundles of hundreds.

"Sure I would've. I'd've taken her nine hundred and handed over my chips—just to see the expression on her face."

"Yeah, and to see what developed," Cyr laughs as Gus stashes $60,000 in cash—12 bundles containing 50 hundred-dollar bills each—in an inside pocket of his jacket.

At the Hilton, a brown check is worth five thousand dollars.

❖ ❖ ❖

Cyr and Gus make plans to meet for breakfast in the Verona Villa—at 1 p.m. the next afternoon. "After church," Cyr says with a straight face.

Gus cracks up. He knows Cyr attends Our Lady of St. Mattress, where he likes the sermons of Reverend Sheets.

World-class chefs whip up anything they want for breakfast—and butlers serve it to them in the Verona Villa. (Gus likes his waffles with fresh strawberries; Cyr likes eggs Benedict with hollandaise sauce. Even if Gus is still sleeping at 1 p.m., Cyr goes up and starts eating.)

Walking to the private express elevator up to Gus' villa, Cyr relates the story of Mr. B and how he'd convinced the two girls that the "whole friggin' city" was full.

Gus asks, "How many rooms *are* available here tonight?"

"A thousand or so. And a dozen suites."

Gus laughs. "A thousand?"

"That's the thing about a three-thousand-room hotel. Even when we're seventy percent full, there's still nine hundred of them left."

"Hey," Gus has a sudden thought. "If the second girl doesn't like the cramped quarters, tell her she can spend the night in my Villa."

"She'd rather have Mr. B spend the night in your Villa," Cyr shoots back with utter certainty.

The elevator arrives and a security guard keys Gus up to the Villas on the 30th floor. Cyr, meanwhile, heads down the back hallway that connects the Villa elevators to the Hilton's high-limit pit. He slides through a side door and strolls toward the lone dice table in the far corner of the room, out of place among all the baccarat and blackjack games. It sounds wrong too: The crap-table cacophony disturbs the typically tense and tempered air of a high-roller room.

Whooping it up at the table are Moe Cohn and a half-dozen of his dice-shooting cronies. The set-up is complete with a full crap crew—two dealers, stickman, boxman, and floorman—and the highest maximums in the dice universe. Cohn is Cyr's new biggest player, with a $10 million line of casino credit. He's the CEO of a major California corporation and he has the gambling gene. Tonight's his first time playing at the Hilton. Cyr has already met him at the airport with a limo and a $5,000 bottle of Chateau Lafite Rothschild; ushered him up to the 13,200-square-foot Tuscany Villa; made sure his credit line was ready at the cage; secured a reservation for eight at Le Montrachet, the Hilton's *tres chic* French restaurant at that time (it no longer exists); and had the crap table moved into the high-limit room (the first time such a thing had ever been done at the Hilton).

A day's worth of details, to be sure—but Cyr's toughest challenge was arranging for Mr. C and his friends to be served by the casino's hottest cocktail waitress. Typically, in a union house like the Hilton, the senior (oldest) drink runner gets the shot at the big players' tokes (tips). But Cyr pulled a few strings and tonight luscious little Lisa is schlepping Chivas and dressing up the place—the only difference between her two-ounce uniform, size four, and a bikini is that it's one-piece.

The hoopla from the players indicates that the table's hot. Cyr stands back a bit at first and watches as Cohn tosses the cost of a new Cadillac across the crap layout. The boxman, Mel, signals Cyr with three fingers pointing up: He's ahead three hundred large.

Cyr's mentors, the old-school Las Vegas hosts and operations bosses, taught him that you don't host a sucker while he's gambling. You don't hang out at the table. You never distract him. You let him play his game. When he's through, you can do all the hosting you want. But Cyr has never subscribed to the conventional wisdom. He's especially irreverent when it comes to the gospel according to the old school. He enjoys hanging around his players at the games. He gets a thrill out of watching whales make bets the size of an average worker's annual wage.

Cyr gets caught up in the love. He cuts into the middle of the table and starts whooping it up and high-fiving Mr. C and his cronies as they make their points.

A phone at the high-limit room's main podium rings. Chester the floorman signals Mel the boxman to send over Steve the host. It's the president of the Las Vegas Hilton, the big boss of operations. He's calling from the surveillance room, where he's watching Mr. C's action. Cyr puts the phone to his ear and hears hysteria at a high volume. "What the hell do you think you're doing, Cyr! Quit high-fivin' 'em! You're bringing *them* luck! You're *jinxin'* us!"

"Yes sir. Sorry sir," Cyr appeases his boss' boss. Thinking: *Yeah, right. He's not counting cards, for cryin' out loud. He's shooting dice. He's playing the field, taking the hardways. He's*

*fading like an eight percent edge and you're sweating a little ac-
tion like a floorman on his first shift. Stop being a bleeder. You're
embarrassing yourself.*

"And tell those dealers to stop cheering when a point's
made!"

"Yes sir." Thinking: *The dealers're only pocketing five hundred in tokes every time a player hits his number. I'll tell 'em to
look real downhearted.*

"In fact, why don't you just disappear. You've done your
job. Now let the bosses do theirs."

"Yes sir." Thinking: *Look at these guys. They're having a
blast. The Hilton's Mr. C's new playground and I'm his new best
friend. This degenerate lost nine million at the Mirage last year.
Sure, I'll leave it to the limp-dick bosses like you—to chase him
away.*

❖ ❖ ❖

Cyr wishes Mr. C continued good luck, quietly. Then he
hurries out of the high-limit pit. Charging into the main casino, he waves at floormen and pit clerks and dealers and
other hosts as he goes. He stops short at a crowded crap table
and puts his arm around the shoulders of a white-haired
player in a light leather jacket. "How they rollin', Mr. D?"

The player turns his head and says, "Up and down,
Stevie, up and down."

Ed Duvall, a.k.a Fast Eddie, is Cyr's second biggest
player, one rung down the leviathan ladder from Moe Cohn.
With a $5 million credit line, it's routine for Mr. D to bet as
much as $80,000 any time the dice roll. A retired Montana
timbermill operator, he's old-school. He can stand at the same
table as long as 24 hours without a break—the guy's a
camel—riding out the cold streaks, pushing the hot hands.
When he gets tired of standing, a floorman brings him a
captain's chair so he can keep playing.

Eddie jets down to Vegas every few months to shoot craps

at the Las Vegas Hilton, MGM Grand, or Caesars Palace. And each time, Cyr or his counterparts at competing casinos cater to Eddie's appetites, lavishing him with the biggest suites, meals at the best restaurants, five-figure shopping sprees, wildly expensive gifts. Cyr has taken Mr. D on trips to Baja, Jamaica, Costa Rica, Hawaii, and a week-long yacht tour of the Greek Isles, all on the Hilton's dime.

Players are power—and tonight Cyr's got it. But he's still seething. Both of the biggest gamblers in town this weekend are at the Hilton. Both are his customers. And he's *still* taking shit from the limp dicks upstairs.

Cyr stands and chats with Eddie. Unlike a lot of whales, Mr. D enjoys kibbitzing while he shoots craps. He trades the lighthearted banter with the best of them. But he doesn't like being questioned about his gambling, which is why he prefers dealers familiar with his style of play.

The point's eight. The good dealers know that Eddie'll place the six and lay a grand on the hardway 8—the high house-edge proposition bet that pays 9-1 if the eight is rolled 4-4, but loses if it's rolled any other way or if the seven comes first. He also likes the hardway 10 for $5,000; if he pops the 5-5 combo, he wins 35 large. (Cyr negotiated the maximum laydown on the prop bets for Eddie; the normal limit is $500.)

The dice fly. "Eight the hard way!" the stickman announces and the dealers get busy. Eddie retrieves a stack of checks from his line and odds bets, plus his hard 8—a big enough payout on the one roll to retire the credit-card debts of the average cocktail waitress.

The crap dealers and bosses at most of the high-limit tables at the big casinos know Mr. D so well that they trust him. One night at the MGM Grand, the same night, in fact, that Mike Tyson bit off half of Evander Holyfield's ear, a lot of tension filled the air as the fight-goers worked their way from ringside at the MGM Grand into the casino. Championship fights are magnets for a menagerie of American culture—movie stars, dot-com moguls, pro athletes, L.A.

gangbangers, and every breed of whale and high roller, along with the square tourists, pikers, and fanny-packers from middle America who happen to be in the gargantuan MGM Grand at the same time. It's an odd and volatile mix.

The night of the severed ear, as 15,000 particularly aroused fight fans made their way through the packed casino, the crowd was startled by a loud bang. MGM executives later explained it away as the pop of a champagne bottle in a nearby restaurant, but many ear witnesses swear it was a gunshot.

Fast Eddie was rolling the dice when hundreds, maybe thousands, of people began pushing and shoving to escape from whatever caused the big pop and the situation quickly got out of control. Slot players clung to their machines, blackjack tables were pushed over, and Eddie's son had to push his father under their crap table to get out of the way of the stampede. In the melee, the table got knocked askew, scattering checks all over the layout.

(A pair of National Basketball Association players were caught on surveillance cameras stealing about $75,000 in $5,000 checks from a blackjack table during the mayhem. MGM management put out the word—discreetly, through their agents—that they expected the money to be returned. The two pro athletes quietly complied.)

After the dust had settled, Eddie turned to the boxman who oversaw his game. "What about my chips?" he inquired, pointing at the mess on the table.

"Mr. D," the game supervisor told him, "what you say you had, we'll give you." And $60,000 in casino checks was returned to him, no questions asked.

"Seven out!" the shooter's roll ends and Eddie groans as the Hilton dealers sweep all the chips into the house's pile.

The cocktail waitress comes by and Eddie orders water. He doesn't drink alcohol when he's gambling, wanting to maintain his focus and discipline, so he downs only Evian or Perrier. The waitresses like him just the same; although he sticks to dollar bottles of water, he always tips at least a red $5 check. Eddie once accidentally toked a waitress with a yellow $1,000 "banana." He didn't take it back. Wouldn't have been right. He's known as a George (a big-time tipper).

Eddie places two brown checks on the pass line for the come-out roll. The shooter rolls a four, Eddie's favorite number. He backs up his line bet with triple odds, six more brown checks.

"Sir, how much *are* those chips?" a bystander asks Cyr.

"Five thousand apiece."

The man calls to his wife. "Hey, honey! You have to see this."

The wife waddles over to the table.

"Check this out—a forty-thousand-dollar bet."

"I can't look at that. It's disgusting," she says and waddles away.

The shooter tosses the dice.

"Four!" the stickman croons. "Pay the line." And Eddie wins enough in little clay discs to buy a new Lexus SUV.

Fast Eddie's riding a hot streak. As Cyr stands watching, Eddie drains the brown checks from the table's rack and the pit boss sends a security guard to fetch another million-dollar box of the $5,000 tokens. Sometimes the boss'll send for three boxes at once, so the game's not delayed.

"How's the lawsuit going, Eddie?" Cyr makes a little small talk as they wait for chips.

"Up and down, Stevie, up and down," Eddie laughs. "Actually," he adds, "it's different this time. My other ex-wives were all excellent housekeepers. After divorcing me, they each kept the house. But not this one."

Eddie lives in the middle of western Montana's Bitterroot National Forest in a relatively isolated compound surrounded by millions of trees. Sleeping Child Hot Springs runs through the middle of his property. The 100-degree water heats the 16-bedroom main house through a system of subflooring pipes. The spring flows through a pool, half as long as a football field, where guests swim and bathe, summer and winter. The dead-end road leading to the house is heated by spring water that runs through pipes beneath the pavement. While snow and ice cover the rest of Montana, Fast Eddie's "driveway" is bare steaming asphalt.

The house is five stories, serviced by an elevator. Each floor is 5,000 square feet, twice as large as a good-sized suburban abode. The first level consists of the recreation area, with snooker and pool tables, a movie theater, and a dice table Cyr gave him for a birthday present. The second level houses the guest rooms, 14 of them, each with its own bath. On the third level is the huge master bedroom with his-and-her baths and one guest room (where Cyr sleeps). The fourth level has the office and library. On floor five there's a big solarium.

The last time Cyr was up to the estate, he was there to give a deposition in the legal dispute between Eddie and his ex-girlfriend, a former $14,000-a-year card dealer at a small Missoula-area casino. She claimed that she and Eddie had a common-law marriage and she wanted millions. He argued otherwise. Cyr testified that he'd traveled with the couple on casino-sponsored trips to the Bahamas, Costa Rica, Greece—and never once heard them speak of each other as husband and wife.

A lot of hosts, the old schoolers in particular, consider their players pains in the ass. Casino marketing executives older than 55 or so might call Fast Eddie a prima donna. He drinks Pabst Blue Ribbon in a glass and wants miniature Mr. Goodbars and Kit Kats waiting for him in his suite. He always gets a window seat on the plane. He likes thin down pillows; the Hilton butlers keep them in a closet, just for him. No incoming calls before 9 a.m. Breakfast is always eggs Benedict or waffles.

If he wants a helicopter to go to the top of Mt. Charleston, the 12,000-foot peak northwest of Las Vegas, it'll be landing on the Hilton roof in 30 minutes, and Cyr and Eddie and his friends will be on top of the mountain in another 30. One hour from a stray whim to fruition. The world at his beck and call, courtesy of the casino.

Fast Eddie loses, on average, upwards of a million dollars a month at the crap tables. Steve Cyr is not unhappy to host him. A player like Mr. D gives him power. Mr. D wants to go to the Greek isles and cruise around on a private yacht? Cyr hosts the trip. Mr. D wants to be picked up in Montana in the Hilton jet and make a four-day detour to Hawaii? Cyr goes with him. Why didn't Mr. D get a dozen ringside tickets to the Tyson fight? Because he only asked for 11 (one for Cyr). Cyr wants to take a few days off in L.A. without being charged for vacation time? He says Mr. D wants his host to meet him there.

Fast Eddie is neither a prima donna nor a pain, at least not in Steve Cyr's ass.

That's Stevie's job—giving the premium players whatever they want. Emphasis on the whatever.

❖ ❖ ❖

Cyr makes a few more rounds. Then, just before leaving the Hilton, he checks in on his whale in the high-limit pit. He notices that Mr. C and his crap buddies are laying back. There's only $25,000 or so on the layout, which means the table's cold, which means they're losing. The boxman, Mel, signals Cyr with all ten, then five fingers pointing down: Mr. C's behind a million-five. Cyr doesn't react, even as he mentally adds $15,000 to the running total of his year-end bonus. He also calculates the night's action so far: from up $300,000 to down $1.5, a $1.8 million swing in … he checks his watch … an hour and forty-five minutes. The Hilton president, no doubt, now considers Cyr a hero, but the players are quiet. The dealers are even quieter. And Lisa the waitress is nowhere to be seen.

Cyr switches on the discretion. "Well, Mr. C," he says,

holding out his hand. "I'm taking off for the night. Anything I can do for you before I go?"

"Yeah, you can light a fire under these bones. Colder'n a whore's heart on a sailor's payday."

"Keep at her," Cyr smiles. "They'll warm up. If you want anything, anything at all, Mel here knows where to find me twenty-four-seven."

"Sure, kid."

Cyr flings open the front doors of the Hilton, tosses the valet a ten-spot, catches his keys on the fly, and roars back to the Hard Rock, to find Jeff Armstrong. He's easy to locate, playing blackjack in the Peacock Lounge, the Hard Rock's high-limit pit. He's all revved up from his stint onstage at the Joint and after an hour at the tables, he's ahead $200,000. Still, he's steamed that a pit boss has just slashed his maximum bet from $10,000 to $5,000, and he lets Cyr know about it in no uncertain terms.

"Whoa, baby! Whoa!" Cyr backs up two steps from the verbal assault and raises his hands over his head. "They cut your maximum? I don't blame 'em. You're short-timin' them. You gotta give them four hours a day, not one. You wanna bet big? Fine, but you gotta give 'em a fair shot at your money. Besides," Cyr moves in and puts a hand on Armstrong's shoulder. "You just played the Joint. You're up a couple hundred. What could be bad?"

The L.A. multi-millionaire smiles, shrugs, sits back down at the table, and picks up his next hand of blackjack.

Arranging for a premium player to perform onstage in the Joint at the Hard Rock. Flying to Montana to help resolve a high-stakes personal dispute between a crap whale and his ex-girlfriend. Standing by as a megaroller dares a libidinous beauty to swap her chips for his. Reorganizing the Hilton high-limit pit to accommodate a private crap table and crew for a titan of southern California industry.

They're all just routine episodes in the life of a Las Vegas superhost.

2

From Salina To Caesars

Steve Cyr was born in 1964. Today, he's 40 and at the top of his trade: He's the casino seducer, holding out the promise of fantasy vacations to prosperous men and beautiful women all intoxicated on the adrenaline of gambling, the aphrodisiac of riches, the aura of self-importance, and, usually, alcohol. Cyr handles them, hobnobs with them, hosts them—and, in the process, relieves them of millions of dollars a year.

It's a career—indeed, a lifestyle—he was practically born to pursue.

Cyr's formative years weren't humble, but they were sometimes a bargain. On the day he was born, the whole doctor and hospital bill came to $138, and insurance covered $110—the least expensive major experience of his life. He lived in little Moundridge, Kansas, population 800, till he was two, then his family moved to the big town, Salina.

When he was eight, his parents bought a Howard Johnson Motel in Salina, smack in the middle of Kansas at the junction of interstates 70 and 135. Steve and his sister Jill, four years older, began helping around the motel immediately; he was such a good worker that by his early teens, he was making $10 an hour, a fortune to a kid his age. Steve Cyr was the first on his block to have a grand in the bank.

The motel had 75 guest rooms and four meeting rooms,

a good-sized facility for Salina, population 50,000. His mother Jean managed the motel. His father Carroll quit his job as the high-school basketball coach to make sure the motel meeting rooms stayed full. He was a mixer and a host. He knew the coaches on the circuit, so all the high-school sports teams that came to Salina stayed at his HoJo. And when he'd hear about other groups coming in, he went after them. He didn't wait to read in the newspaper that they were scheduled. By the time it appeared in print, he had the deposit check in hand. And then he made sure to deliver. He was extremely picky about the presentation of his product—the arrangement of the meeting rooms, the quality of the food service, the treatment of the guests.

Carroll Cyr's son Steve watched and learned.

When Steve was 16, a friend of the family made a suggestion. "You know, my nephew is getting a degree in hotel administration at the University of Washington. With your experience, you'd be a shoo-in." From that point on, he told everyone who asked that he planned to major in hotel administration. In his junior year, a guidance counselor steered young Steve toward the best schools—Cornell, Oklahoma State, University of Nevada-Las Vegas. Rejected by Cornell and OK State, he'd meet his destiny in Sin City by default.

Cyr arrived in September 1983. He wasn't in Kansas anymore. He was in Oz Vegas. It was a land of desert days and neon nights; of valet attendants making $50,000 a year and blackjack dealers pulling down $60,000, most of it in cash; of girls in tube tops and short shorts and high heels and painted fingernails; of guys sizing up prospects, both carnal and career, sex steaming through their veins and dollar signs dancing in their eyes—heady stuff for a 19-year-old farmboy. And this was still in the *old* days, the early '80s, before the big '90s boom when the number of casinos and visitors and valet attendants and blackjack dealers and girls more than tripled.

For that first year, Cyr lived in a ratty apartment near the university. On a visit the following summer, his parents decided to buy him a condo, both as a residence and an investment. Cyr shopped for the real estate. He found a developer who'd gotten into a little financial trouble and was auctioning condos listed for $69,900 at a starting price at $45,000. His parents gave him power of attorney to bid for a unit at the auction. He'd just turned 20.

Carroll and Jean allowed him $52,000. Steve bid on every condo as it came up. He'd call out, "Forty-six thousand!" Then, "Forty-eight thousand!" Then, "Fifty-thousand!" And finally, "Fifty-two thousand!" Invariably, someone upped the bid and Steve had to sit back and pipe down. After a few such rounds, everyone knew that the kid's limit was $52,000. Finally, with only a couple of units left on the auction block, Steve jumped up and shouted, "Fifty-two thousand!" The auctioneer immediately slammed down his gavel and announced, "Sold for fifty-two thousand!" The kid had his condo and the whole crowd cheered.

At UNLV, Cyr took all the gambling-related classes he could: casino management, marketing, and mathematics. His favorite was an advanced gaming class taught by Michael Gaughan, the owner of the Barbary Coast, a small Las Vegas Strip casino between giant Bally's and the Flamingo. The son of long-time casino mogul Jackie Gaughan, Michael lectured the students on the ins and outs of a business into which he, too, had been born.

At night, on weekends, during the day when he wasn't in class, Steve walked and stalked the casinos, looking around, studying what was happening, trying to figure out how to apply the lessons Michael Gaughan was imparting in class, along with those he'd learned growing up in the hospitality business.

One day Michael Gaughan asked him, "Do you gamble?"

Although he hadn't yet turned 21, Cyr replied, "Sure." (In the days before family-friendly Las Vegas and its intensified security surrounding kids in casinos, the unwritten old-school rule for underage gamblers, particularly UNLV students, was that they could play, but they couldn't win. If they hit a slot jackpot or a lucky streak at the tables, they'd get carded and thrown out of the casino.)

"How much is a lot of money to you?" Gaughan asked.

"I don't know. A hundred fifty."

"I want you to go out over the next couple of days and gamble two hundred. Make fifteen- and twenty-dollar bets, a little more than you should with a two hundred dollar bankroll, so you really feel the intensity of each play."

Cyr did it—and the exercise accomplished its intended goal. That was when he first felt the love from winning, then how it segues into greed, and the fever from losing, then how it morphs into fear. Cyr got the only A in the class.

In his senior year, he had to do an internship. But Cyr wouldn't be doing his in the typical bar, restaurant, or hotel. He interned at Gaughan's Barbary Coast. He worked as a clerk in the pit and the cage. He dealt blackjack, craps, and roulette for a week at a time (under supervision and without pay or tokes). He worked at the race and sports books. He sat on the catwalks with binoculars and watched people gamble. He did a stint in surveillance, which, with all the pan-tilt-zoom cameras and silent video monitors and whirring VCRs, looked like NASA to him.

After graduating with a bachelor's degree in hotel administration, he went to work full-time at the Barbary Coast, taking wagers in the sports book. Being paid to sit at a window and watch ballgames, only occasionally interrupted to book a bet, blew his mind.

He was hooked.

❖ ❖ ❖

Cyr entered the industry a few years before everything changed in Las Vegas. He started out as a 22-year-old when the Mirage was just a gleam in Steve Wynn's failing eyes. His timing was such that he was initiated into the mysteries and intricacies and subtleties of player development and was turned out (trained) as a future superstar host by an all-star roster of long-experienced sharp-dressed smooth-talking white-haired men who practiced a decidedly old-school approach to handling high rollers.

The old-timers, men like Jimmy Newman, Johnny Oakes, Guy Hudson, Dan Chandler, Charlie Myerson, Bucky Howard, Joe Rishuti, Minnie Cardella, and many others, were either themselves hard-boiled wiseguys from the days of illegal gambling around the country or had been turned out by the same. Starting in earnest in the '40s, peaking in the '50s, and continuing late into the '60s, Nevada sucked up every serious gambler who'd ever knelt in an alley over a makeshift crap layout in any of the 49 states where gambling was illegal. Once ensconced in the promised land of Nevada, these guys with gambling in their blood came up through the ranks of casino operations—dealers, floormen, pit bosses, shift bosses, as well as cage personnel like cashiers and credit managers—and by the time they reached the ripe old age of 50, they'd gone as far as they were going to go. So they were kicked upstairs into the executive offices and given the job title of casino host.

In the good-old old-school days—the first four decades of wide-open casino gambling in Nevada—marketing to high rollers was strictly a homegrown affair. The VIP system was a procession of pure pedigree. The casino-operations guys knew the players who'd knelt in those alleys alongside them, so they brought with them a ready-made base of customers when they migrated to Nevada, where gambling was legit and everyone could roll the bones standing tall.

The earliest high-stakes players in Nevada casinos were the manufacturers of demon alcohol. The 18th Amendment to the U.S. Constitution, which made federal felons out of anyone who had anything to do with booze, wasn't repealed until 1933, two years after gambling was legalized in the Silver State. So not only did bootleggers supply the illegal hooch to the legal casinos, they turned right around and drank and gambled in them as well. The bootleggers were famous for making cash-only bets; these two-fisted players would no more accept gambling chips, or checks drawn on bank accounts, from a casino than they would from a speakeasy, another gangster, or even their own partners.

World War II, with its tidal wave of black-market products and profits, took the place of Prohibition as the source of millions in untaxed currency consigned to the casino coffers. The war also introduced millions of servicemen to craps, blackjack, and poker, and in the economic boom of the postwar years, the late 1940s and early '50s, veterans vacationed in Las Vegas with discretionary dollars earned as businessmen, professionals, executives, and, of course, crooks of every size and stripe.

These were the original exhibitionist high rollers—a flashy bunch who had little aversion to flaunting or risking their wealth in the casinos. They, too, brought along cash, though they didn't mind exchanging it at the tables for little round clay disks.

Casino marketing through the mid-'60s was a simple matter of a boss vouching for a player; if a boss said his guy was good for it, he was. Or at least he'd better be, because if he wasn't, it was up to the boss to collect. This system evolved into the first organized effort to fill the casinos with qualified players—the junket.

The original gambler junkets began arriving in Las Vegas from the East Coast in the early 1960s. To qualify, a guy had to show $5,000 to $10,000 and be vouched for by another junketeer. The cash was deposited in the casino cage upon arrival and the junketeer could draw chips against it at the table. It was primarily a word-of-mouth system requiring a minimum of paperwork: Other than table markers (IOUs issued by the casino and signed by the gambler), there was little documentation.

The first credit lines, whereby the casino in effect loaned

the gambler his playing stake based on his promise to pay up before leaving at the end of his stay, were laughably small by today's standards. Most were in the $2,000 to $2,500 range. A big player had a $5,000 line. Once in a blue moon, a casino would welcome a $10,000 customer. Two or three times a year, a guy would arrive with $25,000. Average bets in those days were in the low hundreds—$100, $150, $200, up to around $250 per hand of cards or roll of dice.

This was in the days when gambling debts were uncollectable around the country (and the world). So if a guy wanted to skip out on a marker or two, the casinos had very little recourse through the legal system. Oh, they could apply various kinds of pressure, but the best way to avoid getting stiffed for large amounts of money and left holding a bag was to limit the size of the bag.

When oil money from Texas, Oklahoma, and Louisiana began making its way to Las Vegas in the '60s and into the '70s, a new brand of high roller came into existence. Stetsoned wildcatters drove the credit limit up to $50,000 and $100,000 and could bet up to $500 a hand at the Desert Inn, Flamingo, and Caesars. By the time Steve Cyr had earned his degree, the bootleggers, black marketeers, GIs, and post-war exhibitionists were long gone, as were the paltry betting limits and credit lines.

As petrodollars were inflating the casino economy, Howard Hughes was changing the business culture. Hughes had bought up a half-dozen casinos and brought in a new breed of boss to run them—operations managers who'd gotten their training in business, rather than gambling. They viewed their properties as hotels with casinos attached, rather than casinos with some hotel rooms. They left the old-school bosses sitting upstairs in the executive offices, wondering what the hell was becoming of their world.

❖ ❖ ❖

Hilton was one of the first publicly traded corporations to own a Nevada casino. Prior to Hilton's entry into the legal gambling industry, all pointholders (owners) in Nevada casinos had to be individually licensed, which automatically ruled out companies with hundreds or thousands of shareholders. But when Howard Hughes went on his casino-buying binge in the late '60s, he refused to submit to the state's licensing process, which required a personal appearance from the applicant. The reclusive Hughes argued, through spokespeople, that the $300 million with which he was "buying out the mob" should be license enough for the politicians and bureaucrats and regulators. And so it was: The state legislature quickly and dutifully changed the casino-ownership statutes, rushing into law the Nevada Corporate Gaming Acts of 1967 and 1969. This paved the way for Hilton to buy the Flamingo and International (today the Las Vegas Hilton) from casino mogul Kirk Kerkorian in 1970.

Thus Las Vegas began its transition from an underworld-controlled to a corporate-controlled town. Nonetheless, the bosses, whether old school or new, still maintained absolute control over every aspect of the Las Vegas experience for visitors, employees, locals, gamblers, and anyone else who happened to wander onto the scene, just as they had for the past 40 years. This was still long before computers, casino-marketing databases, accounting software, before there was much record-keeping on customers at all. Everything was about *juice*, baby—the personal relationship, the private deal—and the individual details were recorded only in people's heads. Secrets were never shared, for both personal and professional reasons. In terms of the former, a strict code of silence, a natural condition for gamblers and gangsters, prevailed. In terms of the latter, if you told someone what you knew, that person no longer had any need for you.

In those days, the operations guys' authority for issuing players complimentary rooms, food and beverage, and other amenities of the hospitality trade was nearly complete. Any lowly floorman could comp a buffet or coffee shop meal for two. For a room or show, he'd go to the pit boss and say, "We've got a guy over here firing up a couple hundred a hand wants to go to the show." And the pit boss would almost automatically say, "Yeah, okay, give it to him."

Back then, floormen weren't even limited to dishing out comps in their own joints. There were only a dozen or so casinos on the Strip, and most of the bosses knew each other. The floorman could call a boss across the street or down the block to hook up his player with a meal or show at his store. When a boss was finally kicked upstairs after 20 or 30 years in operations, he didn't even have to pick up the phone. He'd have his secretary make the call.

Not every host came up through operations. Some bypassed the casino altogether and went straight from the street to the suite. Rather than years in the gambling pits, these hosts' bona fides were built on relationships with the bent-nose crowd in New York, Cleveland, Miami, Kansas City, Chicago. Charlie Myerson was a perfect example. He'd owned taxicab companies (and was a bookie on the side) in New York City. Steve Wynn, reportedly, grew up knowing Myerson. When Wynn's father, an East Coast bingo-parlor operator, died owing Myerson money, Wynn tried to pay it off, but Myerson told Wynn that a gambler's debts die with him. Later, Myerson went to work for Wynn as a host when Wynn opened the Golden Nugget in Atlantic City. Myerson flew in his big-money players from New York in a company helicopter. Myerson later followed Wynn back to Las Vegas and went to work as a host at the Mirage, earning a reported $450,000 a year.

Whether they came from the street or the pit, these hosts were smooth. They had communication skills. They were liked and trusted by the joints and the players. Their word was their bond. They knew how to make friends with and market to people. It was amazing how many players' names were listed in their black books. One old-timer estimates that

Charlie Myerson had 500 to 1,000 people who referred to him as a "good friend."

But most of the hosts were promoted from within, so the lines between operations and marketing were blurred at best. So the level of service back then was extremely high. A player's casino contact, whether a first-year floorman or a 60-year-old marketing executive, took care of everything. Often a player didn't even have to go to the front desk to check in. Someone brought his room key out to the table. The bosses wanted the players at those tables as long as possible.

Today, if you don't meet the comp criteria of the casino rating system as implemented by Harvard MBAs and tracked by Brooks Brother-clad bosses and audited by tweezer-butt bookkeepers, you can't get a drink at the bar. You can't get a free lunch buffet or the casino rate on a room or tickets to a show. But back in the dark ages of the '60s, '70s, even the '80s, when the old-school bosses had the power of the comp pencil, these were all automatic snap-of-the-finger freebies.

Relationship marketing—one-on-one, handshake, direct. If you were a pit boss or a bona fide casino host (some "hosts" in the '60s and '70s were sports figures, such as Joe Louis at Caesars and Jackie Fields at the Tropicana and Roy Mantle, Mickey's brother, at the Sahara; they were actually glorified greeters, whom the big players liked to meet), you not only knew your customers, you also knew who recommended them, who vouched for them, who was responsible for them. If you said your customer was good for his losses, it was taken on your word alone, accepted without question. If you got burned, it was your ass.

In those days, casino hosts freely shared information on high rollers and their whereabouts around town. They all figured that players would make the rounds and it was just a matter of time before they'd stop by each property to try their luck.

It was all about schmoozing. For example, a floorman's

main function was game protection, but he was secondarily a gofer for the player. Today, they're clerks, paper shufflers. In fact, one of the reasons that the ranks of hosts burgeoned in the late '80s was that the accounting department started overwhelming the poor pit people with paperwork. The emphasis of the floorman's job description switched from casino marketing to casino accounting.

Cyr came up during that transition time, when bosses, buried with paperwork, had less and less time to host. Meanwhile, the hosts were still relying on their established players, many of whom were old or feeble or dying off. And the old-school marketing methodology had few mechanisms for attracting new players. For instance, a host never phoned players at their offices or homes, and especially not at another casino. He never cut into them at the tables. He rarely went after players, period. He let them come to him.

So, many of the newer premium gamblers were falling through the cracks. These players weren't aware that such a thing as a casino host, whose job it was to provide for them, even existed. In Cyr's formative years, plenty of big players came in on their own, paid retail for their rooms, meals, and shows, and fired it up at the tables without so much as a hello from the joint. The floormen were perpetually frantic with other duties, too harried to notify a host up in the executive office that a new live one was hitting it hard downstairs. And for their part, the hosts, who were loath to cut into a player to begin with, were too preoccupied drinking coffee, eating donuts, and reading the newspaper to bother to stroll down to the casino to meet a new high roller.

Even the new players who did know about hosts were afforded a level of service that was less than stellar. For starters, it was up to the gambler to contact the host. A $100,000 player had to call a marketing secretary and put in his request for a room and a ride from the airport. He never heard back from anyone; he just hoped the limo was there at the airport. When he got to the casino, he walked into the lobby and waited in line at the VIP check-in position at the front desk. He had to make his own dinner, show, and golf reservations. And after playing all weekend, it was up to him to find his way to the executive office to sit down with his host, who'd decide how much he felt like comping. If it happened to be the day off of the host whose secretary he'd spoken to, he then had to talk to a completely different host, leaving the gambler to feel like he was begging to be given something in return for his play.

Thus, the handling of high rollers was in a bit of disarray when 22-year-old Steve Cyr was working as a ticket writer at the Barbary Coast sports book by day and haunting the premium casinos night after night, spending hours trying to find his place in the love and fever business, which had captured his imagination and refused to let go.

❖ ❖ ❖

Cyr knew he wanted to be in casino marketing. He wanted to do what his Dad had done all the years he was growing up in Salina: book events and host people. One night in 1987 while prowling the Desert Inn, he noticed a small room off the lobby, next to the front desk, labeled VIP Lounge. Curious, he stepped inside, made a few discreet inquiries, and got a glimpse of a glorious future.

The little lounge at the DI was Las Vegas' first separate check-in area for casino VIPs. As late as the late '80s, high rollers registered for their rooms at the front desk. Perhaps there was a special window at the counter for preferred players, perhaps not. Either way, they were handled by union front-desk clerks on whom the distinction between a nickel low roller and a million-dollar whale was hopelessly lost. The clerk took a credit card, checked the reservations list, and tossed the VIP a key—same as everyone else.

If a million-dollar player happened to say, "You know what? I'd like to eat in the Portofino restaurant tomorrow at eight and I need a golf tee time for Saturday morning and my wife wants to go to the spa, see Tom Jones, and go shopping, so we'll need a limo," the clerk replied, "Well, to make a reservation for Portofino, you dial extension nine. The spa is at extension five. You can talk to the limo dispatcher at extension eleven. The best way to get a tee time is to go out to the pro shop and talk to the starter. And for reservations for Tom Jones, you'll have to call over to Caesars."

The casino might've had a concierge, but there too, the whale had to wait in a line full of shrimp, whether they were hotel guests or just stray crustaceans off the street.

Even in the DI's VIP Lounge, high rollers dealt with union clerks. The only difference was that instead of standing behind a marble counter, they sat behind a wooden desk. Cyr took a good look around and realized that the DI had yet to grasp the full implications of the lounge's potential for handling high rollers. They had the room, they even had an embryonic VIP department, but it was still just front-desk clerks in a private setting.

Young Steve cold-called Mike Sterling, one of the DI marketing bosses, and talked his way into an interview. He walked in, sat down, and 60 minutes later, a 22-year-old ticket writer at the Barbary Coast had himself a job as the first supervisor of the DI's VIP Services department.

Sterling gave him a few secretaries from the executive offices to staff the VIP lounge. Cyr, being Cyr, wanted young and pretty girls for his room, but he had to get around the Culinary Union, which represented all Desert Inn non-casino and non-management job positions and would want to put the senior employees in the cush VIP Services working environment. But Cyr realized that if he staffed the lounge with girls from marketing, he could sidestep the union policies.

Soon after, Cyr and Sterling found that they'd lucked into a few unintended consequences. First, Culinary front-desk employees were making $12 an hour, while the VIP Services hostesses were paid secretaries' wages, only $7 or $8 an hour, not including the tokes they received in abundance from free-wheeling high rollers for their concierge services. Thus, the players subsidized the hostesses' salaries—in keeping with a long-held casino tradition. Second, the hostesses didn't have the union safety net under them. If they screwed up or if a player got mad at them, they were termed (fired); their tokes and job insecurity all but guaranteed a high level of service for the big fish. Finally, to come full circle, since they were young and pretty, the players cut the VIP hostesses plenty of slack, so the whole new system worked smoothly.

(The casino business has always been a man's world. Even in today's otherwise equal-opportunity business climate, the vast majority of big bosses and big players are men and sexism is alive and well in the casino. For example, an old joke in the executive offices goes: Three female dealers are being considered for a promotion to pit boss. The first has a degree in casino management and has worked as a pit clerk, dealer, and substitute "floorman"—yes, women are called floormen—for five years. The second has 20 years of casino experience and a perfect attendance record, and chairs the company's community outreach and charity programs. The third is the sister-in-law of the casino manager, a single mom raising four kids and a dreadful dealer who needs promoting to keep her from messing up. Who gets the job? The one with the biggest tits.)

Once the secretaries were transferred to VIP Services out of the marketing offices, a shift occurred. Now, instead of a secretary working exclusively for one host, all the hosts shared all the secretaries. And they weren't even nearby; they were in the new lounge off the lobby. The old-school guys threw a fit. It was Cyr's first taste of vexation from the old-timers. It would be far from his last.

Cyr, as VIP supervisor, set up a one-stop non-host shop for maxirollers, who quickly taught him what they needed and wanted. For starters, he made sure a limo was waiting at the airport when the premium player got off the plane. On the way back to the casino, the limo driver called in to announce the VIP's arrival, then pulled up to a side door, where Cyr and a bellman were waiting. While the bellman delivered the luggage, Cyr ushered the player into VIP Services, where there was a small table set up with coffee, soda, fruit, and pastries. He made all the reservations for the player's comps—the DI had the high-end Portofino and Monte Carlo restaurants, the Starlight Room featuring the big headliners of the day, the spa where the Rat Pack had relaxed after filming *Ocean's Eleven*, and the Tournament of Champions golf course. He even called the player's host, if he had one, to come down and say hello. If the player didn't have a host, Cyr arranged for him to meet one.

In order to follow through with the premium service, Cyr fought the hotel-side managers for casino blocks (hotel rooms held in reserve for players). In the beginning, he was often stymied in his quest for eight o'clock reservations in the Monte Carlo on a Saturday night or Sunday morning tee times. He cajoled the maitre d's to set aside a certain number of tables in the gourmet rooms for his players. He insisted that the golf starter save spots for the casino. He found that the hotel held out plenty of standard rooms for the casino block, but often sold the suites to paying customers, so he had to take on the reservations department. The only venue in the whole joint that Cyr didn't have to battle was the showroom, where the maitre d' held back the "kings-row" booths. Only when the prime seats weren't filled by players would the maitre d', at the last minute, open them up to the hoi polloi.

Steve Cyr used this time to familiarize himself with the high-roller ropes—the differences in suites, the special handling in the high-limit pit, the connection between bankroll and comps. He learned how all the separate pieces of a resort-casino—the casino, front desk, reservations, limousine, showroom, golf, spa—fit together and worked.

And, of course, he watched what the hosts did and didn't

do. They wore custom-tailored suits, Italian shoes, expensive jewelry. They always seemed to have tans—and the best babes. They got to go to dinner, play golf, and see shows with their players. Early on, a high-powered gambler with a gazillion dollars to burn at the tables came into VIP Services and said, "Kid, where's Johnny Oakes? Tell him to come to my room at eleven tonight, ready to play some serious gin." Steve Cyr, the glorified clerk, thought Oakes had to have the coolest job in the casino and he burned to be a marketing executive himself.

❖ ❖ ❖

But the DI, as far as he could tell, was overrun by hosts, all at least 50 years old. Cyr knew he'd never get a shot with all those geezers in his way. So after almost a year at the DI, he cold-called Danny Angelo, a casino marketing supervisor at Caesars Palace, and got an interview. He admitted to Angelo that he had no experience as a host, but he did have a thousand ideas on how to be one. Angelo was impressed with Cyr's vision and convinced his own boss to give the ambitious kid, who was bound and determined to be a marketing guy *somewhere*, a shot. Not as a mucky-muck table-games host, to be sure, but as a lowly slot host, roaming the machine floor and meeting slot high rollers.

Cyr moved to Caesars and began prowling the casino, hanging around the high-limit slots, cutting into the dollar and five-dollar players. This was before today's slot clubs and player-tracking cards, which quantify a machine player's casino worth, down to the penny, via electronic tabulation; back then the rating system was entirely manual and capricious. Cyr enlisted the change girls. He gave them little Post-It notes to keep track of how much players bought in for. At about $500, he'd get interested.

A natural salesman—ambitious, affable, efficient—and sharp-looking in his power suits and polished shoes—Cyr befriended machine players big and small. He loved his slot jockies, the biggest suckers in the casino. He wanted to comp them to dinner. He wanted to pick up their room charges. He would've given them the moon—if his bosses had let him. But Caesars honchos had Cyr pegged as a loose cannon. And, as they continually reminded him, he was only a slot host, catering to players who still, even in the late '80s, were little more than dog meat in the eyes of operations. "They're just slot sluts," the bosses told him. "They don't count."

Cyr was incredulous. He fumed. He chafed at the bit over the myopic operations bosses, the limp dicks. These guys preferred blackjack and crap players over machine feeders? How idiotic! Slot machines didn't require hourly wages and uniforms and health insurance and vacation pay. Slot machines never called in sick or got fired for stealing. Slot machines held 4% or 5% or 10% or even 25% (the maximum by law in Nevada) of the action. Low overhead. High edge. From the casino's point of view, the perfect gambling device.

In addition, slot players barely knew about comps. They were so appreciative when someone from the casino paid any attention to them at all that they'd be customers for life after one free buffet.

What's more, Cyr instinctively understood the important dynamic of downside risk. What's the most a dollar slot player with a $10,000 bankroll can ding a casino for? Maybe $5,000, $10,000, even $25,000—it's strictly limited by the size of the biggest jackpot. What's the most a $5 video poker player with a $50,000 bankroll can win? Twenty grand, and only by hitting the royal flush, which happens once every 80 hours or so of play. How much can a blackjack or baccarat player with that same $50,000 bankroll nick the casino for? "Who fuckin' knows," Cyr would yell out of his car window, driving home after work, seething at the stupidity of the limp dicks. The sky's the limit! He wanted his slot players treated with at least the same respect as the table-game players. But the bosses barely gave him the authority to comp the snack bar.

That all changed one Friday morning. Cyr was sitting in the conference room, waiting for the start of a meeting on the weekend's action, when a new senior credit host, an older guy named Guy Hudson, walked in. Cyr's eyes opened wide and his jaw went slack. The rule was that every Friday and Saturday, the marketing executives had to wear either dark blue or black dress slacks and suit jacket. Early on, before he understood just how mandatory the dress code was, Cyr had shown up in a dark gray suit. He was immediately written up and sent home to change. But there was Guy Hudson, wearing a snazzy cabernet-colored jacket and lavender slacks. Old-school colors. Cyr gave him two months, three max, at Caesars. Hudson lasted exactly 90 days, then went over to the Hilton. But before he left, he took the young slot host under wing.

Hudson agreed with Cyr about the value of slot players, who'd soon account for more casino profits than all the table games combined. He encouraged Cyr to continue hosting them and gave him comp authority for the buffet and coffee shop. If a slot player wanted a room, Cyr could go directly to Hudson for the nod. Now, he could approach a player and say, "Hi, I'm Steve Cyr and you've earned yourself dinner tonight. Which would you prefer, the Palatium Buffet or Cafe Roma?" He couldn't believe the reaction: Most players either didn't know about comps or thought they were only for high-rolling table-game gamblers and were far too intimidated to ask for one. Cyr responded, "Hey, you're a Caesars-caliber player. Where are you staying? You should stay here with us. At your level of play I can comp your room ..."

One night, a change girl informed him that a slot player had bought in for $5,000 in $5 tokens. Cyr made a beeline for Hudson, who authorized a comp for two to the high-end Bacchanal restaurant. Cyr introduced himself to the player, Mr. E, and extended the Bacchanal comp. Then, excited and shooting from the hip, he asked Mr. E if he'd like to see the

Rainman Suite (where Dustin Hoffman and Tom Cruise hang out in the movie *Rainman*). Mr. E accepted. Cyr ran back to Hudson for authorization and Hudson told him that for another $10,000 buy-in, the slot player could stay in the suite. Cyr gave Mr. E the tour, thereby seeing the famous penthouse for the first time himself—players are power, baby! On an impulse he upped the buy-in to $15,000 and Mr. E didn't blink an eye. He simply pulled three straps ($5,000 bundled in hundred-dollar bills) from his pocket and Cyr had his first big sale.

Caesars' high-limit slots weren't far from the crap pit. Cyr hung around the crap tables long enough to notice that the floormen were often too busy to pay much attention to players who qualified for comps. He went to Hudson.

"What happens," he asked, "when a guy walks in off the street, buys in at the crap table for five grand, and loses it right away? The floorman's supposed to comp him, but he doesn't have time. And the hosts don't bother working the floor. So a guy who could lose forty or fifty thousand a year walks out the door.

"Why don't you call me a 'cash host' and set me loose on the tables as well as the slots? If I cut into someone who already has a host, I'll back off. But I'll bet you I can hustle a lot of medium rollers who we're otherwise losing."

Hudson liked the idea, but he also knew that new ideas often took a long time to implement in the casino business—maybe as long as it took for a boss to recognize the opportunity to take credit for it. So while he didn't let Cyr loose on the spot, he did prepare him for the cash-host position by walking him through the process of hosting table-game players.

"Say you cut into a crap player, Mr. F, or he walks in the door and asks to see a host. The first thing you do is find out as much as you can about him. You talk to him. You get a feel for what kind of player he is. Is he just trying to weasel comps, maybe a room or two tickets to the show, or does he crave the action? You love it when he says, 'I'm looking for fifty thousand in credit. But when I lose the fifty, am I gonna be able to get more?' Likewise, when he says, 'How much can I bet?' it's a dead giveaway. Not: 'Do I need to stay at the hundred-dollar table to get my room comped?' But: 'If the table limit's a thousand, can I spread two hands at a grand each?' He's just given away the game. You know he's a gambler and you can take him.

"Then you walk Mr. F over to the cage. The casino needs a copy of his driver's license, his Social Security number, a blank check from his checking account so they don't make a mistake on the account numbers, and a copy of a credit card or two. They all go into his credit file.

"Then, as long as he's standing in front of you and has asked for a line, you call Central Credit. 'Central,'" Hudson explained, "is the casino-credit reporting agency, the TRW of the gambling industry, which is hooked up to casinos all over the world—Atlantic City, Europe, the islands, Down Under—and you get a credit rundown. Central tells you that he's got a fifty-K line at the Hilton and eighty-thou at the Desert Inn. So you know that he's 'good pay.' The single most important credit information you can get on a guy is his track record.

"Then you want to establish his maximum line. You tell him, 'Mr. F, I'm going off duty soon, so I'll be leaving. I'll be back in the morning. What's the maximum you want us to hold you to tonight? How much is enough till I see you again tomorrow?'"

"'Well, how about that fifty grand?'"

"You say, 'Are you sure? I'm going home and I don't want to get a call at three in the morning that you want another fifty.'

"'I think fifty should hold me. I'm not planning to lose it all, you know.'"

"You give him the fifty and go home.

"Now listen to me, Steve. This is important. Hosts often

get calls at home at three in the morning. Are you a heavy sleeper?"

"Sleep? You're kidding me, right?" Cyr scoffed.

Hudson eyed him critically, sizing him up differently all of a sudden. "You don't need to answer this, but I have to ask it. Why don't you sleep?"

"Excitement, baby! All this action revs me out of my mind. I'll stay here all night to be around it. Phone calls at three a.m.? Bring 'em on."

"All right, then," Hudson continued, satisfied that Cyr's sleep habits were due to adrenaline and not amphetamines. "Your phone rings, waking you up. The first thing you want to know is, 'What time is it?'

"You hear, 'Three-thirty,' from a voice at the casino.

"Obviously, you know it's about Mr. F, but you ask anyway. Then you say, 'Tell me what he looks like.'

"You hear, 'He looks like he's had way too much to drink. He's lost up to his credit limit.'

"You ask, 'Has he gone through his TTO?' TTO stands for 'this trip only' and refers to an automatic ten to twenty percent extra advance on a credit line that pit bosses are authorized to extend to a player who's maxed out. You understand?"

"Yes, sir."

"Now you hear, 'Yeah. He demanded I call you and get the other fifty you talked about.'

"So now, your guy's down sixty thousand or so and he wants another fifty. It's a tough moment for a host—especially right after being woken up. The good hosts prefer not to give their gamblers more firepower. The guy might get hot and win back his sixty, and another sixty to boot. Me, I want to take the sixty and go back to sleep. I like to lock it up. I've already won it, so I take it. Tomorrow's another day.

"So you say into the phone, 'All right, here's what I want you to do. I want you to put your arm around him and walk him back toward the elevators. Tell him I'll be there at nine a.m. and I don't want him losing any more money to-night. Tell him he'll thank me in the morning.'

"The wise casino host, not to mention the wise credit executive," Guy Hudson, senior credit executive at Caesars, drummed into Cyr's head, "knows one thing: It's the player's responsibility to set his own limit, and it's the casino's responsibility to hold him to it. It's that simple. The last thing a host wants to do is damage his top players. If he's got a deal going with his man for fifty thousand, plus another five or ten grand, that's the way the deal's supposed to go down. In the heat of the moment, it might pain you to maintain the line and it definitely stings the player to be held to it. But in the morning, both you and your player will know that the right thing was done."

Cyr learned later, of course, that it's often not so cut and dried. There's also a time to be aggressive. Not greedy or fearful, but confident.

Greedy: Maybe my guy'll lose the second $50,000 and then I'll be an even bigger hero.

Fearful: Maybe my gambler'll get mad about being held to his line. If he swims away, I might never find another fish like him again.

Confident: If he's an established customer who's come in, played a half-dozen times, and paid off his markers, and I know he's solid, I can take a reasonable shot with an extra fifty. Maybe he's got $1 million in the bank. Maybe he's chasing his losses and will keep losing. Hell, he might even go over to the DI to tap into his credit there, win, and pay us with their money.

By 1990, Cyr's mentor Hudson had been in the business 20 years. After two decades in the trenches, he had a sixth sense about what a player would and wouldn't do—how much he'd lose, how much he'd win, how far to string him out, so that the casino could not only collect it all, but the player could walk out the door smiling, knowing he'd gotten a run for money he could afford to lose.

Hudson was old school, so he was constitutionally inclined to be conservative (thinking long term), as opposed to aggressive (giving into the greed or fear and getting all you can *now*). He lectured Cyr, "You never want to bury anyone. That's the worst thing you can do to a player. You always want repeat business. Is it New Year's Eve? You want him to come back for the Super Bowl. And two weeks after that you've got your Sweetheart Party for Valentine's Day. A month later is the NCAA Final Four college-basketball championships or a St. Patrick's Day event. In a twelve-week period, you're banging a guy six times. If you burn him out at your joint, he'll go somewhere else. See to it you keep the suckers well within their ability to play and pay.

"Remember that term, Steve," Hudson emphasized. "Play and pay. In time you'll come to appreciate that it's the secret of success in this business. The idea is to have every gambler in the world sending you money every month—it's like being on the gambler's payroll. Good steady players are annuities. The casino can collect a set amount, month after month, year after year. Why break them?"

Hudson tutored Cyr, and though he wasn't authorized to green-light this eager kid to try out his cash-host idea, he also figured Cyr wouldn't wait for permission anyway. And sure enough, it wasn't long before he made his move. One night, he cut into a crap game as if he'd done it a thousand times before and said, "Hey, I'll comp his dinner." The floorman was grateful and the player was grateful and what the pit boss didn't know wouldn't hurt him. Now the marketing department, rather than operations, was hosting a fish—as it should be. And he was Steve Cyr's fish.

But the marketing bosses still recognized only two kinds of hosts: slots *or* tables. They called Cyr on the carpet, told him he was out of control—giving tours of suites, comping crapshooters, promising the Bacchanal to mere slot players—and what did he have to say for himself?

What Cyr said (which is better lost in the mists of history) got him termed. He knew he was right, that the limp dicks couldn't see the future when it was banging them over the head, so he didn't waste time pouting. He went back to the Desert Inn and re-sold himself to Mike Sterling as a cash host—something Sterling had neither heard of nor imagined. But Sterling recognized a good idea. He also knew how Cyr worked—always selling, always closing—so he gave him another shot.

The kid had no fear of approaching anyone—slot players, crap players, blackjack players. "Hi, I'm Steve Cyr and I'm a host here and my job is to take care of you." And he didn't just hand a big player his card and hope he'd call. He introduced the player around, to the dealers, bosses, maitre d's, concierges. He showed him the suites. He checked up on him in the restaurant and showroom, making sure he was getting the service a big fish deserved.

Of course, he was still putting on something of a show—playing, rather than being, the part of a cash host. He hadn't even turned 25 yet. And some of these table-game players took him into scary territory.

The first time he watched a player lose $15,000 making $100 bets at a blackjack table, he was so pop-eyed that he had to call home to tell his Dad. And a week later, when a guy dropped $25,000 in an hour at the crap table, Cyr got physically sick to his stomach. More than a year's pay, right over the table! But the Steve Cyr show went on and he turned cockier as he went, until one night he didn't even introduce himself when he approached a guy at a dice game. All he said was, "Hey, you're a Desert Inn kinda player and I just bought you dinner at Portofino." Then he handed him the comp, shook hands, and walked away, thinking, *Am I cool or what!*

He wanted the players to ask the dealer or floorman, "Who was that masked man?" He wanted *them* to want to know *him*. He wanted them to chase after him. He wanted the dealer to say, "That's Steve Cyr. He's the man."

And when they did track him down, he wanted them to feel like they'd made it to the juice—because now they knew Steve Cyr.

3

Storming Barron's Joint

One of the first items on Steve Cyr's agenda when he got to Las Vegas as a 19-year-old was to join an athletic club. He'd played football, basketball, and tennis in high school and he intended to stay in shape. He gravitated to the Sporting House, at that time the largest athletic club in Nevada.

One of the first people he met at the Sporting House was Denny Mason. Cyr beat up Mason one on one at basketball and Mason said, "Hey, I don't want to go up against you anymore. I want you to be on my team." But it wasn't so much Cyr's playing skills that impressed Mason, it was his attitude. Cyr could trash-talk with the best of them and that's what Mason, a telemarketer by trade, instantly liked about him. For his part, Cyr learned quickly that Mason was a gambler who could put four-figure cash deposits in cages all over town.

Someone mentioned to Cyr that Mason was in telemarketing. It went in one ear and out the other. But he remembered it one day toward the end of his second stint at the Desert Inn, when Mike Sterling called him into his office with an idea: "Steve, I want you to take on a big job for us. I want you to hire four or five people and be in charge of the telemarketing operation at the Desert Inn."

"You got it!" Cyr responded. "And thank you for your confidence in me, Mr. Sterling. I won't let you down."

After work, he rushed over to the Sporting House and found Denny Mason.

"Denny, you're in telemarketing, right?'

Denny nodded.

"Well, the DI just put me in charge of telemarketing. Denny, what *is* telemarketing?"

"Well, Steve, it's selling things over the phone."

And whack! Another nail was hammered into the old-school casino-marketing coffin.

It didn't happen overnight, to be sure. In fact, Cyr had barely touched index finger to telephone dial before he was fired again after mouthing off to the wrong boss for the last time. From the DI, he went back for a second round at Caesars as a slot host, tramping the floor and greeting the walk-ins, the intimidated, and the comp-ignorant. He also made a point of meeting as many unhosted blackjack and crap players making $25, $50, and $100 bets as he could. He wasn't brazen about it, but neither was he covert. Knowing and hating the Caesars system, he was well aware his days there were numbered no matter what he did.

He worked the brutal swing shift, 8 p.m. to 4 a.m., and one night at 3:55, when all he wanted to do was go home and collapse, a floorman paged him. Cyr went to the blackjack pit, where the boss pointed out a well-dressed middle-aged player firing up $5,000 a hand. *Huge* money.

This gambler had refused for hours to give his name to any number of floormen, bosses, and hosts. This was at a time in the history of casino gambling when Uncle was less intrusive into citizens' financial dealings, so players were able to remain anonymous if they so chose. Today, anyone who buys in for more than $3,000 in cash is subject to government scrutiny. This is the trigger point at which the casino must submit a Suspicious Activity Report to the Treasury Department if it appears to a floorman or boss that a player is trying to circumvent cash-reporting requirements. At a cash buy-in of $5,000 or more, a floorman must approach a player and warn him about Regulation 6-A, which requires the casino to demand government-issued identification—"Your paperz, pleez!"—from anyone who exceeds the $10,000 cash maximum. At $10,001, if the player agrees to supply ID, the house must submit a Currency Transaction Report by Casinos (CRTC) to the IRS. If he refuses, he's tossed out on his ass. But this wasn't about government regulations. Cyr's mission was to cut into this $5,000-a-hand player, get his name, and make sure he became a Caesars regular before he walked out the door.

Six hours later, at 10 a.m., the player, up $400,000, called it a night. Cyr didn't have his name yet, but he was still there, stalking him. The player told Cyr he was going to the restroom, but ducked through the side door and into a waiting limo. Cyr quickly commandeered a bellman and a luggage van, then followed the limo to the private-plane terminal at McCarran Airport. There, he got lucky. Twenty bucks to the ground crew bought him the player's name, Al Franco, and the name of his construction business in Phoenix.

When Cyr returned to Caesars, the bosses immediately called him into a meeting. He was expecting to be commended for taking an extra six hours of his own time to identify the gambler who'd just walked with nearly a half-million of their money. Instead, they termed him: unauthorized use of a company vehicle.

On the way out the door, he bumped into Guy Hudson and told him what happened. Hudson responded that he was leaving too, going to work at the Hilton, and told Cyr to hang tight. "Don't worry, kid. Something'll turn up."

A few days later, Cyr was talking over his employment prospects, or lack thereof, at the Sporting House with Denny Mason. "Call my guy Joey and tell him you're gonna be his number-one salesman," Mason suggested. Cyr did and Joey hired him on the spot to sell vitamins over the phone.

The deal was a year's supply of vitamins for $799 and the telemarketers made $200 a sale. Cyr's personal goal was two or three sales a day, 10 to 15 a week. So what if he had to call 500 people to do it? Soon he was making $10,000 a month, talking on the phone all day, and honing the skills that would help usher in the future of Las Vegas casino marketing.

Six months later in March 1990, Guy Hudson summoned Cyr to the Hilton and hired him.

❖ ❖ ❖

Guy Hudson arrived in Las Vegas in 1962 from Ft. Worth, Texas, where he'd worked as a teller at the Continental National Bank. He got a job at the Bank of Nevada, then at the Mint casino downtown, toiling in the cage as a cashier. In 1967, Hudson was hired as a cage cashier by the casino boss at the Flamingo, with whom he played golf on occasion. Guy earned $25 a shift, plus a free meal. He worked at the Flamingo for two years, learning the casino credit business from guys like Artie Newman and Marshall Burger; both had migrated to Las Vegas in the late '50s after working for years at casinos in Havana. When Kirk Kerkorian opened the International in July 1969, Hudson was hired on as the day-shift cage supervisor. He was 34 years old. A year later, after Kerkorian sold the International to Hilton, Hudson was working for the large hotel company.

In 1971, Hudson returned to the Flamingo Hilton as the vice president in charge of casino credit. For the next 12 years, he played an integral part in the Flamingo's expansion from 600 to 2,500 rooms and from $2 million to $40 million in annual profits. In 1983, he had a disagreement with his boss over a year-end bonus and left, going to work for Steve Wynn at the Golden Nugget downtown. After six years at the Nugget, he left to work at Caesars where, as Cyr had realized the moment he saw him, Hudson didn't fit in. Luckily for Hudson, the Hilton had an opening for a senior credit executive and he went back to his old company.

By that time, the Hilton had jumped into the high-roller

business in a big way and needed some fresh blood in the marketing department. The old-school hosts, Hudson saw immediately, were pulling down big-time salaries for what was essentially semi-retired status. And Steve Cyr was the only twentysomething Hudson knew who not only had the gumption and guts, but at least a little casino marketing experience, to step in and do the job.

Hudson sold Cyr to Lee Skelley, Hilton's casino manager, and Pete Castiglia, Hilton's slot marketing director, by telling them that they could steal Caesars' ballsiest young slot host (Cyr hadn't worked at Caesars for months, but Hudson knew that bosses liked to steal hosts from other properties). Hudson regaled them with stories of the kid's sales exploits: It didn't matter what Cyr sold—cars or vacuum cleaners, pizza or toilet paper, real estate or casino gambling—he'd sell more than anyone else in the world and Hudson made sure the Hilton bosses knew it.

"He'd make a great carney," Hudson told Skelley and Castiglia. "He'd have been Barnum or Bailey, either one. That's the kind of raw aggression, killer instincts, and raging imagination this kid has."

In addition, Hudson told them, Cyr was a worker. In Las Vegas in 1990, if you showed up to your job on time and stayed the whole day, you were already doing better than half the employees.

Even though his starting salary as a Hilton slot host was a mere $24,000 a year, Hudson knew full well that Cyr would show his stuff soon enough. He never, however, expected him to start showing it on his second day on the job.

The day before he was scheduled to report to work at the Hilton, Cyr flew to Phoenix on his own dime to harpoon his Caesars high roller, Al Franco. Franco turned out to be an extremely successful contractor who handled large construction projects all over the Southwest. Cyr cold-called him at his office. Franco remembered Cyr from his big night at Caesars and was impressed that the kid had tracked him down. He agreed to fly into Vegas and visit him that very weekend at the Hilton.

On his second day of work, Cyr was yawning and fidgeting through his training as a slot host when he was paged to the front desk to greet Al Franco. He had to grab Hudson to set up Mr. F with a credit line, a room, and meals. Franco lost $164,000 at the blackjack tables that weekend and on Monday morning, Lee Skelley and Pete Castiglia were eyeing the brash newcomer, wondering how the hell a slot host got hooked up with a blackjack bigwig.

Meanwhile, Cyr was prowling the casino floor like a hungry jackal, cutting into slot, crap, blackjack, even baccarat players, acting like he owned the joint. "Hi, Steve Cyr at your service. Can I buy you dinner tonight at Benihana?" Or, "Can I take you to dinner at Le Montrachet?" Or, "How about two tickets to Wayne Newton?" Or, "You've never seen our suites? When you're done playing, have me paged. I'll give you the whole tour." Always selling. Always closing.

By the end of the first week, it was clear to the bosses that Cyr was ballsy, and too confined in his role as a slot host. Problem was, there was still no such thing as a floor or cash host at the Hilton, and they were reluctant to rock the old-school boat too hard. So the day his business cards, the ones that read "Steve Cyr, Slot Host," came back from the printer, Cyr was promoted to "Director of Casino Support Services," a department of one, and given a desk in the marketing office sitting behind Johnny Oakes.

Johnny Oakes started his casino career in the early '50s at the Sahara, as usual, in operations as a cage cashier. In the late '60s, he moved over to the Flamingo, then the International. By the time Steve Cyr showed up, he'd been the most popular Hilton host for 20 years, except for a short interlude at the Desert Inn, where Cyr met him. After getting into a beef with Barron Hilton, who fired him, Oakes went to work at the Desert Inn for Mike Sterling. A short time later, Hilton relented and brought him back. Mike Sterling himself arrived shortly thereafter to work in the Hilton's fledgling international marketing department. It was pure serendipity that Cyr and three of his mentors—Hudson, Oakes, and Sterling—all found a home at the Hilton at the same time.

With his own desk upstairs, Cyr's hunger for players turned ravenous. Fresh from the vitamin boiler room, Cyr begged Skelley and Castiglia to let him get on the phone and hunt table-game players. Even though dialing for gamblers had been taboo since Thomas Edison, they agreed. They were already aware that the kid was relentless in his approach to work and life. They recognized that he was selling *them* as much as the players. They knew he'd hound and pester them till they gave him the green light. They also suspected he'd find it wasn't as easy to recruit high rollers as he thought. It might be a good lesson for him: knock off some of the cockiness, make him eat a little crow.

Cyr went back to his cubicle, got on the phone, and called Denny Mason. He said, "Denny, if you come down here right now, I'll give you a credit line of forty thousand. You can take up to ten thou right off the top. Also, I'll buy you a nice dinner at Le Montrachet."

This was the first Mason had heard of casino credit lines. He'd always been a strictly play-and-pay kind of guy. If he didn't have the money and wanted to be in the action, he took a cash advance on his Visa card. And now his basketball buddy was telling him he could sign a table marker and receive $10,000 in checks, then mosey over to the cage, cash out, and walk. Didn't even have to gamble. Had 30 days to pay it back. Interest-free.

Denny made a beeline for the Hilton, filled out all the bank and credit forms, and signed on the dotted line. Cyr called the bank, which verified that he had six figures in his account. Then he went back to Skelley and Castiglia— "Okay, here's a forty-thousand-dollar player. Everything checks out. He wants to come around tonight and have dinner."

The whole transaction took less than an hour.

Cyr returned to his desk with the comp and Denny said, "You know, I've got a friend who'll love this deal. You've met him—Doug, from the Sporting House." Denny called Doug, who made a beeline for the Hilton and filled in the paperwork. Everything checked out. Cyr went back to Skelley and Castiglia— "Okay, I've got another guy who's good for forty-thou and he wants to have dinner tomorrow night."

Within the first two hours of getting the go-ahead as a table-games host, he'd produced two five-figure players. And that was in addition to Al Franco, the bigwig who'd come over from Caesars on Cyr's initiative. Now the Hilton casino and marketing bosses didn't have to wonder what Guy Hudson was trying to pull. They recognized a cobra-charmer when they saw one. Skelley and Castiglia knew they could direct the kid to do anything: "Go out and catch this poisonous snake. Don't get bit. Just put a chain on it and bring it in."

They increased Cyr's salary by $12,000. It was a 50% raise. After two months on the job, he was making $36,000.

❖   ❖   ❖

The next thing Cyr did was have a long chat with Johnny Oakes, whom he sat near in the marketing office. Oakes, one of Las Vegas' original snake charmers, was a great people person. He'd never met a player he didn't like. Players would tell other players, "If you're going to Vegas, stop in and see Johnny Oakes." For decades, he didn't have to do a thing—except sit there and let high rollers come to him.

Cyr asked Oakes where he might get leads on players. "Are there any lists of gamblers with credit lines at the Hilton, but without established hosts?"

Oakes shrugged; he didn't know from lists.

Cyr couldn't believe his ears. "You mean, nobody's working any old leads?"

Oakes suggested he check the marketing database.

So Cyr approached the Hilton information techs, the keepers of the credit files, and had them run a list of customers who lived in Southern California, had lost at least $10,000 lifetime at the Hilton, and hadn't been to the casino in two years. The list came back with more than 1,000 names. Bingo!

Why hadn't these players been back? Lots of reasons. Hosts left, taking their gamblers with them. Even if a host didn't swipe his players, many were simply forgotten. Hosts also burned out or nickel-and-dimed players who were too pissed off to return. And plenty of players were unhosted walk-ins who applied for casino credit, lost $5,000 or $10,000 or $15,000, had a floorman comp a coffee-shop dinner, and walked out again, without ever meeting a marketing guy. For whatever reason, 1,000 profitable players had taken their losing ways elsewhere.

To narrow down the possibilities, Cyr went back and asked the computer guys to give him a more detailed list, including three qualifiers used by hosts to assess a player's worth: game choice, game strategy, and theoretical loss.

As for game choice, casinos prefer gamblers to play craps, roulette, and baccarat over blackjack. The former trio are negative-expectation games, meaning the house has a built-in advantage on every bet. Hence, the more hours played, the more money the house makes.

In most cases, the house makes its money by paying less than true odds on winning bets. This results in an edge that's working on every spin of a wheel, roll of the dice, or deal of the cards. For example, they rake about a penny and a quarter off winning $1 banker or player bets at baccarat, a penny and a half off $1 line bets at craps, around a nickel off $1 bets at roulette, and 30¢ or more off $1 bets at keno.

A tight crapshooter who sits on the pass and come lines and takes full odds (a house advantage of less than 1%) is less valuable to the casino than one who plays the field (5.6%), hardways (9%-11%), and other bad-odds propositions on the dice layout. The casino loves these longshot suckers, as well as roulette and baccarat players. The bosses and bean counters even have a fondness for blackjack players who rely heavily on hunches. A poor-strategy 21 gambler, or one who plays one of blackjack's new derivative formats (such as a single-deck game with a 6-5 payoff for naturals), may buck a house edge of 2%-3%.

When this blackjack sucker is making 60 or more $500 bets an hour, he has a "theoretical loss" or "theo" of upwards of $750 an hour ($500 per hand times 60 hands times a 2.5% edge equals $750). This is how the house quantifies his value. Conversely, a solid 21 player who employs basic strategy (a set of inviolable playing decisions based on the total of the gambler's cards against the dealer's up card) might be giving up as little as .2%, thus having a theo of a mere $60 an hour ($500 per hand times 60 hands times the .2% edge equals $60).

Obviously, Cyr was looking for losers—and he found them easily, by crunching the relevant data from marketing's player files. His second list consisted of every player from the first list who had at least a $10,000 credit line and at least a $200 average bet, played craps, roulette, baccarat, or poor-strategy blackjack, had an average theo per trip of $6,000, and hadn't been to the hotel for one year. It contained 375 names.

Then he went through the Central Credit files of those 375 players. He looked at dozens of them a day, paying particular attention to monthly income, mortgage and car payments, credit-card debt, and, especially, the amount of money owed to competing casinos. He made lists of players with credit lines in the low fives ($10,000 to $25,000), mid-fives ($25,001 to $75,000), high fives ($75,001 to $99,999), and low, mid, and high sixes (early on, Hudson wouldn't let him touch seven-figure players). He developed a sort of shorthand by which he could size up a player with information from four categories: credit line, average bet, largest loss, and largest win. He compiled the 50 most promising prospects—and he never again worried about where his next player would come from.

Hitting the telephone, he waded though the walls of secretaries and assistants and wives and answering machines. His initial goal was just to get the player on the line. He might not close him immediately, but he could sell him. Every gambler who'd take a phone call from Steve Cyr was potential money in the bank. Every phone call brought him closer to the close. Every "no" got him within striking distance of a "yes." After all, these were gamblers and he was offering them the run of the casino candy store.

Oakes, Hudson, Skelley, Castiglia all heard Cyr calling and calling and calling, capturing players, booking a new $25K or $50K or $75K guy every day, like clockwork. They could see that he was breaking the taboos and developing a new way of hunting whales in the desert, and they let him. The day his business cards, the ones that read "Steve Cyr, Director of Casino Support Services," came back from the printer, the bosses made him a bona fide "Casino Marketing Executive."

❖ ❖ ❖

Although his $36,000-a-year salary was a mere third of what he made as a telemarketer, for the first few months he didn't care. He was learning the lay of High Roller Land. But after a while, he started to suspect that the old-school hosts hung around the office all day, clinging to their traditions, simply because they couldn't be bothered to do the job. They sat by the phone like the Maytag repairman, waiting for customers to ring, because they had neither the know-how nor the balls to cold-call a new gambler and get him in. The worst relics begrudged making an appearance in the casino for any reason, even when a stray player happened to fall through the door.

In their defense, the older hosts had spent the past 10 or 15 or even 20 years in a stagnant market. Las Vegas in the '70s and '80s was in the doldrums, barely managing to hold its own, especially after gambling was legalized in New Jersey in 1977. There weren't too many new domestic players showing up (it was the casinos' international marketing departments that were bringing home the bacon).

And although Cyr couldn't realize it at the time, a 26-year-old hotshot running around in a frenzy 10 hours a day made the slower-moving 55-year-olds look like slugs. But it didn't mean their brains weren't clicking. A holdover host might have sat in the marketing office or stood in a pit looking like he was about to keel over, yet he could reel off 20 things that were going on around him (including what Steve Cyr was doing).

Of course, while they could *see* what Cyr was doing, they didn't necessarily *understand* it.

At a marketing meeting, an old-school rep actually wondered aloud where the kid found all these players. For the first time, Cyr lost it. "They're in the fuckin' database! They're right there! You want some of these names? How many? Here! Call 'em!"

At the same meeting, another relic bragged that he'd bagged a player the previous weekend at a $100 blackjack table. "Big fuckin' deal!" Cyr was on a roll. "The guy's already *in* the joint! He walked in on his own because he saw a billboard or heard about Le Montrachet or wanted to see Wayne Newton. Tell you what, Ned. Call this guy, Mr. G, who told me on the phone an hour ago that he hates the Hilton, that it's boring and has nothing to offer, and see if you can get *him* in."

The old hosts were under attack, but they couldn't change. They slinked back to their offices and waited by their phones. And then, when a customer did happen to call, wanting to stay in a Classic Suite on the 29th floor, one of the silver-haired slugs would check him on the computer and say, "Gee, I'm sorry, Mr. H. I know you've got a hundred-thousand-dollar line, but you've got to be at two hundred to stay in a Classic. Unfortunately, you fall a hundred grand short."

Cyr would overhear this and go back to the database. He'd learn that the Classic Suites were running at about a 20% annual occupancy. The hosts were not only leaving the rooms empty, they were actually chasing off a big player, just because some limp dick told him it was a $200,000 credit line or no suite.

He'd do the arithmetic: 365 days in a year, at 20% occupancy, let's see, those suites are empty almost 300 nights. Why? Because the bonehead bosses wouldn't budge off the criterion.

He kept pushing. He'd check the reservations on Thursday after lunch, knowing that if a Classic Suite wasn't booked by then, it would sit empty all weekend. Why? Because if an established domestic player hadn't reserved by Thursday, he wasn't coming. And international players didn't fly in from Japan or Malaysia or Saudi Arabia on a whale whim. So Cyr unilaterally lowered the criterion, called his fence-sitters—guys from California or Texas just waiting for a good reason to show up that weekend—and said, "If you come in tomorrow and bring fifty Gs, I'll give you the Renaissance Suite for two nights."

Cyr was daring the entire executive staff to say something to him. He didn't care. Even if someone did get up the gumption to confront him, he was loaded for bear. "What's the value of a fuckin' suite? Twenty-two hundred dollars a night? Think again! It's nine p.m. and you haven't rented it? The value is zero. Nada. Zippo. Zilch. How much does it cost you to give it to a player, *any* player? Nine dollars an hour—which is what a union maid makes to clean it. There's no debt on the suite; the building's been paid for ten times over. Don't tell me we're better off leaving it empty unless a two-hundred-thousand-dollar player can stay in it. It costs thirty-six dollars to clean. And meanwhile, the guy I put up there lost eighteen K over the weekend. The proof's in the pudding, baby."

For Cyr, there was no such thing as bad publicity. He didn't give it a second thought when he got chewed out or written up or if another host said something derogatory about him to the bosses. He laughed when he heard them crying, "How come all we ever hear about is Steve Cyr, Steve Cyr, Steve Cyr?"

Cyr snickered. "How come that's all you hear? Because I'm out there workin'!" Sure, he was pushing the envelope, but the numbers didn't lie. He was bringing in the sheaves while the relics were resting on their laurels.

It didn't matter a bit to him when a supervisor from another property called to complain that he'd invaded his property looking to steal players. On one occasion during his first few months at the Hilton, Cyr heard that a big player, Mr. I, was heating up a dice table at the Stardust. So he high-tailed it over there, and though he was caught a little short with only $200 in his pocket, he headed straight for the high-limit crap game.

He stood next to Mr. I, bet on a few rolls, then leaned in close. "If this shooter sevens out, I'm tapped."

"Don't worry, kid," the high roller told him. "The night's young. We'll get 'em in the end."

Moment-of-truth time: "Well, Mr. I, I have a confession to make. It's true about this being my last bet, but I'm not really a dice player. I'm Steve Cyr from the Hilton and you're either gonna love me or hate me, but I've got a limo and a bottle of Dom waiting outside, and a Classic Suite on the twenty-ninth floor, if you'll come over and gamble at my house."

"You're shittin' me!" This kid losing his last dollar to get him over to his own casino so tickled Mr. I that he cashed out, went to the Hilton, and proceeded to lose $43,000.

The next morning, the head host at the Stardust called one of Cyr's bosses and complained that he'd poached a player right out from under their noses. The boss made all the appropriate apologetic noises, then called in Cyr and, trying mightily to stifle his amusement, said, "Just don't get caught again."

Another time early on, Cyr heard about Mr. J, a high roller from Birmingham, Alabama, who always played at the Desert Inn. He telephoned VIP Services at the Desert Inn, claiming to be Mr. J and telling a hostess he wanted to make sure she had his correct address and phone number on file. "I don't want mail going to my ex-wife, honey," he said, sounding like Colonel Sanders. "What address and phone number do y'all have for me?"

After getting the contact information, any other angle shooter would've thanked her and rung off. Not Cyr. He proceeded to tell her that her information was wrong, then gave her a batch of bogus numbers. The correct data was being deleted from the Desert Inn marketing computer while Cyr cold-called and closed Mr. J—another customer in the burgeoning black book of the hell-bent young host.

❖ ❖ ❖

Steve Cyr whirled around the Hilton like a Persian dervish, both impressing and horrifying his old-school bosses and the holdover hosts.

But the kid still had a number of lessons to learn, some painful. Guy Hudson was on hand when Cyr hosted his first quarter-million-dollar loser. This particular evening, Cyr's megaroller, Mr. K, lost the $250,000 fast; it was the limit of his credit and he demanded more.

Cyr wanted to take him to a half-million.

Hudson, in charge of credit, told him no. "If he loses the rest of the half-million, it'll bust him out. That's all his money. And you'll have big trouble collecting."

But Cyr was too overcome by the half-million moment to listen. The player went to dinner, Hudson went home, and Cyr hit up the swing-shift credit manager to double Mr. K's line, which he promptly lost. And lo and behold, it *was* all the money he had in the world. Mr. K was flat broke and he left without paying up. (Later, Mr. K sued, necessitating a countersuit from the Hilton.)

This incident was instructive in three critical areas. First, Cyr not only didn't realize, but he simply couldn't *believe*, that anyone would gamble more than they could afford to lose. He didn't understand chasing losses, steaming, going on tilt, none of the ways that gamblers go haywire.

Second, at that point in his career, he believed players when they said, "The hell with you. If you don't give me more credit, I'm never coming back!" The old-school hosts like Oakes had told him to believe it; for them it was true. Customers used to be loyal to the hosts and the joints. When a customer said, "I'm never coming back," he meant it. (Today, Cyr just laughs every time someone threatens to walk away forever. They all come back. They can't help it, he claims; they're degenerates.)

And third, he gained a deeper respect for Hudson's expertise and he never, ever, went around him again.

That Monday morning, Hudson sat Cyr down and reminded him of the two sets of three magic words that every conservative host should live by: "lock it up" and "play and pay."

"You're in the big leagues now, Steve," Hudson hammered home. "These aren't dollar slot players or twenty-five-dollar blackjack bettors. If a small-timer loses his checking account, his savings account, the kids' college fund, the wife's trust fund, his house, his car, his watch, that's his problem. But a big-time degenerate with a quarter-mil in casino credit? That's the casino's problem.

"The sad thing," Hudson coached, "is that you can't, at the end of the day, protect the customer from his own weaknesses. How many casinos are there within walking distance right on the Strip?"

"Lots."

"And how many big players have high credit lines at each one?"

"Plenty."

"So when some guy stumbles through the door and he's firing high and away and you know he's got a problem, you can get concerned. You can ask him where he's been, then make a quick call to that property and talk to a host who'll tell you, 'Yeah, he just lost a hundred fifty, which is fifty more than he can afford.' And when he asks you for credit, you can try to protect him by refusing.

"But you also know that he'll probably just walk next door and a hungry host over there won't be so morally minded."

Hudson had worked with dozens of hosts around town who enjoyed burning out players. Totally greedy. Mean-spirited. The casino industry attracts them like moths to a flame. Some hosts like nothing more than to seduce players, bust them out, and forget about them. On to the next victim, the next high-rolling sucker.

Like the player rep at a casino down the street who took Mr. L, a high roller with a $100,000 credit line, all the way up to $800,000, a hundred grand at a time. Mr. L was drunk and on tilt. The host didn't break him—Mr. L had plenty of money—but, Hudson lectured Cyr, it was the wrong thing to do. It was irresponsible. It was immoral. The host wanted to show his bosses how much money he could take this player for. But it came back to haunt him.

Mr. L called his old friend Guy Hudson and asked about his options.

Hudson told him, "Fax me copies of all the paperwork." Then he set up a meeting with the owner of the host's casino, whom he knew. He showed the owner the documentation, with the times the markers were issued and how they went up by $100K one right after the other. "This is outta line," Hudson argued. "You know it, I know it, and the host knows it. My guy's good for it, but if you don't show him some speed, he could make it difficult on you."

The owner and the player got together and worked out a settlement. Hudson didn't even work for that casino. But now he had the undying loyalty of a player who knew that even though it was Hudson's job to get him to lose in his own joint, he was still looking out for him.

Before Hudson, practically any host in the Hilton marketing department could authorize a credit line: Take the player's financials, verify them with the bank and Central Credit, then give him whatever he wanted. Indeed, when Hudson first got to the Hilton, if a player stumbled through the door and had a valid driver's license, Hudson himself would almost automatically give the guy a $10,000 line of credit.

But he soon learned that the Hilton's hosts weren't responsible for collecting when their players lost. That was solely up to the collection and legal departments. The hosts didn't have to work off the collections, so they had no reason to care how much a guy lost.

As soon as Hudson snapped to this, he began making the hosts come to meetings and answer some pertinent questions. "How come this guy hasn't paid? How come this guy's late? How come this other guy's late? They're all your guys." He made the hosts responsible for the losses. He knew from long experience that casino receivables can quickly get out of control if hosts aren't accountable for collecting.

Hudson lectured Cyr, "It's a delicate balance for a host to try to maintain a business relationship with his players on the one hand and be their friend on the other. But it can be done."

In the end, he explained, it all boils down to personality. Hudson's temperament was diametrically opposed to that of the senior casino managers up and down the Strip who didn't like to fraternize with the customers. These bosses rarely went to dinner, played golf, or stood around the tables with the players. They might've been reserved, but they probably pretended to be more introverted than they actually were in order to keep their player relationships on a strictly business basis. That way they didn't have to fade the contradictions inherent in the gambler-host dynamic. They kept the hosts between themselves and the players.

Hudson, conversely, believed that the contradictions were manageable and, incidentally, he liked to have a good time. He enjoyed going out with the customers. Not to other hotels; he'd never take a customer to another joint—which would break another cardinal rule of old-school hosting. But he liked dining with them and playing golf with them and accompanying them on trips. He still counts a number of his players among his close friends, which is another reason he was not about to let them get buried—not by the bosses, the hosts, or anyone. At the Hilton, when one of his underlings overextended one of his friends, Guy Hudson, senior vice president of casino credit, got upset, which meant that heads would roll.

❖ ❖ ❖

Steve Cyr was in his element. He'd found his calling. He was working in the casinos, at a career he'd prepared himself for, it seemed to him, all his life. He was in the thick of the action—the high-stakes gambling, the five- and six-figure deals, the limo rides and luxury suites and gourmet meals. He was matching wits with megarollers. He was learning to manipulate the greed and fear of his players and to manage the love and fever in himself. Every moment on the job seemed superheated—and, perhaps inevitably, it spilled over into his personal life, rendering the line between the two thin and blurred.

He drew inspiration from others like him. Checking into an L.A. hotel, he immediately noticed the bellman, who was either a luggage performance artist or on methedrine, or both. This hyper baggage handler picked up Cyr in the hotel lobby and led him to his room, double time, rapping like a ma-

chine-gun the whole way. About the hotel. About the neighborhood. About the weather. About the other bellmen. At
the room, he opened the door with a flourish, ushered him
in, hoisted the suitcase onto the luggage rack, hung the garment bag in the closet, closed the blinds, cranked up the a/c,
turned on the bathroom light, the whole time tapping out a
staccato tour of the room.

Cyr, a connoisseur of the congenial con, pulled a wad
from his pocket and started riffling the single dollar bills.
The bellman quickly grabbed the remote, turned on the TV,
and started showing him how to use the onscreen hotel di-
rectory and channel guide. When Cyr exposed a fiver, the
bellman offered to run to the liquor store for a bottle or two
or the diner across the street for some take-out. Finally, Cyr
flicked a sawbuck off the roll and walked the crazed bellman
toward the door, who by this time was whispering, "Girls?
Boys? You name it, I deliver. Just ring the bell desk ..." while
grabbing his luggage cart and hustling into the hall with ten
bucks for a two-minute act. Cyr knew he'd seen an artist at
work and made a mental note about his own act.

He also realized he *needed* bellmen. Cyr began haunting
the competing casinos, talking to luggage handlers, security
guards, cage cashiers, VIP hostesses, dealers, floormen, pit
clerks, hosts, cocktail waitresses. Any front-line employee
in a position to know anything about big players could become a node in a network of casino moles he might orga-
nize. He approached them, introduced himself, passed out
business cards, and told them any information that helped
him hook a big fish would earn them dinner for two at
Benihana, or possibly Le Montrachet, or even two tickets to
Wayne Newton. Always selling, baby, always closing.

The downside was that he had to go back to the limp
dicks and browbeat them into setting him up with what's
known as a CNC, or comp non-casino account, to pay off his
moles. At his peak, Cyr was writing $10,000 in mole comps *a
month.*

While waiting to pick up a player at the airport, Cyr noticed several limo drivers standing around holding signs with players' first and last names on them: The Mirage Welcomes Mr. Gnossos Pappadopoulis. Caesars Palace Welcomes Mr. Hank Stamper. The Tropicana Welcomes Mr. Switters. He walked up to the limo drivers, handed out twenties, and asked how high their passengers bet. One driver might say, "I don't know, but I'm taking him to the back Mirage entrance"—the high-roller drop-off area for the villas. Another might offer, "This guy's staying in the Genghis Khan Suite, so he's probably the biggest player in the joint tonight. But he's a stiff: never tips." A third might have the whole story, "He brings two-hundred fifty Gs with him. His average bet is twenty-five hundred. He can lose it all, but if he gets ahead a little, he stops. His date of birth is February twenty-sixth, nineteen forty-six." This driver? Cyr would hand him his card, write him a comp for four to Benihana on the spot, and invite him to call if he ever considered becoming a host.

Every time he went out to the airport, he came back with at least two or three new leads. With the player's first and last names, the casino, and a brief description, he could cold-call the mark and try to lure him over to the Hilton for dinner.

His voracious appetite for hot leads extended to Hilton's other hosts as well. Another unwritten rule held that as long as a host's customer had come in within the past year, the player was untouchable. But once that year was over, he was fair game. So Cyr returned to his good friends in the database department, spread around a little cash, got print-outs of the other hosts' players, and went looking for customers who hadn't shown up for 10 months. He selected the prime candidates, studied their Central Credit files, and at eleven and a half months performed telemarketing magic to bring them back to the Hilton—as *his* customers.

Suddenly, the other hosts started seeing Cyr with their

players. Cyr would shrug and say something like, "He told me you never returned his phone calls and were murder on the comp criteria. He's been playing over at the Tropicana where he *liked* his host. Besides, I waited a year before I went after him."

Once he'd perfected this particular player-development technique, he stopped abiding by the one-year rule. If one of the relics got lazy or did something to piss him off, Cyr went after his players with a vengeance. If the other host complained to the bosses, Cyr might get written up, but the host risked getting termed for the slug that he was.

Cyr even badgered the bosses for leads. He nipped at Oakes' and Hudson's heels like a yippy dog. And why not? They knew all the big players. If a new high roller asked to see Johnny Oakes, Oakes might discreetly slip him to Cyr. A few years away from retirement, he didn't want to make waves, but he did want to see the kid do well. If it'd been a few days since he'd gotten a lead, Cyr would tail Oakes around the casino till the old host got fed up and said, "All right already! Come on in," and he'd give him a couple of leads. Not only did Cyr have his names and numbers, he could also invoke the magic words, Johnny Oakes, when he cold-called the customer.

❖ ❖ ❖

In 1990, at the age of 26, over the course of his first year as a bona fide casino marketing executive, Cyr single-handedly added more than a million dollars to the bottom-line profit of Hilton Corporation. That was *after* all the deductions for his players' rooms, food, airfare, and other comps, including the CNC payoffs to his moles. Yet he was still green enough, and the mystique around the 50- and 60-year-olds in the office with their debonair airs was still mysterious enough, that he continued to wonder whether everyone was doing better than he was.

One evening early in 1991, in his never-ending quest for customers, he decided to paw through trash cans to see what he might find. What he found was a report requested by Barron Hilton himself, Chairman of the Board, with a list of all the hosts, their bottom-line profits, their pay, and their percentage of profit-to-pay.

Cyr found that he'd generated a $1.4 million profit to date, while making $36,000 a year. One of the holdovers, who'd worked at the Hilton since the day it opened ("And you're still a fuckin' host!" Cyr laughed at him), was making $125,000 in salary and had $220,000 in bottom-line profit—a pitiful net-to-salary ratio.

Obviously, he couldn't let anyone know he'd seen the report. Still, he was livid and on an impulse the next morning, he went into the office of the big boss of casino operations, Jimmy Newman, and told him he was quitting. He said he could sense that he was doing better than most of the geezers combined, but he was still low man on the payroll pole. Then he walked out and went home, planning to go over to the Golden Nugget or Flamingo the next morning. But later that day, Newman called. "Well, we've talked it over and decided to raise you to fifty-two thousand. Isn't that great? You're all of what? Twenty-six years old and making twice your age in salary—a grand a week!"

Cyr drove back to the office and pretended to be satisfied, knowing full well that the worst of the relics were still making double what he was. But he went right back to hustling. He liked the Hilton, especially working with Oakes and Hudson. Also, $52K really was big money for a 26-year-old and he figured he'd get used to it for a few months— knowing he could and would walk out again, then name his salary when they begged him to come back. Most importantly, though, he didn't relish even a one-day interruption of his march to become the best host who ever lived.

4

Turning the System on Its Head

In 1978, the debut of gambling in a derelict seaside resort in south Jersey ended Nevada's nearly 50-year monopoly on legal casino gambling. Before then, if you worked any job in a Nevada casino, you were considered a novelty, an object of curiosity. But if you were a dealer, floorman, or boss and told people anywhere outside of Nevada what you did for a living, you were accorded a status just short of movie (well, maybe TV) star.

In 1986, eight years after New Jersey got gambling, Steve Cyr announced to his family that he intended on making a career in the casino industry. His mother, Jean, warned, "You'd better like Las Vegas, because the only other place to work is Atlantic City."

Three years later, the industry changed forever. The Mirage, which opened in 1989, was the Big Bang of modern gambling. Steve Wynn's volcano-erupting, white-tiger-exhibiting, high-roller-vacuuming four-star megaresort manifested an immediate national interest in casino gambling, giving rise to riverboats in Iowa, casinos in historic mining towns in Colorado and South Dakota, hotel-casino strips on the Mississippi Gulf Coast and in Tunica, two huge Native American casinos in Connecticut, a dozen major Native operations in California and hundreds of small ones around the country, not to mention a relentless mushrooming of new megaresorts in Las Vegas.

The specific and direct changes that Steve Wynn wrought in Las Vegas involved architecture, spectacle, entertainment, and service. Wynn's volcano erupted on the half-hour, right on the Strip. A 20,000-gallon aquarium sat behind the front desk and a 100-foot-high glass dome allowed natural light, rare for a casino, to brighten the gambling tables. Wynn stole Siegfried and Roy from the Frontier, gave them a 1,700-seat showroom, and charged an unheard-of $72 per ticket.

Everything about the Mirage glowed with Steve Wynn's personal charisma and vision. Including the profits.

Wynn, in the process, also changed the face of the whale business. He built state-of-the-art high-roller villas with private entrances, along with a couple hundred mini-suites. His high-limit pit was one of the most lavish in the world. He coaxed superhost Charlie Myerson out to Las Vegas to handle East Coast high rollers. He raided the ranks of Caesars hosts, putting them under contract (host contracts didn't exist prior to the Mirage).

The floodgates were open.

Two months later, the Rio debuted in Las Vegas, catering to a growing class of wealthy young partiers who flocked to the casino to ogle the string-up-the-ass cocktail-waitress uniforms. And six months after that, the 4,000-room Excalibur opened directly across the Las Vegas Strip from the Tropicana, which alone had held down this intersection, now one of the busiest in the world, for 32 years. Suddenly, the bosses at Caesars, the Desert Inn, the Tropicana, the Hilton, and Bally's woke up, sniffed the air, and said, "Holy shit! We'd better start marketing."

But back in the dark ages of the early '90s, no one studied to be a player-development representative. Not even UNLV had a class in high-roller hosting. Only the senior operations managers and a remaining handful of wiseguy types dared aspire to the vaunted status of casino-marketing executive. In all the upscale joints, the hosts were the most glamorous employees. Though they didn't work too hard, they strutted around like kings, making cameo appearances in the casino with their big-money players, chatting briefly with the bosses. They were well-dressed, relaxed, smooth. Most were George. People genuinely respected and liked them; the dealers, floormen, and bosses thought, I'd sure love to do what *he* does.

Then Steve Cyr burst onto the scene. The Hilton pit personnel saw him 20 times a day, every day—either making arrangements for incoming players, introducing at-hand players, or waving goodbye to departing players. He sat and kibbitzed with his gamblers as they played. He made sure they were having fun. He coaxed them to tip more. He always livened things up. The dealers, bosses, waitresses, hostesses, clerks, maitre d's, bellmen, valets, and limo drivers all saw Steve Cyr busily, often frantically, being a casino-marketing executive. He was like *ten* old-school hosts combined.

He'd have one guy—Mr. M, say, a plumbing-supply wholesaler from Dubuque who'd never been to the Hilton—coming in with $75,000. It might've taken three months to close him over the phone, but finally Cyr seduced him with two tickets to a prizefight. As soon as Mr. M called back with arrival information, Cyr launched into action: He arranged limo pick-up at the airport, put in a suite request (and often defended his player, almost to the death, at the suite meeting, where the hosts fought over the limited accommodations available), ordered up a fruit basket and bottle of champagne from room service, and made dinner, show, golf and spa reservations.

Then he had to establish Mr. M's credit: Get him to fill out the faxed credit app, check his bank references and account numbers, pull his Central Credit file, determine his credit limit, and decide on the TTO.

When the weekend rolled around, it was showtime. On arrival day, Cyr dressed to kill—lucky black boxers peppered with little white dice, white dress shirt with 14-karat-gold dice cufflinks, power suit, tasteful tie, and black shoes polished to a high shine. He headed for VIP Services, where he grabbed the suite key, made sure it was set up, and met the limo driver. He'd greet Mr. M at McCarran with the limo—the old-school hosts never dreamed of meeting a player at the airport.

Back at the hotel, when Mr. M brought up the subject of checking in, Cyr scoffed. "What? You're a VIP. You don't stand around in line in the lobby like the low rollers." Then they'd go directly up to the suite. Waiting there were the fruit, champagne, and two tickets to the fight.

Everything was handled. Everything was smooth. And there was one last move: getting Mr. M into the casino. At the proper moment, Cyr would say, "Listen, Mr. M. I don't know if you want to fire it up now or later—I can take you to lunch or dinner and get you a massage—but I need to know what time you're gonna make me look like a superstar." Now it was Mr. M's turn to live up to his end of the deal, which meant risking those seventy-five Gs.

During the visit, Cyr checked up on Mr. M's play and comps. He called him at least once a day. He might congratulate him on his hot streak or commiserate with him over his losses. He might ask if there was anything he could do. Or he might have to bust Mr. M's balls about not showing the casino enough speed ("My boss is breathing down my neck. I gave you the suite and the ringside tickets. Now you need to play a little …"). Or he might have to call him on the carpet for being a comp whore ("Don't ask for another bottle of Cristal! You're killing me on these comps. My bosses are all over my ass …").

Mostly, though, the daily call meant that he'd be listening to about an hour of gambling stories. After all, the number-one thing gamblers love to talk about is gambling.

"Goddamn it, Steve! I was stuck fifty-thousand, fought tooth and nail back to even, and then I got creamed! Down sixty. Why? All because I wasn't on that fuckin' hard four!

I'm *always* on that fuckin' hard four! But I was playin' scared and didn't want to risk it. And wouldn't you know, that fuckin' hard four came up, I dunno, like six times in a row. ..."

"Damn, Mr. M! Maybe you should've been playing roulette," Cyr might rejoin. "We had a roulette player beat us out of a hundred and five Gs last night. A roulette player! Can you believe it?" Maybe it even happened, but Cyr'd say anything off the top of his head to hold up his end of the conversation.

"No! How'd he do that?"

"Who knows? He just loaded up his favorite numbers and got lucky. How else would someone win at roulette?"

Or, "Boy, did you see that line on the Super Bowl? You gonna lay the five on the Giants? Or you gonna take the Bills and hope Kelly doesn't have to leave the game early?" Slinging the lingo always warmed up a gambler.

Cyr invited Mr. M to dinner too, mainly because he didn't want him to go to another property, but also to befriend and sell him. If he and Mr. M hit it off, Cyr might meet him at a Hilton bar after the fight. Or even a Caesars bar. This was taboo by old-school rules—hosts *never* entertained their players off their own property—but Cyr didn't let that stop him. If he did, that would mean he could never take a player to a topless club! The two might even end up at Cyr's digs. Millionaires hanging out at his modest little two-bedroom condo, Cyr would marvel.

At the end of the trip, Cyr and Mr. M settled up the markers; Cyr also made sure that Mr. M's comps didn't exceed their agreement. Then the host would put the player in the limo to the airport and wish him a safe flight home.

When Mr. M got home, Cyr followed up, calling him to make sure his trip was satisfactory and sending him a thank-you card.

Finally, he had to collect any money owed on outstanding markers. He'd sweat it for 30 days, then go into collections mode till the debt was retired.

All this for one player.

Sometimes Cyr hosted two or three or four players over the same weekend. Five was his limit. He tried six once and nearly had a nervous breakdown.

Then it started all over again on Monday morning—the cold-calls, the deals, the details.

And so the young dealers and floormen now had a new style of host to watch—and be envious of.

❖ ❖ ❖

Meanwhile, Cyr kept thumbing his nose at the old school.

In 1991, the Hilton opened its VIP Services department, complete with a lounge and front desk. But in the eyes of the operations bosses, high rollers still weren't created equal: Slot players—the Rodney Dangerfields of the casino—weren't allowed. Cyr had to resurrect his old argument to get his machine Monstros the respect they deserved.

"My guy is feeding three-coin twenty-five-dollar machines!" he yelled at the bosses. "Do the arithmetic—six hundred spins an hour at seventy-five dollars a spin is no different than an hour of blackjack at seven-fifty a hand! Did you get that: *seven hundred and fifty a hand.* Only, my guy loses three times faster. *I'm* telling him he's welcome in the VIP lounge. If he isn't, *you* kick him out!"

❖ ❖ ❖

Cyr mined more high-roller ore from "bill-backs," the charges for big players from competing casinos coming over to see a headliner at the Hilton. When Wayne Newton or Engelbert Humperdinck or Tom Jones appeared in the show-room, the Hilton booked 10 or 12 bill-backs on an average weekend. A Mirage executive would call over to Hilton VIP Services and say, "Mr. N is coming over to see the show with his wife and two friends. Bill the tab back to me personally."

Only three or four executives at a casino could authorize bill-backs and they always specified the limit, usually $500 or $1,000, but it could go as high as "unlimited." Cyr liked the bill-backs, but he *loved* the unlimiteds.

Every weekend Cyr scanned the bill-back list and zeroed in on the best prospect for poaching. Mr. N, for example. The first item on Cyr's bill-back agenda was to grab Mr. N's tickets to the Wayner at the box office, duke the showroom maitre d' a twenty to reserve a king's-row booth, and personally instruct the VIP Services hostess to page him when Mr. N's party of four showed up.

Then the act started. "I'm sooooo sorry, Mr. N," the hostess told him. "There's no problem, don't worry, but I'll have to call Mr. Cyr."

Mr. Cyr, of course, already had the four tickets in his suit pocket. He delayed a few minutes, just to the point where Mr. N would be a little concerned. Then Cyr walked in and said, "Mr. N! How are ya? Remember me? Steve Cyr? I met you at the Mirage a few years ago."

"Sure, Steve, sure I remember." Of course, Mr. N couldn't possibly remember. Cyr'd only learned of Mr. N's very existence a few hours prior. Still, few gamblers ever risked embarrassing themselves by not "remembering."

"I don't know what happened; the Mirage must've forgotten about you. But I'm personally walking you right to the front of the show line. Kirsti, call down to the showroom and order up two bottles of Dom for Mr. N and his friends."

Now he had Mr. N thinking that, first, the Mirage had screwed up and second, that Cyr was a hero. On top of making everything right, the young host was also doling out $300 worth of champagne (for which the Mirage, of course, was paying full retail on the bill-back).

Meanwhile, Cyr's mole at the Mirage had already supplied him with the guy's vitals, so Cyr could run his Central and get him credit. After going to the cage and requisitioning four $500 promotional chips, he moseyed back to the booth in the showroom and said, "Hey, I feel really bad about you having to wait at VIP. Here's a couple thousand. After the show, go take a shot on Steve Cyr." Finally, at this point, he handed Mr. N and his friends his business card.

After the booth, the champagne, and the $2,000 in chips, Mr. N looked like a big wheel in front of his friends, who now couldn't wait to play off the free money at the tables. There, Cyr cut in again, carrying another bottle of Dom. Filling their glasses, he said, "You know, Mr. N, as a courtesy I arranged for ten thousand in credit for you, in case you get comfortable here and want to keep playing." Then he'd launch into his spiel about the great restaurants at the Hilton, and Tom Jones appearing for a month, and the Super Bowl party coming up. Always selling. Always closing. If Mr. N agreed, Cyr'd give him a tour of the suites. And if Mr. N was suitably impressed, Cyr might actually get him to move from the Mirage to the Hilton. He'd say, "C'mon, let's go get your bags and put you in the Hollywood Suite."

Meanwhile, the cocktail waitresses kept plying the group with expensive champagne. Soon, they got to a point where they were too embarrassed just to use up their free play and blow, so Mr. N signed a marker. Maybe they even had cash.

In the end, it looked like Cyr had given them four tickets to the Wayner, four bottles of Dom, and $2,000 in free play. Mr. N shook his hand, thanked him for a wonderful evening, and promised to call him soon for a return engagement. But Cyr hadn't *given* them anything. Mr. N lost $30,000 and became a Hilton customer in the process.

All while on loan from the Mirage of an evening.

❖ ❖ ❖

One weekend Mr. O put $50,000 cash in the cage, signed a marker for $5,000, and proceeded to go on a monster run. He wound up cashing out $125,000 at the cage and bought back the marker—but left the casino without retrieving the

$50,000 he'd put on deposit. Cyr waited for him to come back for his money, or at least to call about the extra cash, but after two months, Mr. O was a no-show. Cyr phoned to remind him about it. "Why don't you come in next weekend? You don't even have to bring any money. You've still got fifty large in the cage."

"I do?"

Cyr couldn't believe it, but Mr. O had forgotten completely about the $50K! He reasoned that if someone didn't remember leaving tens of thousands in cash in the cage, he must have *lots* of money.

He went to the accounting department and asked for a list of gamblers whose money had sat in the casino's vault for six months or longer. The list held more than a dozen names. Those were the easiest sales calls he ever made and more than a half-million dollars in forgotten cash, just sitting in the cage, went back into action—under Steve Cyr's host number.

(Cyr learned later that the operations guys didn't appreciate this move. They'd hoped that the half-mil would remain forgotten "forever." In the old days, before photos and signature cards and credit cards and Social Security numbers and thumbprints were demanded as proof of ID, when a gambling man's word was his bond, a casino marketing executive would take a friend to the cage to pick up the money: "This is Mr. O. He wants his deposit back." And the cashier would hand it over, just like that. The friend would sign Mr. O's name and the money was his—to split, of course, with the host. So much for a gambling man's word.)

❖ ❖ ❖

Cyr also discovered another entire class of valuable gamblers that was being utterly ignored by everyone—except the collections department. These were players whom the holdover hosts and operations bosses considered "trouble gamblers," players who were late in paying off their casino debts.

After scanning hundreds of casino-credit applications and Central files, Cyr noticed that the profile of a particular type of player emerged time after time. These were guys who had to struggle to pay off their markers, but settled up on gambling debts before making the monthly mortgage payments. They probably couldn't get a $1,000 credit line on a MasterCard or afford shoes for the baby, but they paid off the casino. And once they were clear, they'd come right back in, sign new markers, and the cycle would begin anew.

Poring over Centrals and watching Guy Hudson and the other credit managers, Cyr developed his own sixth sense for recognizing the classic play-and-pay gambler. This was a rare case of Cyr adopting an old-school technique, established by the legendary casino operators—Benny Binion, Moe Dalitz, Jackie Gaughan, Sam Boyd, and other old-timers—who could determine whether a player was a good or bad risk simply by talking to him. They didn't crunch credit applications through accounting programs. They didn't need a clutch of CPAs to figure a guy's value. They didn't have data from Central Credit to evaluate his total losses and average time of debt repayment. Rather, they jotted down a number or two on a scrap of paper and carried it in their jacket pockets until they had it committed to memory. Then they burned the paper and the information became what was called "graveyard": You either took the secret to the grave or, if you repeated it, the secret might take *you* there.

The casino accountants turned their noses up and thumbs down at Cyr's play-and-payers. But for once, the operations bosses actually approved of one of his marketing tactics. After all, these were *gamblers*. Even though they might be late in paying off old markers and their casino credit was cut off, they still craved the action. They could be taken for more. So Hudson and Oakes dialed Cyr into the subtleties of seducing the trouble gamblers and the nuances of the play-and-pay deal. They had to gamble for cash, not credit, and they had to pay off their outstanding markers with a portion of any winnings. Sometimes Cyr would offer to match their front money with an equal amount of casino credit—if he wanted the players badly enough. It all added up to the same result: It kept the suckers and losers in action.

❖ ❖ ❖

One day, Cyr overheard an Asian host talking to a marketing boss about giving a Malaysian whale $100,000 in promotional chips to come over from Caesars and play at the Hilton. This seemed like a fortune to Cyr—two years' salary. But the Hilton was merely matching the free $100,000 in chips with which Caesars was luring the whale and, as the Asian host explained, the $100,000 was merely the whale's first bet.

In addition, Cyr knew all about "show-up money," often used by sawdust joints to attract low rollers. These small, old, and usually seedy casinos, mostly located in downtown Las Vegas, handed out little funbooks full of coupons for discounts, meal deals, and gambling promotions, including cash, such as a free roll of nickels or three free dollar tokens. For a whale, the free $2 or $3 turned into a hundred large.

A short time later, Cyr was trying to convince Fast Eddie D, the crap whale, to give the Hilton a shot, when it just flew out of his mouth: "Hey, if you come over tonight I'll give you twenty-five grand when you walk in the door."

Eddie agreed and Cyr had to run to Jimmy Newman for permission to requisition five $5,000 promotional checks from the cage. When the boss raised an eyebrow, Cyr told him, "It's his first bet." Newman smiled and signed off on the $25,000. Fast Eddie lost a half-million at the Hilton crap table that night.

Show-up money quickly became a powerful harpoon in Steve Cyr's whale-hunting arsenal. Of course, he didn't expect the casino bosses to okay every request for walking-in-the-door promotional checks, so he had to find other lures.

❖ ❖ ❖

Up until that point, only international whales were extended discounts on their gambling losses. The casinos offered 5%, 10%, up to 15% discounts on losses of $1 million or more to big kahunas from Japan, Hong Kong, Taiwan, Malaysia, Indonesia, and the like. But the only cash a casino returned to a *domestic* player was reimbursement for airfare. If a player qualified (by the size of his average bet, the total amount of his losses, or some slush in his comp account), the casino picked up the cost of his plane ticket. But that was all. Even if he'd flown in from L.A. on a $129 round-trip and lost $50,000, he received exactly $129.

One day some credit manager at some casino finally gave in to some host who was arguing in favor of a rebate on losses for a big domestic player. "Tell you what. Give him five percent of his loss, but make sure you call it airfare reimbursement so I can deduct it from his comp account and not have to justify it as a rebate to the CFO."

Thus, though the player's airline ticket cost only $129, the host could return $2,500 worth of "airfare" on a $50,000 loss. This was manna from heaven to Steve Cyr. Now he had *all* kinds of cash to play with. Five percent of his biggest player's losses might amount to $5,000 or $10,000, which he could rebate in whatever way his player preferred: before gambling just for showing up or after gambling as a rebate on loss.

As he was hosting Mr. P from San Diego, who dropped $100,000 at the baccarat table, Cyr got to thinking about the Hilton's casino jet. Mr. P was entitled to five grand for a $150 round-trip ticket from San Diego. Cyr knew full well that it was far cheaper to pick him up and drop him off in Hilton's Hawker. Hilton owned the business jet outright and the pilots got paid whether they were flying or not. A little jet fuel and voilà—a $4,500 saving.

But oh no. You couldn't send the company jet for a $100,000 player. Half a million. Maybe.

So a few days later he went down to the airport and simply jacked the Hawker. On the authority of his own signature, he hopped the Hilton jet to Phoenix to pick up none other than Al Franco, the high-rolling contractor. "Listen, Mr. F. I'm picking you up in the Hawker, so don't bust my balls about airfare reimbursement." Franco was thrilled and Cyr saved the Hilton nearly $10,000 that day on Franco's $200,000 loss.

Of course, the bosses threw a fit: unauthorized use of a company *aircraft*. Cyr had to quit again. For the second time, he walked out and went home in protest. Newman called him back again, with a raise in salary to $75,000 and a $25,000 signing bonus. But Newman was also tired of Cyr quitting to make a point and this time he insisted the host sign a contract, the first host contract ever issued by the Hilton Corporation. It spelled out his term of employment, raises, bonuses, vacations, and comp and credit authority. Newman knew how valuable Cyr was and wanted him all locked up. For his part, Cyr viewed the contract as a kind of tenure, a stable foundation from which to keep stretching the limits, with relative impunity, of the whale hunt.

❖ ❖ ❖

In Las Vegas, 1993 was the Year of the Great Race. Following the first wave of megaresorts—Mirage, Rio, Excalibur—that ushered in the "new Las Vegas," the second wave materialized with three giant properties racing to open first. By the time the dog days of August 1993 rolled around, the 2,500-room Luxor, the 2,900-room Treasure Island, and the 5,000-room MGM Grand were all nearing completion, all poised to open within six weeks of each other, all positioned to cater to the growing high-roller trade. The Rio had already expanded once, the Stratosphere Tower was rising, New York-New York was about to set a new standard for architectural theming, and the Hard Rock Hotel-Casino had just broken ground. By then, casino gambling had also spread to Louisiana and Missouri, and was threatening to invade Illinois, Indiana, and Windsor, Ontario (across the river from Detroit). Competition for players was intensifying like never before.

By that time, the Hilton had been in the international whale business for nearly seven years. The Hilton had catered to the high-end baccarat crowd since it opened in 1969, but it wasn't until 1987 when VP of Casino Operations, Jimmy Newman, installed an international marketing department, that the joint began going after some of the serious wealth created by the Asian boom of the mid-1980s. Newman hired a few operations guys who'd gained experience in baccarat rooms around town and lured Mike Sterling, Cyr's old marketing boss from the Desert Inn, to run the department.

At the same time, Newman remodeled the 29th floor of the Hilton tower into nine suites, called the Classics. Decorated in various themes and occupying 1,500 to 2,500 square feet, they were more than adequate for the old-school domestic players, as well as smaller fish from across the Pacific who wanted to try on the Hilton's new international marketing efforts for size. But by summer 1993, with the Great Race in full swing, Newman needed whale-sized digs to compete.

He went to Barron Hilton and told him he wanted to spend $40 million or so on three supersuites to accommodate his Asian high rollers in a manner to which they weren't accustomed in Las Vegas. He wanted to renovate the entire 30th floor, the penthouse level, to create three Sky Villas totaling 40,000 square feet at $1,000 per foot—by far the most expensive remodel in Las Vegas history. Newman told Hilton he expected the Sky Villas to set the standard for whale lodging for years to come.

It took Newman eight months to talk Hilton into springing for it. Newman finally convinced him by guaranteeing that he'd have the Villas paid off by whale losses within six months of opening. The construction crews were put to work. They worked round the clock to complete the job by New Year's Eve 1994 and the Sky Villas proved so popular with million-dollar players that they were paid off with casino winnings in *three* months. All $40 million.

A new era in high-roller hosting had been inaugurated. Overnight, the world's whales fixed their sights on the Hilton and its new accommodations and Steve Cyr, with nearly four years as a Hilton host under his belt, had access to the keys.

❖　❖　❖

The suite meetings, where the hosts vied for the top-floor lodging for their players, had always been intense, but suddenly, they turned into cutthroat free-for-alls. They took place at the Hilton before every major event: New Year's Eve, the Super Bowl, Chinese New Year, Valentine's Day, the Jimmy Newman Golf Tournament, the National Finals Rodeo, heavyweight prizefights, and big concerts such as the Rolling Stones. Whatever the occasion, 10 or so hosts expecting a total of 40 or so players fought over 16 primo suites. How did they keep 40 high rollers in the air at the same time? With a greaseboard, an erasable marker, and skill at arms—juggling, that is.

The hosts maintained progress reports on all the players who claimed they'd be coming in. The list was continually updated to account for cancellations and changes in schedules, down to a week or so before the event. Then the marketing executives and bosses got together and duked it out, each advocating for his own players.

The decisions were made based on a number of factors. First came the needs of the international hosts, whose Asian or Arabian whales always had first dibs on everything. Next came the needs of the marketing-department supervisor, who generally had to handle orders from the operations bosses for their wives (and/or girlfriends), friends, and players. After that, the dominant domestic host, who generally had the dominant domestic players, held sway. Last in line were the lesser domestic hosts, who begged and pleaded for left-over crumbs and morsels.

From 1993 on, Steve Cyr was the dominant domestic host at the Hilton. He was the most aggressive and fearless and creative, thus his were always the biggest non-Asian play-ers. He also made it a point to be the best prepared for the suite meetings, which usually enabled him to shoot down whatever argument might be brought up against him, no matter how furiously the shit might fly.

"Well," host Fred puffed up at the suite meeting before, for example, a Tyson fight, "we've made a million dollars on my Mr. Q."

"Sure," Cyr countered, "but that's since 1977. How much is that a year? Fifty grand? My guy Mr. R has been coming for less than a year and we've already made a half-million on him."

Host Ted chimed in, "Fine, but my Mr. S lost a half-mil-lion on his last trip. *He* should get a Villa over both of them."

"Except," Cyr rebutted, "he's from Connecticut. He comes once a year, twice if you're lucky. And you have to pick up his airfare and his wife's airfare and his son and daughter-in-law's airfare, plus all the other happy horseshit. And his two previous times here he *won* a million. My Mr. R's from San Diego and comes up with his girlfriend every other weekend."

Host Fred wasn't done advocating for Mr. Q. "Doesn't a long-time player count for something? He's been a loyal cus-tomer for twenty years."

"Well, Fred, it says here right on Mr. Q's Central," which Cyr had with him, anticipating this argument, "that in the last seven years, his largest loss has been forty thousand. I've got Fast Eddie D coming in for this fight. His *average bet* is your guy's largest loss."

Now it was the turn of host Ed, whose smugness never failed to annoy Cyr, to hold forth on behalf of Mr. T. "I got you all beat. My Mr. T has a two million line and bets fifty-thousand a hand."

"Mr. T is a big bettor, but he's also a perfect-strategy blackjack player," Cyr argued. "He's too tough. He'll only lose fifty, and he knows how to win. He's dinged us for a quarter-mil several times. My guy Mr. R is a slot whale in the middle of a monumental slide into oblivion. He loses thirty-five or forty-five thousand a *month*. He's coming in for the fight *and* the Super Bowl *and* the Sweetheart Party in February. His losses alone will pay for that tricked-out Mustang we're giving away at the Valentine's party."

Cyr'd cited Mr. R just to shoot down host Ed. The slot whale in fact *wasn't* coming in for the fight, but Ed didn't know that. Meanwhile, to guard against another host pulling the same move on him, Cyr often called players whom the other hosts claimed were coming in. "Mr. T? Steve Cyr from the Las Vegas Hilton. Ed here tells me you're coming in for the fight next weekend."

"What?" Mr. T was surprised. "I don't know where he got that. I'm not coming in for the fight."

With the facts in hand, Cyr would pounce on Ed at the suite meeting. And Ed wouldn't only turn red. Ed would be dead.

Cyr, being Cyr, couldn't resist kicking the corpse. Suspecting that Ed might have invoked Mr. T to try to lock up a Villa for a smaller fish, he pushed further. "So who do you *really* wanna stay in the Villa, Ed?"

Hoping against hope that Cyr would relent or a boss might take pity on him, Ed said, "Mr. U."

Such a revelation would be met with stony silence. Everyone knew Mr. U was not only a minor $500-a-hand blackjack nerd, but he was a stiff to boot. Some thought he was a card counter. Cyr would look away. Perhaps host Jed, instead, would pick up the thread. "Mr. U's an asshole. I'm sure I speak for everyone in this room when I say no matter how much he brings, stick him in a standard room, sign side, no drapes."

(As far as room requests were concerned, players familiar with the building usually wanted a high floor facing the golf course or a low floor facing the pool. "Sign side, no drapes" meant a room facing the huge Hilton sign, flashing on and off all night—"Hilton," "Hilton," "Hilton"—and no drapes to shut it out. Or worse, sign side, no drapes, and close to the elevator or vending machines, which were noisy day and night.)

Once in a while, Cyr would look at the Eds in the suite meetings and actually feel a little sorry for them. They'd promise an undeserving player a Villa, when it was unlikely he'd get a Classic Suite or even a lanai king on the third floor by the pool. But the sympathy was usually short-lived; it was Ed's own damn fault for promising to begin with.

For his part, Cyr took the opposite tack of the lesser hosts and tried not to promise anything to anyone, even though most of the time he knew he had things all sewn up. Up until the very last minute, he'd tell even his biggest fish, "I don't know if I can get you a Villa tonight. I'm trying, but the whole world is showing up for this fight." He preferred his players to be pissed off initially, over the phone, then pleasantly surprised when Cyr "came through," rather than to believe that all was well, only to be negatively surprised at the moment of truth. It was important to Cyr to be the hero, not the goat, in his player's presence.

Of course, sometimes even Cyr's players didn't get a Villa. No matter how dominant Cyr could be in a suite meeting, the international hosts' hold on the supersuites superseded even his. Even if a $5 million Asian whale in town wasn't staying at the Hilton, a Villa had to remain vacant on the chance that he'd come over from the Mirage or Caesars.

Sometimes one would sit empty for a week, while the whale frolicked at the MGM.

The international host is under enormous pressure to protect his turf. First, he gets only one or two chances a year to host a whale, while Cyr can lure his mini-whales anytime. In addition, culturally, Asian hosts have to be hypersensitive, taking strict care not to offend their players, by covering every possible contingency, including keeping Villas open indefinitely.

In such cases, Cyr might get impatient and press the issue. "Hey, Leung! Larry Flynt's coming in and I've got to have that Verona Villa."

"No no, my guy's coming in *tonight*."

"That's what you said yesterday and the day before yesterday and the day before that. I'm taking the suite and if your guy does show up, I'll move Larry."

But Asian whales weren't the only reason Cyr might not get a Villa. Sometimes too many of his own players wanted to show up for an event. His three biggest players were always bigger than everyone else's, but maybe a new guy, someone he'd been on the phone with for months, also wanted to attend a fight. Now Cyr had a tough decision to make: Should he be loyal and give the Villa to the veteran? Or should he go with the new guy to get some fresh blood in? He typically leaned toward the new guy. The veteran, he reckoned, had been overcomped a hundred times and would come in regardless of the accommodations. For lots of guys, their weekends in Vegas were their whole social life, while others were just stone-cold degenerates who'd take what they could get.

Cyr also liked to downgrade one of his big kahunas a bit, just for the sake of appearance. He couldn't come through with a Villa *every* time; if he did, his guy would know he was always blowing smoke when he told him, "I'm *trying*, but it's gonna be tough."

The bosses had the final say on who got the Villas, who got the suites, and who got bupkis. But ultimately, it boiled down to which of the hosts had the biggest Dick (or Tom or Harry).

❖ ❖ ❖

The limited availability of suites was only one part of the battle. There were also the skirmishes over tickets to the fights. The Hilton might spring for 50 tickets, but only eight ringside. So now the pecking order had to be reviewed again. Eventually, the ticket list got hammered out, with players' names next to numbers one through fifty. But it usually wasn't final until just minutes before the opening round. The night before the fight, a guy in the top five might need two extra tickets for a couple of unexpected guests. So now two names had to be cropped from the bottom of the heap and everyone else bumped down a couple of rungs. Or a guy no one even expected to show up that weekend might lose $75,000 and start browbeating everyone in sight for two tickets. Now two more names would have to be dropped—and some poor sap of a host had to break the bad news.

And then there was the reserved-games problem. Perhaps Mr. V wanted his own roulette table in the baccarat room to accommodate his entourage of seven, while Mr. W also wanted a private roulette table. So a baccarat table would have to be moved out to fit in the other wheel. Meanwhile, Moe Cohn, Cyr's biggest crap whale, needed his own dice table and crew in the baccarat room. And a couple of Asians who liked it quiet wanted their own baccarat table in the back, farthest from the main casino. That could be handled, but now there wasn't enough room for a lower-limit baccarat table for the guys who wanted to bet only $500 to $5,000. By rearranging, another table was squeezed in. But as soon as the last seat at the last table was accounted for, someone else would call up asking for his own game.

Cyr also fought with the maitre d', because everyone wanted to eat at exactly the same time, 7 p.m., in exactly the same place, Le Montrachet. And he duked it out with the limo dispatcher, because everyone wanted to take a stretch over to the fight at 9 p.m. And he went hand-to-hand with VIP Services over spa times, because the spa guy didn't hold as many places as he should have and the wives and girl-friends couldn't get in when they wanted to.

Then he found himself being yelled at by the customer who didn't get the suite or tickets he was expecting. Or he had to yell at the high rollers who came in late Friday night, played golf on Saturday morning (over which he had to fight with the golf-course starter for tee times), then went to the spa, had dinner, and headed for the fight: "So when are you gonna gamble?"

A couple of hours before the fight, Cyr's cell phone started ringing with one call after another. Charles Barkley's stuck a hundred and wants another hundred. Fast Eddie just called and the Hawker's landing. Are you gonna meet him at the airport? Larry Flynt's bitching from the Villa because the butler didn't get the coffee right and where're the cigars? Mr. Y wants to go to dinner with you, then to a topless club. And Mr. Z is screaming that he's still waiting for his two tickets to the fight.

Cyr, the eye of the storm, the maestro of the maelstrom, got it all done. He handled it personally. He delegated. He browbeat. He bullshitted. He broke rules. When he had to, he robbed Mr. Y to pay Mr. X. He strutted around the Hil-ton, making sure everyone knew about it. "Hey, I'm the man. I got the power. You want two tickets to the fight tonight? Depends on the whether."

"The weather?" Mr. W asked.

"Yeah. Whether or not I decide to give them to you."

❖ ❖ ❖

Although he was now earning in the high five figures a year, Cyr was trying to keep pace with his players, many of whom could gamble the equivalent of his yearly take-home pay in an hour. He sold his old condo, bought a new house, and saddled himself with a hefty mortgage. He carried credit-card debt of $50,000-$60,000. He couldn't help overspending—it was part of the life. Twenty-nine-year-old Steve Cyr, pulling in $1,200 a week, would take out a player and his wife and foot an $800 tab for caviar and champagne. He'd take another couple of his guys to topless clubs and throw money around like he was picking it off trees. His dry-cleaning bills were astronomical. And he gambled a little himself.

One of his customers, Mr. V, was a twentysomething Southern California trust-fund real-estate investor who started out betting a couple hundred a hand right after he turned 21 and only a few years later was playing for $10,000 a throw. Mr. V called Cyr at home one weekend and asked what he was doing.

"I'm mowing the lawn," Cyr told him.

"No, really. What are ya doin'?" Mr. V just couldn't fathom that his high-powered casino host would cut his own grass.

5

The Office Orangutans

After five years as a Hilton host, Cyr was the top-earning marketing executive on the property; the next highest earner was a distant second. The old-school hosts were retiring, getting termed, or going to other casinos where they didn't have to compete with hotshot young kids pushing the high-roller envelope. He was now making $100,000 a year.

Then, in late 1996, Hilton absorbed Bally's in a $3 billion friendly takeover. But in a curious twist, the Bally's management team absorbed the Hilton casino and in short order, a Bally's hatchet man began to implement the kind of top-to-bottom shakeup for which the casino industry is infamous.

The new president of the Hilton came straight from Bally's and in rapid succession fired six vice presidents from Cyr's office, including Guy Hudson. He also termed all the holdover hosts; Johnny Oakes only avoided his pink slip by retiring. (More than one of the hosts later sued the Hilton for wrongful termination. Hilton lawyers simply claimed that the hosts' production was too low and trotted out the profit-to-earnings paperwork to prove it. The hosts lost.) Coincidentally, Cyr had been away from work on his regular days off while the Hilton's marketing house was cleaned. He left on a Saturday night and when he returned the next Tuesday morning, it was like a neutron bomb had hit the joint: All the offices in his department (except his) were completely tenantless.

Cyr sat in the gutted Hilton marketing department, totally on his own. All the senior employees who'd watched his back and covered his ass when he'd bitched at the pit bosses or front-desk clerks or box-office ticket agents, or was drunk up in a suite with a player while he was on duty, or was stealing other hosts' players, were now gone.

Worse, Cyr was certain that he too was on the chopping block. All the Bally's bosses had to do was buy out the last six months on his contract. He was so sure of this fate that before lunch that Tuesday, he called his travel agent and booked a package trip for a week in Cabo San Lucas, leaving that Friday.

Well, Tuesday went by, then Wednesday. On Thursday, Cyr took a look around. He saw that the Hilton was still shell-shocked, with all the executives keeping their heads down, trying not to expose their necks to the hatchet. *Fuck this*, he thought. *What do I have to lose?* He walked right up to the new president of the Las Vegas Hilton, introduced himself, and said, "I'm your best producer. I'm hosting Larry Flynt here next week."

The president looked him up and down and said, "Young man, I don't think you'll get Flynt through these doors. But if you do, you'll have my attention."

Next, Cyr went to Jim Bradshaw, the new senior vice president directly under the president, and asked for help. "Give me a hundred large in promotional chips and I'll bring in Larry Flynt."

Bradshaw flinched. "A hundred thousand?"

"What the hell?" Cyr responded. "It's his first few bets."

Bradshaw agreed. That weekend, when Larry Flynt pulled up to the Hilton's front door in a limo, Cyr was there—rather than in Cabo—to greet him; Jim Bradshaw—the boss of every dealer, floorman, pit boss, casino manager, casino host, and slot host—was there too.

Seeing Flynt convinced Bradshaw that this self-pro-claimed best producer might be just that. He handed Cyr a yellow legal pad and told him, "Write down what you need to make you happy here."

Cyr jotted down a few incidentals, along with a single demand that would make or break the deal: He would answer only to Bradshaw and only Bradshaw could terminate him. Cyr told Bradshaw he refused to fade all the vice presidents who were coming in to replace the fired staff. He didn't want to be a vice president himself, but he did want a new title that placed him above the rest of the hosts: senior casino marketing executive. "Otherwise," he threatened his new boss, "I'll sit out the six months left on my contract, then go to the Rio or the Mirage or New York-New York and take every one of your players with me."

Bradshaw loved hearing that kind of confident trash talk. Cyr couldn't be cocky enough for the new boss, who promoted him to senior host (his fourth title at the Hilton). He raised Cyr's salary to $150,000, bumped his credit authority up to $250,000, added an annual bonus based on a percentage of his players' losses, and gave him stock options.

There was more. He handed Cyr the reservations log and said, "Steve, you can book whoever you want in the Villas and suites."

He also handed him the Hawker reservations log and said, "Steve, go wherever you want in the company plane. You don't even have to ask me."

He handed him a set of keys and said, "Steve, the biggest office in the marketing department is yours."

And he told him, "Steve, we've got to hire a whole new set of hosts. Tell me how many and who. And get yourself a secretary."

Suddenly, all the handcuffs, which had hobbled Cyr for nearly a decade at the DI, Caesars, and the Hilton, were removed. Up till that time, in his best year he'd won $5 million from his players. Now he began winning a million a *month* for the Hilton.

Cyr was in charge of the show, and things were beginning to get fun.

❖ ❖ ❖

Tina Jones was 22 when she showed up at the Hilton looking for a job. She figured to get hired as a receptionist, secretary, or assistant, but her goal was to climb the organizational ladder, trade up in lifestyle, and live the corporate Las Vegas dream. Personnel sent her upstairs to the casino marketing office to be interviewed by ... Steve Cyr.

Cyr knew what he wanted and Tina Jones seemed to fit the bill. She was young, confident, and ambitious. While he was joking with her, she slipped and said, "Shit!" That sold him on her (and her on him). He was in the process of hiring a dozen or so "orangutans," and he needed an assistant who wouldn't get all huffy if someone said something a little off-color or politically incorrect. He simply couldn't have a priss in an office full of apes.

Her first morning, Tina reported for work promptly at nine, got to her desk, parked her purse, and checked the first item on her to-do list prepared by Cyr: "Phone messages. Instructions in booklet in desk drawer." She grabbed the manual, figured out the answering machine, and listened.

"Steve! It's Doug. Mr. U is on his way in the G Three. Is the limo at the airport? He's in the Conrad Villa, right? Eric's his butler, right? If not, you have to tell whoever it is that Mr. U needs to have his yogurt drained through a cheese-cloth—he spreads the top creamy part on his toast, or some such craziness. Call me on my cell!"

"Hey! Steve! This is Jim. Sorry, but you can't have the Conrad Villa tonight. I've got Mr. T up there. You'll have to stash your guy in a Classic for the night."

"Steve? Kenny here. Just calling to let you know that I FedExed the check for eighty-five thou yesterday. You should have it this morning. I'm paid up! You promised me fight tickets, my brother. Call me!"

"Cyr, you son of a bitch! You let me down, man. Twenty-five thou. That's all I needed. You knew I was good for it. I've always been good for it. But instead you embarrassed me. Well, last night was the last straw, asshole! I'm going over to Luxor."

"Cyr, where's that requisition for your helicopter trip to the Grand Canyon today? I can't sign off if you don't bring me the form."

"Steve? Nick. You're not gonna believe this, but Mr. S wants brown sugar in his toilet water. I'm not, uh, shitting you. What should I tell him?"

And there were six more strange messages from strange people. Only one or two even bothered to leave their names, and none supplied a return phone number. Tina realized that she should probably be taking notes, so she figured out how to play back the messages and started trying to write each one down on a little pink message slip. G Three? Conrad Villa? Fight tickets? Twenty-five thou? Grand Canyon? Yogurt and cheesecloth? Sugar in the toilet? It was a foreign language!

Then the phone started ringing in real time. She listened to live people, all men, yammering about situations she couldn't even begin to fathom.

"No sir, he hasn't been in this morning. I don't know when he's expected. No, I don't know where he is. No, I couldn't tell you anything about six tickets to Starlight Express. I can take a message. Yes sir, I'll make sure he gets it."

And, "I'm sorry. I don't know anything about Mr. Cyr stealing a player from Caesars last night. I can leave him a message."

And, "No, I don't have Mr. Cyr's cell-phone number. To be honest with you, this is my first day on the job. Me? Twenty-two. What? Oh, I'm five-foot-four. Tina. *You'll* call him on his cell? Hey, you know the number? Can you give it to me? Thanks! Well, I look forward to meeting you, Mr. R."

When she got through with the phone, she checked her list. "Download all the e-mail." She printed out eighteen messages.

Back to the list. "Write thank-you letters to Mr. Q and Mr. P—use Thank You template in Letters folder on PC."

After formatting the letters, she stopped to take a breath. It had felt like a 45-minute whirlwind. But when she looked at her watch, it was 12:15. The job was a dream.

That didn't mean it was a picnic. Everyone she dealt with seemed to be in some stage of panic, chaos, or emotional, financial, or logistical distress. On her third day at the Hilton, Mr. P called and told Tina that Steve had promised him five tickets to the World Wrestling Federation match at the MGM Grand Garden. But when he showed up at the Will Call window with his four kids, the tickets weren't there. What's more, the show was sold out. Tina Jones had one irate player on her hands and she couldn't track down Cyr. Thinking fast, she grabbed some petty cash, ran over to the MGM, found a scalper, paid the price, and solved the problem. After that, Cyr trusted her.

Tina paid close attention to everything going on around her and her confidence grew. Soon, she knew what needed doing without being told, and understanding what players wanted became second nature.

It didn't take long to discover the perks of working for Steve Cyr. Players often wanted to do something nice for their favorite host, but Cyr didn't always have the time or inclination to accept. In those cases, the next best thing was to do something nice for his assistant. Tina was 22 years old, living in a hovel, driving a heap, yet all these rich guys were giving her flowers, gift certificates, casino chips, trips to California. And everything, all over town, was comped. Dinners, shows, limo rides—everything!

It wasn't *all* roses and chocolate. Tina also became an object of envy and pettiness. She'd go down to the box office to pick up a dozen tickets to *Starlight Express*, the Andrew Lloyd Webber roller-derby musical, and run headlong into resistance.

"Hi, I'm here to pick up Mr. O's tickets for Steve Cyr."

"Oh yeah?" a 21-year-old female clerk might scowl. "Who are you?"

"I'm Tina Jones. I've worked here for eight months. You've seen me a dozen times. I have a beeper, a name tag, and here's my employee badge."

"Well, we can't give the tickets to just anyone who comes down here and asks. I'm sorry. You'll have to bring the form."

Tina would go back upstairs and tell Steve that she'd just wasted a trip to the box office. Then he'd have to run down— not call down, but storm down to the box office—so he could rip into the clerk, preferably in front of her boss.

It wasn't just the box office. It was the hostesses in the VIP office. It was the restaurant-reservations staff. It was the other marketing secretaries. All the girls were jealous. Most of the young women who worked entry-level at the Hilton, hundreds of them, wanted to trade places with Tina. To them, her job was to sit back and be spoiled. And in a way, it was true. Steve, his orangutans, the players—they all spoiled Tina one way or another. What a life. What's more, she had freedom. And why wouldn't she? She was assistant to the ultimate free-spirit—Steve Cyr.

It was non-stop madness for two years. Tina had never imagined a world such as the one casino marketing executives inhabited. None of her friends believed her when she tried to describe it. She had to take them along when she could, just to prove it was true.

❖ ❖ ❖

By early 1997, the Hard Rock, Stratosphere, Monte Carlo, New York-New York, and a half-dozen neighborhood casinos had opened in Las Vegas. The competition for players— and player reps—was cutthroat. A lot of host wannabes tried to step up. New marketing executives were hired for a skill they already possessed, such as telemarketing, a second language, or sales experience. Or they came up the traditional way through operations, picking up a piece of the host trade here as a dealer, a piece there as a floorman, another piece perhaps as a pit supervisor.

Cyr's experience—growing up in the motel business, earning a degree in hotel administration with an emphasis on gambling, helping set up one of the first VIP Services departments, working in a vitamin boiler room, and doing his time as a slot and cash host—was a fortuitous training ground for the big-time ass-kissing and hand-holding, seducing and fleecing, involved in handling high rollers. Every other host, however, came from a different background and had different experience.

As soon as he was set loose to hire his own hosts, one of the first prospects Cyr went to bat for was Ray McIntosh, who'd dealt craps at the Hilton for nearly 20 years. McIntosh had climbed the company ladder, all of one rung, up to boxman, the low-level suit who supervises the crap table, one of the most boring jobs in the joint. Cyr and McIntosh got to be friendly and one day Ray confided in Cyr. "I'm so crispy fried, I'm gonna blow my brains out if I have to sit box one more shift. C'mon man, make me a host!" And he did.

Cyr head-hunted Nick Ippolito, a friend and slot host from his Caesars days.

He found Doug Bean working in VIP Services; Bean spoke Japanese and could handle Asian whales.

And Robert Coury was a floorman from MGM who cold-called Cyr and impressed him as a natural-born player rep.

He also hired a few telemarketing guys with no casino experience whatsoever. One had never even been *in* a casino before. He had no clue and even less interest in what went on in the business, but he was a "Ma Bell motherfucker," as Cyr put it, and a quick study to boot, feeding the orangutans player after big player.

With the exception of Nick Ippolito, Cyr shied away from traditional hosts. When word got around that a bomb had just wiped out the Hilton casino-marketing department, reps from other properties showed up in droves. Cyr asked them about their players and they'd pull out long sheets of green-bar computer paper generated from a marketing database; the applicants had rarely met or even spoken on the phone to anyone on the list. When he asked for stories about how they'd stolen a big player from a competing casino, they just looked at him. Cyr would laugh and say, "You're a greeter, a maintenance host. I need casino marketing executives. Come back when you've got some players."

Cyr went on a hunt for supersalesmen. One day on his way to work, he stopped off at the Cadillac dealership and asked to see the top car salesman. They got to wrangling and Cyr almost talked him into getting out of the car business and going into the casino business, but the guy wanted $50,000 more than Cyr could pay. The reason he liked him, though, was that he almost talked Cyr into getting out of the casino business and going into the car business.

Above all, Cyr knew instinctively what made a good host. To select a potential player-development rep, he counted on the same sixth sense he relied on to size up a player. First and foremost, a host had to be a people person. Volcanoes and pirate shows and casino spectacles don't move people. People move people. Hosts are people motivated and motivating.

Second, he had to be capable of working in the pressure cooker of high-stakes gambling—juggling players, casino politics, and moral ambiguity.

Cyr could tell if someone would be able to handle all the bullshit that goes with the player. Though most high rollers didn't get to where they are by happenstance—they play the game of life better than anyone else and thus are the winners of life's gambles—some of them just couldn't cut it outside the business world. They might be bulls in the boardroom, but on the street? Not a lick of common sense. And it wasn't uncommon for their wives and girlfriends to be a bit clueless, which made for more dicey dynamics. The host had to smile and bow and scrape, all the while wondering why (and silently bemoaning the fact that) the customer was rich and he wasn't.

Also, the host is the *only* one who knows the whole story. He doesn't tell his player the whole story. He doesn't tell his boss the whole story. He walks a tightrope between the two. He often has to lie to both. Maybe he agrees to some outrageous proposition to capture a big player, knowing full well that he can't sell it upstairs. When the customer shows up, the host has the 20-minute limo ride to make it right with him. If he can't, he has two minutes to cajole and threaten and scream to make it right with his boss.

A host has to simultaneously befriend and betray his players. He has to pretend he's on their side, while he grinds every last dollar out of every last sucker he can. He has to remember that his bonus checks are based on losses.

On top of everything, there's a paradoxical hurdle a break-in host must overcome. The host's job is to bring in high-rolling customers, but most new hosts don't know any high rollers. Unless, that is, the break-in has a 31-year-old hotshot boss who turns him on to the new-school scheme of things, then tosses him the keys to the casino candy store.

❖ ❖ ❖

Robert Coury was one new-school host who rose through the casino ranks in the old-school fashion. He came to Las Vegas in 1977 from New Brunswick, New Jersey, at age 21 to go to UNLV. He lasted one semester. Coury knew someone who knew someone and wound up getting juiced into a job at the Tropicana. He was told that if he put in a year or so as a security guard, he could break in as a dealer.

Coury was savvy and ambitious and figured out early

how the game was played. A few weeks into the job, a casino manager sent him to the airport to ship a package via air freight. It was a long tube with something light, green, and felty rolled up inside, and Coury deduced that it was a crap layout. At the time, with casino gambling legal only in Nevada, interstate shipping of gambling-table layouts was against federal law.

At the air-freight counter, the clerk asked him what was inside. Coury had to think fast.

When he got back to the Trop, he told the boss, "Next time you want me to do something illegal, at least warn me about it first."

"What did you tell the air-freight people?" the boss asked.

Coury handed him the receipt listing the contents as fishing poles. After that, the bosses shunted more of their dirty work his way, such as shipping slot machines out of state and, on one memorable occasion, delivering $100,000 in nickels to a house on the outskirts of the city. The weight of the coins ruined the shocks and struts of the company van, and almost ruined Coury's back moving the boxes into the garage. He wondered, naturally, where the nickels were going from there, but he knew better than to ask.

This was a time when only women could begin careers as dealers on the fabled Strip; even then they sometimes had to render a little body tax unto a big boss to get and keep the job. Men had to break in downtown; they could get a job on the Strip only if they knew someone. After eight months in security, Coury had accrued enough juice to move up to dealerhood.

He dealt at the Tropicana for a few years, then at Bob Stupak's now-defunct Vegas World. From there, he worked his way up and became a boss at the Sahara and Boomtown (now Silverton), finally landing a job as a floorman at the MGM Grand.

But Coury's dream had always been to be in casino marketing. Ever since he worked at the Trop, he'd aspired to become a table-games host. In those days, he used to watch Minnie Cardella, one of the top Las Vegas hosts of his time. The hosts were always the hippest dudes in the coolest job, but Cardella was king and Coury wanted to be like *him*.

As a floorman at the MGM, with 20 years in casino operations under his belt, Robert Coury knew what he had to do. Unlike plenty of other floormen and pit bosses who were on the make or a power-trip, or were burned out or ignorant or greedy or lazy, Coury was simply a good soldier—protecting the games, filling out paperwork, and rating players. But he also made it a point to befriend the big gamblers. He talked to them. He asked where they lived. He exchanged business cards. He took notes in the pit. He kept files. He remembered names, faces, and details. After a while, many of the high rollers would play only in his section.

He also cultivated hosts.

Floormen have to have hosts on their side. The power struggles in the pit are ferocious. Despite the flashy atmosphere, pit jobs are deadly dull, an assembly line of repetitious and relentless tasks. The never-ending boredom and player emotion, along with intense heat from surveillance and security, a hierarchy of bosses that's nearly military in its rigidity, and the capricious ease with which employees can be fired, engender petty jealousies, spotlight incompetence, and foster an environment of distrust, dislike, and disgust. On top of all that, sexual tension tinges nearly every relationship in the pit. Floormen, lowest on the pit-boss totem pole, must often navigate a political minefield to execute the simplest transactions.

A typical scenario. A beautiful woman sits down alone at a table. A floorman moves in on her, he introduces himself, and makes small talk. When he sees that she isn't wearing any rings, he might want to impress her by comping her to dinner that night. But if this floorman has to request the comp from a shift manager who's been power-tripping him for years, he's got a problem. "You're just trying to get laid," the shift boss might say. "Forget it." And if the floorman has *already* offered the woman a comp, now he's humiliated.

However, if the floorman can call a cooperative host, he's got a much better shot at it. "Hey, I've got a gorgeous lady here. She's only betting greens, but she's dressing up the joint. She sat down at an empty table at four this afternoon and guys have been firing it up all around her ever since. I don't think she's a hooker. I'd like to buy her dinner."

The host, if he's smart, will not only cut the comp, but he'll also sign over three more blank tickets for the floorman to use at his discretion in the future. With the host as an ally, the floorman can be confident in making the move on the woman. It works out for everyone. The woman's happy, because she gets dinner. The host is happy, because she might turn into a good customer and the floorman now owes him a favor. And maybe the floorman actually does get laid, which was the object from the start. (The only one who's not happy is the shift manager, who *wanted* to humiliate the floorman.)

Coury spent three years as a floorman at the MGM. When he felt ready, he applied for a job in player development. He got interviewed twice, once by a friend in the marketing department, but in the end, they blew him off. He was just a floorman. What could he know?

So he loaded a Ziploc bag bursting with players' business cards into his briefcase and wound up in an office at the Las Vegas Hilton, sitting across the desk from ... Steve Cyr.

"I want to be a marketing executive."

"Oh yeah? What've you got?"

Coury dug into his Ziploc, pulled out a card, and handed it over.

Cyr took a look at the business card of Mr. N, a player from Seattle. On the back was a hand-written notation: "$2.5 million line. $25,000 a hand."

Cyr whistled. This was a major player, even by his standards. He thought back to all the wannabe and greeter hosts he'd interviewed who didn't have shit. Now, here was a guy who'd gotten friendly enough with a player to exchange business cards. He'd collected his data on the spot and taken the time to write it down. Cyr eyed the bag, bulging with business cards. "You could make an entire career off that bag of yours."

"That's what I'm hoping to do."

"Hell, you could make a career out of this one guy."

"Well, he's my biggest player."

Cyr cold-called the number on the card. "Mr. N! Steve Cyr from the Las Vegas Hilton. I know you like to play at the MGM Grand, but if I could have two minutes of your time, I'll give you, oh, about twenty-five thousand reasons to come give us a play."

"Look, buddy," Mr. N responded. "I don't know who you are or how you got my name and number, but don't waste your breath, because I'm happy at the MGM."

"I don't doubt it, Mr. N. MGM's a great joint. But, well, for one thing, you play in the main pit, don't you? I'll level with you and tell you that I got your card from a floorman over there. Here at the Hilton, a guy giving us your level of action gets his own table, his own pit, his own damn room! And that's just for starters."

"Like I said, you're wasting your time. I'm stickin' with Kerkorian."

"Fine, fine. Just wanted to introduce myself to you. And to tell you that I'm gonna be up in Seattle tomorrow; that's why I called. I'm meeting with another player and taking in the Supersonics game. How 'bout if I stop in and buy you lunch."

"I don't do lunch. I work through lunch. I get in here at seven a.m., work my ass off, go home, then do it again the next day."

"And can't wait to get to Vegas, I bet."

"True enough."

"Can I just show up around lunch time?"

"I suppose, but let's just put it down as an appointment on my schedule."

"Great! How about noon?"

Mr. N laughed. "All right—but don't come here in a limo expecting to get me to go out for lunch."

Bingo. Cyr hung up the phone, called his travel agent to book him a flight to Seattle, then found a limo company and reserved a stretch Lincoln, asking the reservations clerk about a good place for lunch. (The next day the Cyr tsunami rolled into Seattle and in the backwash, Mr. N wound up at the Las Vegas Hilton—that very same night, thanks to the Hawker.)

Coury sat patiently till Cyr was done making the Seattle arrangements. Then he said, "I've also got Mata Hari."

Cyr's eyebrows arched. He was all too familiar with the nickname of one of the most notorious female blackjack suckers in the state. The story went that her first husband was a general in the Indonesian Army who sent her to the U.S. in the early '70s with a suitcase full of diamonds. He himself never made it. She liked to play at the MGM, because that's where Robert Coury was. He was the only one who'd put up with her and give her the type of attention she needed, *positive* attention. Everyone else—dealers, floormen, bosses, hosts—hated her, and no one could seem to hide it. Mata Hari insisted on a private game—just her and a dealer—every day. That could be accommodated. The problem was she was a holy terror when she lost. She tore up cards, threw chips at floormen, and screamed in Indonesian. And she lost all the time, often upwards of $50,000 a session.

When she pulled into the valet parking area in her $100,000 Mercedes, the valet guy called the casino manager and said simply, "*She's* here." Then the casino manager called the pit boss, "*She's* here." Then the pit boss called the pit clerk, "*She's* here." Finally, the pit clerk told Coury, "*She's* here."

Coury, as a matter of course, would have her private game all set up by the time she arrived at the pit. He had the patience to sit with her and soothe her and tell her, "It's all right. Take it easy. Stay calm." Without him, she'd get upset immediately and start steaming. With him, she could play a reasonable game.

Cyr didn't care about her rep. *So what if she's a lunatic?* he thought. *We can give her a private game 24 hours a day, 365 days a year! What's a dealer cost—$52.50 per shift? Coury here can sit with her till she shrivels up and dies. She's local, so she doesn't need airfare. She doesn't need a suite. She doesn't even need a limo. Meanwhile, she'll swell the Hilton's bottom line by half a mil a year.*

Then Coury gave him the key to bagging Mata Hari. "Her birthday's next week. Invite her here for a party, give her a private game, let me sit with her, and she's yours."

And with that, Robert Coury was finally on his way to following in the footsteps of Minnie Cardella. By not paying attention, the MGM had forced Coury's hand and sent him to the Hilton with a number of MGM's top players.

Coury was passable on the phone, making cold calls and convincing players to come in to gamble. But his strong suit was relationship marketing. As soon as he got one-on-one with his customer, it was fast-friends time. He didn't rush. He didn't apply pressure. He didn't double-talk or bullshit. Instead, he continued to practice the interpersonal skills he first learned as a security guard at the Tropicana and honed on the floor at the MGM. He listened to his players. He liked them.

Take the $500-a-hand blackjack player he met in his second week as a host. Within the first hour of knowing each other, the guy was already telling Coury about his high-rolling colleagues and his wife was looking to set him up with some of her single friends. (The single and successful Coury had a special cachet with the women he encountered. Even Mata Hari told him she'd pay him $100,000 a year to marry her daughter.)

Like Cyr, Coury had found his niche as a player rep. He

had a blast hosting mostly middle rollers; because he was so personable, his forté was the $25,000 to $75,000 player, guys who were entitled to most, but not all, of the comps that Cyr's heavies got. Though he often pretended to, Cyr rarely had to refuse a request—no matter how outlandish—from his players, who could have practically anything they wanted. But the lower-level gamblers in the Coury inventory walked a finer line. Occasionally, they had to be told no, and Coury was the guy who could do that best.

❖ ❖ ❖

Then there was Doug Bean. Bean is a member of the Church of Jesus Christ of Latter-day Saints. Because Bean's church is opposed to gambling, many players wondered how he reconciled his racket with his religion. For Bean, it wasn't an issue. He considered himself a salesman. Players came to Las Vegas casinos. Hosts marketed casino perks to players. Bean didn't ask them to do anything illegal or something that went against *their* religion. And he didn't gamble himself.

In the midst of his college days as a music and theater major at Brigham Young University in Provo, Bean fulfilled his two-year Mormon-mission duties in Japan, where he learned the language in order to proselytize.

In the early '90s, a fellow missionary suggested that Bean move to Las Vegas and use his language skills in the service of a casino that catered to high-rolling Japanese. Levitating on a bubble economy at the time, the Japanese were flocking to the gambling capital for fun and anonymity. Bean decided to give it a try and landed a job as an entry-level VIP Services clerk at the Las Vegas Hilton, starting at a salary of $30,000 a year.

The fresh-faced Bean found himself treading water in the vast Las Vegas sea of dreams. He took a look around and noticed that his Japanese customers got their biggest bang from baccarat, and that baccarat dealers made $80,000 to $100,000 a year, mainly on huge tips from the big whale-sans. He figured he had an edge by being able to speak to the players in their own language, so he learned how to deal the game.

While training, Bean succumbed to the temptation to play, parking himself at a mini-baccarat table one night at the Rio with a $100 bankroll. Initially, he felt the love—the excitement of gambling, the thrill of winning, and the greed of wanting to win more. But after pressing his bets, the fever reared its sweaty head and he busted out. The fear overcame him and the next thing he knew, he was at a casino cash machine.

(This is an ATM machine with a vengeance. When you get money from a cash machine off a credit card in a casino, you pay upwards of 5% of the cash advance, which goes to the casino. Another 3% is sucked off the top by the credit-card company for the cash-advance fee. Then you pay 5% more than the usual usurious interest to the credit-card company for interest on the cash advance. The machine also collects the names and addresses of people who seemingly can't control their gambling habits—to sell to direct-marketing companies.)

Bean withdrew another $100 to chase his losses. He got lucky, earning back his first $100 and winning another $300 to boot—then gave up gambling for good. But now he knew first-hand how addictive and disruptive it could be. He actually dealt baccarat a few times, but he didn't like that either, so he scrapped the whole idea.

But he took to being a host just as Cyr had foreseen. And together, the two of them went after big international players.

In one instance, an old BYU roommate of Bean's wife was dating a guy whose mother was friendly with a woman who worked as a secretary in the international marketing office at Caesars. Word got passed from the friend to the mother to the son to the girlfriend to Mrs. Bean to Doug and ultimately to Steve about a Malaysian high roller, Mr. M, who liked to bet $50,000 a hand at the baccarat tables at Caesars. It turned out that the high roller had gone to high school with a guy who owned a non-descript Oriental eatery just west of the Las Vegas Strip.

For three months, Cyr and Bean ate at the restaurant at least a couple of times a week. (It was the first time Cyr tasted sushi, a food he actually learned to like. Previously, the Midwestern corn-fed farmboy had been deathly afraid of anything that wasn't meat and potatoes.) The owner of the restaurant regularly saw Cyr and Bean sitting at the same table in their expensive suits and finally asked who they were. The three became friendly. After a number of scary scaly meals, Cyr and Bean had insinuated themselves into the good graces of the restaurateur, though they still didn't have an angle on what they could do for this friend of the high roller to get him to owe them a favor.

One day Bean was talking about taking his children swimming. The restaurateur mentioned that his kids didn't know how to swim, but he wanted them to learn, if only for safety reasons, since almost every house in Las Vegas has a backyard pool.

Cyr saw an opening and dove in. "Hell! We've got some fantastic swimming instructors over at the Hilton. We'll get you a lanai suite on the third floor, right by the pool, and one of our instructors will teach them how to swim right there."

The restaurateur agreed. Problem was, the Hilton didn't have any swimming instructors, so Cyr and Bean had to go into full scramble to hire, at their own expense, an outside teacher for the day. They found one at the YMCA, paid him $100, and gave him a Hilton T-shirt to wear. Then they reserved a lanai suite, explaining to Bradshaw that it was all for the *friend* of an international whale.

The restaurant owner and his family showed up the next

Sunday afternoon. The kids learned to swim and Cyr and Bean got access to Mr. M.

The first time Mr. M came to the Hilton, he lost $999,800. One of the casino bosses tossed $200 of his own money on the table and told the dealer to drop it so the loss would roll over to a million. In that moment, both Cyr and Bean "popped their cherries" (this only happens when a host wins a million *in one session*, not when he surpasses a million lifetime). The whale, a senior official in the Malaysian government—a public servant—had a million cash to lose over a weekend.

Bean later went to Malaysia to visit Mr. M. When he arrived, the plane, a commercial airliner, stopped before the gate and the ground crew pulled up one of the little ladders. Bean alone deplaned. He was ushered by three army officers into a huge limo waiting on the tarmac to whisk him away. Then the plane continued to the gate. He never went through customs or immigration.

Some tension existed between Bean and the Asian player reps, who typically feel that Caucasian hosts should stick to their own kind. (Asian hosts have also been known to have their own side deals with players, obscured from the casino bosses by the language differences. They hate it when a white guy can talk to one of their players in his own language.) The problem was exacerbated when a number of Japanese high rollers took a liking to Doug. One decided to put him to his own litmus test. He paged Bean and asked him to come up to his room. Bean knocked on the door and from inside, the high roller called out, "What time is it?"

Bean called back in, "Two o'clock."

"Afternoon or night?"

"Afternoon."

"All right."

"That's it?" Bean asked.

"Yes. That's it."

Apparently, he passed the test, because soon thereafter, the Japanese high roller was flying Bean around America while he visited horse farms in search of top thoroughbreds, relying on the Hilton host to translate and interpret American business and social customs.

Bean also hosted Mr. L, a Japanese billionaire-banker whale. Mr. L had been visiting Las Vegas since the 1970s. For more than 25 years, he came once a year for a couple of weeks, and as he grew richer, his limits got higher and his bets got bigger. So did his entourage. When Bean hosted him, his retinue consisted of 40 people, including his dozen or so children and grandchildren. The youngest, a five-year-old, had his own Visa card—his grandfather owned the bank.

From the 1970s through the late 1990s when he retired, Jimmy Newman, the most powerful executive in the Hilton company aside from Barron Hilton, handled Mr. L personally. Of course, a herd of hosts often hovered a holler away, including Bean, who eventually took on Mr. L—and everything that came with him.

One time the Japanese banker was scheduled to arrive in Las Vegas a few days after Bean's first daughter was due to be born. The baby was late and Bean was going nuts. He called the obstetrician and said, "Look, man, you've got to induce! Deliver this baby so I can host my whale!"

Another time, a couple of younger members of Mr. L's entourage took a red Hilton limo to an In-N-Out Burger on West Tropicana. They loved the place and told their grandfather about it. The next day, the whole entourage hit In-N-Out. It took 12 red limos—every one the Hilton had—and Bean had to stand out by the ordering box, fading the height of summer heat in his dark suit and necktie, translating burgers, fries, and milkshakes for 40 Japanese in a dozen Hilton limos. Bean could only imagine what the long line of lunchgoers thought about the Hilton limo parade ahead of them—until the first car, with Wisconsin license plates, pulled up after waiting in the line. Bean was still standing at the squawk box, loosening his tie and wiping the sweat from his neck, when a Grandpa Kettle-type leaned out of the car window and said, "Son, this is the classiest burger barn I've ever seen."

Bean wanted to do a good job for Mr. L. First, he was Jimmy Newman's customer, and if the whale put in a good word with the boss, it helped his cause. Second, it didn't hurt having a billionaire banker in his Rolodex. And third, with luck he'd get a handshake. A handshake from Mr. L was usually good for five figures. Not five *fingers*. Five *figures*.

Unlike Cyr, Bean never intended to remain a casino host for long. He regularly picked his customers' brains to find out how they became successful, thinking that perhaps some of it might rub off on him. Bean knew that at some point in his casino career, it would become too aggravating to minister to millionaires while he was making $100,000 a year.

❖　❖　❖

Dan London was a longtime Las Vegas casino marketing executive who never lived in Sin City. Instead, he worked out of an office in the City by the Bay. He was a "branch guy," as opposed to a "property guy" like Cyr, who had an office inside the casino. London's job was to target Bay Area gamblers on behalf of whatever casino he happened to be shilling for at the moment. First it was the Tropicana, then it was the Las Vegas Hilton (later he worked for the MGM Grand).

There's a world of difference between branch and property hosts. All a property guy has to do to bump into customers is hang around the casino cage. A branch guy is away from the casino, in San Francisco, Chicago, San Diego, Hong Kong, Taipei, wherever. How does he find his customers?

When he first started working for the Tropicana in 1988, London owned a Bay Area sports bar that pretty much ran itself. He knew little about casinos, but he was a salesman. He understood the secret of moving people. First and foremost in business is customer relations. A close second is the deal. Deals move people: credit lines, minimum and maximum bets, comps, discounts on losses. Players can gamble anywhere—Vegas, Reno, Atlantic City, the Bahamas, Macau, Genting Highlands, even Moscow. What keeps them coming back to a particular casino, though, are the relationships and the numbers.

London's first months on the job were tough, to say the least. The Tropicana marketing bosses just threw him out there without training, leads, or so much as a good luck. He reported for work bright and early every morning dressed in his suit and tie, then sat at his desk staring at the telephone, which never rang. He had to get creative in a hurry.

His first idea was to drive to South Lake Tahoe and cruise the casino parking lots, jotting down California license-plate numbers. When he returned to San Francisco, he enlisted a couple of cops who hung out at his bar to run the tags and get the names and addresses of the vehicles' owners. He cold-called them, visited their businesses, and if he learned that they were big-time gamblers, sent them fruit baskets—anything to establish a relationship. It didn't work, and after a month of futility and failure, he gave up on the tactic.

Then one night he was heading home when he walked past the marketing office for Caesars World—at that time the parent company for Caesars Palaces in Las Vegas, Lake Tahoe, and Atlantic City—in its own building near his office at Fisherman's Wharf. He stopped outside the door, wondering how he might get a peek at the list of Caesars' big-time northern California gamblers. Then he noticed the dumpster sitting behind the Caesars World office building. Inspiration struck.

By staking out the building, he discovered that two nights a week the janitor arrived promptly at 7 p.m. He cleaned for a couple of hours, then dropped a half-dozen garbage bags into the dumpster on his way out.

The night London made his first dumpster play, it was foggy and windy. He pulled his car into the parking lot behind Caesars World and cut his headlights. The foghorns moaned mournfully out on the bay and the wind howled. Spooky.

He got out of his car and looked around. He shivered—whether from the cold and damp or fright, he couldn't tell. He approached the dumpster and opened the lid. A rat jumped out, landed at his feet, and scurried away into the shadows. London's heart pounded.

He grabbed the Caesars World trash bags, tossed them into his trunk, and tore out of there. At home, he donned rubber gloves and began sorting through used coffee filters, candy wrappers, soda cans, pizza boxes, apple cores, dirty tissues—and potentially precious paperwork. He searched for computer lists, phone messages, anything that might identify Caesars' local high-end Bay Area customers.

Little turned up that first night. Little turned up for a month. But London was desperate. He was obsessed. Twice a week at 9 p.m. like clockwork, he sat waiting in his car in view of the Caesars World dumpster. After the janitor dumped the trash and split, he opened the lid, kicked the bin to flush out the rat, and hauled home the garbage bags.

One night he noticed something. A Bay Area gambler had lost $50,000 two weeks earlier and a memo was sent out from the player's casino, in this instance Caesars Las Vegas, to the San Francisco branch office. A copy of the memo, complete with the player's name, address, and phone number, had found its way into a garbage can, a garbage bag, and the garbage dumpster, then onto Dan London's kitchen floor. Bingo. Based on this "action report" on a bona fide player, he could now call the customer, promise him the moon, and woo him to the Trop.

There were more leads to come. Every time a Bay Area player lost $50,000 or more at a Caesars casino, the local office received a similar memo, a copy of which, two weeks later, spilled out of a garbage bag at Dan London's feet.

Though London had no telemarketing experience, neither did he have any fear of cold-calling customers. After all, the marks were gamblers. Out of the blue they'd hear from this host running down a long list of luxuries that were theirs for the taking. All they had to do was show up.

Dan London began acquiring customers for the Tropicana and earned the nickname "Public Domain" (he researched the garbage laws and found that once someone dropped trash into an outside receptacle, anyone can legally go through it).

Six months after he began intercepting the Caesars office trash, London had to go out of town, but he was loath to miss even one appointment at the dumpster. He went to a close friend for help: "Jimmy, you gotta pick up the garbage for me. Go to the dumpster at the Caesars office. The rat'll jump out, but don't worry; he's used to it." Jimmy shuddered, but he did the deed for Dan.

When he got home, London dug through the pizza crusts and tea bags and hit the jackpot. Buried in the haul that he might have missed was the master list for Caesars' best northern California gamblers, a total of 1,300 names. Company executives had apparently developed a new computer format and tossed out the mailing list from the old one. London finally had all he needed.

Shortly after, Hilton had an opening for a branch guy in its San Francisco office and recruited him. Working for the Hilton now, he and Cyr spoke on the phone occasionally. One day Cyr told him that he'd be in San Francisco that week on personal business. London picked him up at the airport. They started talking and Cyr couldn't believe how little London knew about the property he worked for. He'd visited the Hilton when he was hired, but he'd never been given a tour of the suites. He always requested a third-floor lanai room with a king-size bed for his players, because that's where he'd stayed and found it acceptable. But he didn't know, for example, that there were only six kings on the third floor. London might put in a request for two of them for his players over a weekend, then wonder why neither got one.

"Listen, Dan," Cyr said. "Come to Vegas next week and I'll show you around."

When London arrived, Cyr blew his mind. He had no idea about the Classic Suites on the 29th floor, let alone the Sky Villas on the 30th. He didn't even know he could requisition a fruit basket or a bottle of champagne to leave in the room with his business card.

Cyr put London through his unofficial player-rep training program. He made London traipse through all the suites, same as he did all the other orangutans. He made him eat at the restaurants, once with a big player, Mr. K, in tow. He called it "Supping with Steve." London watched Cyr toke the maitre d' $20 just to reinforce their deal that any of his players could walk right in and sit right down, even at eight o'clock on a Saturday night.

He listened to how Cyr talked. "Hey Mr. K, after dinner, you're not gonna embarrass me, right? You're gonna fire it up, aren't you?"

He learned that it was all right, necessary even, to harangue a player. He was amazed when Cyr told Mr. K, "All right, I comped dinner, but you gotta pick up the toke." A lot of the hosts were afraid to go to dinner with their players, afraid they might have to leave the gratuity, which was often $50, $75, even $100. Cyr's way eliminated the financial concern.

London hadn't known about any of it. But after the Cyr Tour, his player losses increased by a factor of five.

They went up again big time after London attended a few classes at the Steve Cyr School of Telemarketing.

6

Telemarketing the Marks

When Steve Cyr arrived in Las Vegas in 1984, he was so green that he didn't know what juice (the Las Vegas term for power) was. Thus, he didn't know that he didn't have any. But by 1997, after a half-decade at the Hilton, he *was* the juice.

Most weekday mornings, he sat at his desk, wearing a PBX-operator-type headset with earphone, mouthpiece, and wire between the two, dialing for players and making judicious use of his juice.

"Mr. J? STEEEEVE CYYYYR from the Las Vegas Hilton. When're ya gonna get your ass back to Vegas and make me look good?"

"Len, old frien'! STEEEEVE CYYYYR from the Las Vegas Hilton. I've got the Hawker coming out to Omaha next Friday to pick up another player. Wanna be on it?"

"Barney, baby! STEEEEVE CYYYYR from the Las Vegas Hilton. Everything's set. You've got a Classic Suite both nights, eight tickets to see David Copperfield at Caesars, and I'm picking you up myself from the airport in a Hilton limo."

"Mahmoud, my man! STEEEEVE CYYYYR from the Las Vegas Hilton. Your buddy Tony's coming in this weekend. He's bringing cash and a couple of girls. I got him a two-bedroom suite and four tickets to the fight. He wants *you* to *be there*."

"Mr. I? STEEEEVE CYYYYR from the Las Vegas Hilton. We've got you booked into the Del Coronado. You'll heli-

copter from LAX to the Del and check in. I've got a couple
bottles of Cristal waiting for you, plus a box of Cohibas, those
cheddar-cheese pretzels you like, and a bowl of M&M's—
only the green ones. Have a ball. Next weekend, though,
you're coming to the Hilton to pay me back."

"Larry and Liz! STEEEEVE CYYYYR. Super Bowl
parteeee! You're set up for a half-million, plus twenty K in
chips and a fifteen percent discount on losses. But hell, you
never lose!"

"Chris! STEEEEVE CYYYYR from the Las Vegas Hilton.
Am I your fuckin' hero or what? Here's the deal ..."

"Mr. H? STEEEEVE CYYYYR from the Las Vegas Hilton. You want it? You got it. Just come to *Vegas*, baby."

❖ ❖ ❖

You learn quickly how to sell to gamblers. And it's easy,
because first, you're selling what they're dying to buy anyway—casino candy. And second, it's all done over the phone.
There are no visuals—no body language, no facial expres-
sions, no twitches or tics or tells. It's all tone and terms and,
of course, telemarketing.

The lead is the main thing and Cyr had his leads coming
from all over the place—database lists, his crew of orangutans, other high rollers, and his network of moles at the tables
and in pits, cages, executive offices, suites, porticos, bell
desks, limos, and strip clubs, not to mention dozens of other
nooks and crannies scattered all over town.

How did Cyr inveigle so many casino informants?

The vaunted old-school code of silence among gamblers
and casino workers still remains in effect, to a certain extent.
There's a definite us-and-them mentality in the casino business. It's the rare gambler who trusts a non-gambler. It's the
rare casino boss who'll talk about his world to the straight
sector. Even the laborers in the casino trenches know it's
usually in their best interests to keep their mouths shut.

The code isn't, to be sure, as strict as it used to be, when casino trade secrets were graveyard. As in all businesses, information is power. And information, even in the close-knit casino culture, is usually for sale.

You're a limo driver. You pick up Mr. G at the airport. You already have a pretty good inkling that he's a VIP (you're picking him up in a 22-foot-long car, after all), but his girl-friend confirms it as she exudes excitement about staying in a Palazzo Suite at the Rio. You can identify a bona fide high roller. It's a salable tidbit.

You're a Rio bellman. You know Mr. G is going into a Palazzo Suite. So you know he has to be a half-million dollar player.

You're a hostess in VIP Services. You have the keys ready for the Palazzo Suite when the bellman comes in to schlep Mr. G's bags.

You're a cashier at the cage who gets Mr. G's credit ready. You know his credit info, bank balances, how much he owes, and to whom.

You're a pit clerk who knows Mr. G wants a private crap table.

You're a shift boss who tells every crap dealer, "Mr. G's playing tonight. Fuck up and you're fired."

Dealers call dealers all over town and everyone knows that a high roller's coming in. Even butlers who sign confi-dentiality agreements and are sworn to secrecy occasionally give up a valuable detail. Nothing's sacred.

Steve Cyr is often the highest bidder for information. Once he gets the name of a premium player and a descrip-tion (the valet might say, "He drives a Ferrari"; the pit clerk might say, "He bets five thousand a hand"; the stripper might say, "He dropped a grand in fifteen minutes"), the Cyr Sys-tem goes into overdrive.

The player's Central Credit file reveals enough to deter-mine if, and how, to approach him. Then comes the phone call.

The first challenge is to bulldoze through the barriers of

inaccessibility these high-powered players erect to protect their privacy.

"Hello, is Mr. F in?"

"May I tell him who's calling?"

"Steve Cyr from the Las Vegas Hilton."

"I'm sorry. He's in a closed-door conference."

"I know. I'm supposed to talk to him during the conference."

The Mr. F's of the world are rarely in a closed-door conference; typically, they're sitting alone at their desks. But one time, Mr. F actually *was* in a closed-door conference and made the mistake of taking the call and putting it on the speaker phone. "Who's this?"

"Mr. F, this is STEEEEVE CYYYYR from the Las Vegas Hilton."

Mr. F practically leaped onto the phone; he couldn't pick it up fast enough. "What the fuck is this? How the hell did you get through?" he whispered into the mouthpiece.

"I got ten thousand reasons for you to come see me at the Hilton this weekend when you're staying at Caesars."

Mr. F couldn't capitulate on the spot, but Cyr'd gotten his attention. "Jesus! You've got some kind of balls. What's your number? I'll call you back."

Another trick: "Good morning. Mr. Evergood's office."

"Hi, who's this?"

"This is Bonnie."

"Bonnie! It's STEEEEVE CYYYYR from the Hilton. Is Roger in?"

Now Bonnie's thinking: *Do I know this guy? Maybe I'm supposed to. He sure seems to know Roger.* She says, "Yes, but he's in a meeting."

"Okay, I can hold for him."

"Well, it's gonna be a *long* meeting."

Cyr looks at his watch and it's 8:45. "Well, Roger wanted me to call him at eight-thirty, but I'm running a little late today. I don't want him mad at me."

"Would you like to leave a message?"

"Of course."

It isn't perfect, but it's something. Cyr would never say, "Just tell him Steve Cyr from the Hilton called." Weak. Instead, he'd say, "I'm holding those five-thousand-dollar Tyson tickets"—or front row for Kool and the Gang on New Year's Eve or the helicopter to the Grand Canyon—"that he requested."

That makes Bonnie think again: *Damn, Roger must really want this.* And she doesn't want Roger mad at her, either.

"I'm gonna be giving them away to *someone* today, so he needs to call me."

Now Bonnie's under prime-time pressure.

"Hold a moment, please."

She buzzes Roger and says, "I've got Steve Cyr from the Las Vegas Hilton on the line. He says he's got those tickets to the Tyson fight you requested."

Eight out of ten times, Roger takes the call. "What did I request?"

"Hi Roger. Listen, we talked two months ago at Caesars. You said you'd never stay at the Hilton unless I got you ringside tickets to the Tyson fight. I got 'em for you. They're right here in my hot little hand. I'm looking at Section Seventeen, Row B. Can't put you in Row A. That's where Barron Hilton sits. What time can my limo pick you up at the airport?"

Cyr always leaves messages offering an opportunity. More often than not, "opportunity messages" earn return phone calls.

Once he gets the gambler on the phone, the odds are in Cyr's favor. Whether they realize it or not, these gamblers are just dying for an excuse to hit Vegas and play. The right phone number's the key. A direct line to the customer is the closer; it practically clinches the deal all by itself.

One way to do it fast is to lead with questions that have affirmative answers. "You're gonna be in town this Friday, right?"

"Right."

"You're a dice shooter, right?"

"Right."

"Does it work for you if the first ten thousand dollars is on the house?"

"Hell yes!"

"I'll have the limo pick you up at nine o'clock, okay?"

"Okay."

❖ ❖ ❖

Cyr always has his pitch ready and he never deviates from it, because then he sounds different. The customer picks up on that right away and stops trusting him.

He knows he has 10 seconds to make the customer believe he's his best friend or he'll lose him. He *never* starts a pitch with, "Hi. My name is Steve Cyr." What that really says is, "You don't know me, but you should let me waste your time while I attempt to sell you something." It's the kiss of death.

Instead: "Hey, Mr. D! It's STEEEEVE CYYYYR from the Las Vegas Hilton. Got a smokin' deal for you. Let's discuss it over dinner at Le Montrachet, on me of course. How's eight o'clock?"

And then, he's prepared with a rebuttal for anything Mr. D might come back with.

"Well, I don't have time to come over for dinner."

"Ya gotta eat, don't ya? I'm gonna have a limo pick you up and drop you off. It's only fifteen minutes extra out of your night."

"Well, I'll have to check with my wife."

"Hey, we're gonna give your wife a surprise shopping spree. Don't tell her or you'll ruin it!"

"Well, I've already got dinner plans for both nights."

"Fine. Forget dinner. But I've got *twenty-five thousand reasons* for you to come over to the Hilton, if you get my drift.

Now, are you gonna run over here on your own two feet to get those reasons, if you get my drift? Or would you rather I send that limo for you?"

"Well, I don't get your drift, son. Why don't you spell it out for me so there's no misunderstanding."

"Mr. D, in Vegas, you're a star. And we're gonna give you an appearance fee. You know how they pay Robert Redford ten grand to show up somewhere? We're gonna give you twenty-five just to walk in the door."

The money line is the power line. The deal closer. No further rebuttal necessary. Not one player in a hundred can resist free loot. Even if a guy gets offered just $1,000 or $500, he'll come over to collect. It works on all levels. Low rollers get $20, $10, $5, even $2 in "bounce-back" cash coupons in the mail and they can't run to the casino fast enough.

Cyr keeps pitching. He keeps selling. He has a rebuttal for anything anyone could think of to say. Mr. D is the one in a hundred who says no to twenty-five Gs? Turns him down flat? No sweat. Mr. D's a waste of time. Cross him off the list. On to the next sucker.

❖ ❖ ❖

A limo mole calls up and reports that a Mr. C is staying in an MGM Grand suite for the weekend. For that, the driver takes down a Cyr-issued lunch comp for two at the Hilton buffet. Cyr gets on the horn and calls a floorman mole at the MGM. Since the floorman has access to the pit computer, he can give Cyr the one other piece of vital information he needs: date of birth. For that he comps the floorman dinner for two at the Hilton coffee shop. With the DOB, he can go right into Mr. C's Central and find everything he needs to know about him—address, home and office phone numbers, a $50,000 line at Luxor, and a $10,000 loss at the Frontier in February '97.

"Hey Mr. C! STEEEEVE CYYYYR from the Las Vegas Hilton." Cyr might track him down at MGM Grand while he's there or at his home or office the week after. "We met earlier this year when I worked at the Frontier. I remember it was around Valentine's Day."

"Sure, I remember," Mr. C buys right into Cyr's lie, not wanting to admit that he doesn't remember. "I was with my girlfriend. It was our first trip to Vegas together. Had a great time."

"Ah ha. So you lost ten thousand, but you got the girl. ... Did your wife find out? Ha ha."

"Ha ha."

And a connection is made. From there it's a hop and a skip to, "Wanna really impress your girlfriend, Mr. C? Come on in a week from Wednesday and I'll give you two nights in a Classic Suite. Usually you need a hundred-thousand-dollar line to stay up there, and if Larry Flynt or Michael Jordan shows up, I'll have to bump you down. But that's unlikely. For those two nights, you and your babe can enjoy yourselves in real style."

Mr. C bites and Cyr's brought in a $50,000 player for the cost of a room that would've been empty anyway. It's an excellent second-tier catch for the whale hunter.

❖ ❖ ❖

The next time, it's a bellman at the Mirage who calls and says, "Mr. B is staying in one of our villas. His luggage tags say he comes from Chickasha, Oklahoma." The bellman gets dinner for two at Benihana.

A week or two later, Cyr gets out his Rand McNally Road Atlas, studies Oklahoma for a few moments, then gets Mr. B on the phone.

"Mr. B! STEEEEVE CYYYYR from the Las Vegas Hilton. Listen, sorry to bother you, but a friend of mine from the Mirage mentioned you the other day and said that you lived in Chickasha. When I was in the service, I was stationed at Fort Sill. I used to drive through Chickasha all the time on my way to Oklahoma City. And there was this hamburger place. They had the best bacon cheeseburgers I've ever eaten. What the hell was the name of that joint?"

"Oh, you mean Bill's Burger Shack? Best burgers in Chickasha, that's for sure."

A lesser host might laugh or trip himself up, but Cyr doesn't miss a beat. "Yeah! That's the place. My mouth is starting to water. Is it still there?"

The connection is made and Cyr does a little more telemarketing magic and one more high roller is on his way to the Hilton.

❖ ❖ ❖

Another ploy. A dealer at MGM calls and tells Cyr about Mr. A, a big player and an even bigger drinker who sat at her table the night before. Cyr asks what table she was dealing at and she tells him the one closest to the coffee shop. For this she gets two tickets to *Starlight Express*.

A month later, Cyr gets the guy on the phone and says, "Hey Mr. A! STEEEEVE CYYYYR from the Las Vegas Hilton. I met you about a month ago at the MGM Grand. You were playing at the table where you can smell the food from the coffee shop. I handed you my card and you promised you'd call."

But Mr. A doesn't bite. Instead, he says, "I don't know you. I don't have your card. And I never said I'd call. What kind of crap are you trying to pull?"

"Well, I'm not surprised you don't remember. You were pretty, uh, happy when we were chatting. I was the guy on third base, making the dealer bust and saving your butt. You do remember Claire, the dealer, don't you? Blond, big tits, rings on every finger?"

"I remember *her*. It's you I'm having trouble with."

"Hey, no sweat, Mr. A. I'm a pretty average guy. All I wanted to do was treat you and your wife to a nice weekend at the Hilton. I've made a reservation for you for the twenty-third and twenty-fourth in the Renaissance Suite. I'll call you back on Monday to re-confirm and get your flight info so I can have a limousine meet you at the air-port. Here's my phone number if you think of anything else I can do for you."

❖ ❖ ❖

It used to be considered unethical to call a player at home. This taboo died hard and fast as soon as Cyr started using the phone to steal players from the senior hosts who still abided by it. But even when old-school marketing executives had to start calling players to compete with the new-breed of telemarketing hosts, they still never did so on a weekend. Cyr, however, just couldn't lay off Sundays. He worked Sun-days. He also reasoned that it's the one day almost everyone is home. He'd call up and say, "You know, Mr. B, I was think-ing about you on my way home from church."

❖ ❖ ❖

Not even death stops a single-minded host like Cyr. He goes after the widow.

"Hello, is this Mrs. C?"

"Yes."

"Hi, this is Steve Cyr from the Las Vegas Hilton. Is Mr. C at home?"

"Uh, no, he isn't."

"I used to work at the Desert Inn and I knew Mr. C over there. It's been a couple of years since we've seen you or your husband."

"Well, John died eight months ago."

"Oh! I'm so sorry to hear that, Mrs. C. John was such a great guy. I enjoyed being his host every time he came to town."

Cyr doesn't know John from Adam. It's an old lead he got from somewhere, a phone number he's finally getting around to following up on. He's bluffing, coming right off the top of his head. "He was one of my favorite players. You used to come out to Vegas with him, as I recall, didn't you?"

"I certainly did. John never went anywhere without me."

"And you used to like to play the hundred-dollar slots, didn't you, Mrs. C?" Cyr takes a shot in the dark to see if she's a player.

"Well, honey, the hundred-dollar slots were a little rich for my blood, but I did get a thrill out of the twenty-five dollar machines."

Bingo.

"Do you still come out to Las Vegas?"

"I haven't since the funeral, but you know what? My girlfriends and I were just talking about taking a trip out there …"

"Well, here's what I'm gonna do. I'm gonna fax one of my business cards to you."

If she doesn't have a fax number, Cyr might FedEx a single business card. He wants to get something in a player's hands right away, within the hour; later today's too late; tomorrow it's lost. Actually, he wants to fax Mrs. C the credit paperwork to sign, then have her fax it back, all while the two of them are still on the phone.

"And I'm gonna book a reservation for you for three weeks from this Friday. That should be enough time to make your plans, shouldn't it? When you get my card, call me back and we'll get all your girlfriends set up too. How's that sound?"

"That's very thoughtful of you, young man."

"Least I can do for John. I sure am sorry to hear about him, Mrs. C. But we'll take good care of you in his memory."

❖ ❖ ❖

Gamblers had no chance against Cyr. He could outtalk them, he could outthink them, he could dance around them like Muhammad Ali in the ring.

He was inexorable. He was like the tides. He wouldn't let up. He rarely gave up. It was the customers who gave in. They had to. The only way to get him to stand down was to say yes. He was closing the deal before the poor suckers could open their mouths.

No one in Vegas could verbally hammer away like Steve Cyr.

❖ ❖ ❖

Cyr and his fellow hosts frequently played the Round Table game. Six or eight of them got together at Cyr's office, the one Bradshaw gave him, which he outfitted with three phone lines, a conference table, a couch, a TV/VCR, even a little humidor. Six or eight orangutans could fit in the office, sitting at the table around the phones. They smoked cigars and played poker for $5 and $10 while one of them cold-called a player. The others listened, then critiqued the call when it was done.

One time at the Round Table, Nick Ippolito explained that he'd been after Mr. D, a slot whale. His home phone was on file. Nick called him and left a hundred messages over a six-month period, but it was on the answering-machine phone, which no one ever picked up. Mr. D never returned Nick's calls. No one had his private home number, which he actually answered, or his work number. His Central Credit file didn't have them. Finally, someone picked up the home phone and Nick managed to get Mr. D's direct line at work. Now he needed to know how to handle it.

Since he'd phoned this guy and left tons of messages with nary a response, Mr. D obviously didn't want to talk to Nick. But he probably didn't want him leaving message after message on his voice mail at work, either. So the group decided to give Mr. D a nearly foolproof reason to phone back: Nick would piss him off. Who cared if he called because he was mad? At least the guy would be on the other end of the line. If he told Nick to buzz off, fine. Cross him off the list. Next sucker. But maybe he'd take just enough rope to hang himself. Or maybe he'd even appreciate an obvious, though gentle, con.

Nick called Mr. D's office and got his voicemail. He left this message: "Mr. D, this is Nick Ippolito from the Las Vegas Hilton. You've got to do me a big favor—save a guy's job. Spare his life, actually. You *know* me. I've left dozens of messages on your machine at home, inviting you to everything under the sun. All you had to do was c'mon in, have some fun, play a little. You're playing everywhere else around town. Or you could've just told me thanks but no thanks, and I would've stopped buggin' ya.

"Trouble is, for the past few weeks, all my big slot players have been winning. You wouldn't believe how these bad boys have been rakin' it in the past ten days or so. Half my players are cleaning my clock. The other half, like you, won't return a phone call. I'm on kind of a losing streak here, Mr. D, if you know what I mean. And now my boss, Steve Cyr, is gonna fire me. Today. I can't get fired, Mr. D! I've got three kids. My mother-in-law lives with me. My wife's gonna leave me—and she's not gonna take the kids or her mother with her! You gotta help me out here! Please, *please*, call me back!"

Mr. D, it turned out, did have a sense of humor. He called back and eventually agreed to play at the Hilton—though not before Nick had to use the power line, the deal closer: free loot.

This episode gave Cyr an inspiration. A couple of mornings later, he called a player Robert Coury was having trouble closing and said, "Hi, Mr. E? STEEEEVE CYYYYR from the Las Vegas Hilton. I'm Robert Coury's supervisor. I'm looking at your file and I don't see a reservation for Super Bowl weekend. What happened? Didn't he call you? He did? Well then, I don't have to fire his ass for not *calling* you, but I do have to fire his ass for not *getting* you here ..."

It worked. And from that, he got the idea to call back the same players he himself couldn't close the first time. He used his telephone voice-changing device and pretended to be his own supervisor, threatening to term himself if the player didn't show a little speed. Then he called back as himself, begging the guy not to let him get fired.

❖ ❖ ❖

Cyr'd had his sights set on Moe Cohn for years. He knew he played at the Mirage, that he was a personal friend of Steve Wynn's, and that his real name wasn't Tom Smith, like it said on his player's ID card. Everyone was in on that particular secret, but his real name? No one—not the valets, bellmen, dealers, floormen, pit clerks, not even the pit bosses—knew.

The Mirage pit personnel gave him markers on the rim, which means he paid off his losses at the end of his visit. And he had two player cards, one under Mr. S for the pit, the other under his real name for the cage. Word on the Strip held that he'd never play anywhere but a Wynn joint. But Steve Cyr never believed the word on the Strip.

Eventually, Cyr sweet-talked a Mirage cashier and traded a couple hundred dollars in comps for two words: Moe Cohn. Cyr tracked him down at his office in California and started cold-calling him.

"Hey, Mr. C! STEEEEVE CYYYYR from the Las Vegas Hilton. Say the word and I'll send Barron Hilton's G Three to fetch you, put you up in a Sky Villa, and throw a private dinner party for twenty on Saturday night—"

"Stop calling me or I'll sue your ass for harassment!"

Cyr called him once a week for more than a year until one day he just laid it on the line. "Look, the Mirage is playing you for a sucker. Did you know that?"

"Huh?"

"When you lose a million at the Mirage, how much do you pay off?" Cyr didn't wait for an answer. "I'll tell you how much: a million! Why are you paying an extra hundred and fifty grand?"

"What are you talking about?"

"I know you just lost two million at the Mirage."

"How do you know that?"

"What difference does it make? You lost two million and you paid the *whole* two million. With me, you'd only pay a million seven. We give you a discount on the loss."

"All right, look, kid. I'll make you a deal. I'm gonna call the Mirage and ask about the discount. If you're lying to me and I find out, this is the last time you ever call me. Agreed?"

"All right, but if I'm not lying, you come in and play at the Hilton."

"Hang on." Cohn put Cyr on hold. When he came back, he said, "Well, my host tells me they only discount losses for international players."

"Right. So you're a politician from Indonesia and you get a discount, but you're a stand-up domestic business guy and you get nothing? I'll give you fifteen percent on losses right now. And I'll double the table limits that those pussies at the Mirage hold you down to. And ..." Cyr took a shot in the dark, knowing Cohn's proclivity for privacy, "I'll put the crap table in the baccarat pit and give you your own crew."

Cyr closed the crap whale. One night later on, Moe Cohn made the biggest laydown Cyr had ever seen: $240,000 on a single roll of the dice.

❖   ❖   ❖

The cold-calling, the phoning for fish, the dialing for degenerates—it's all just the first phase of the massive amount of telephone work in the life of a casino host. At the height of his tenure at the Hilton, Cyr spent hours every day on the phone, only a portion of which was calling people he didn't know. The rest of the time, he was talking to existing players (many of whom he'd hooked through a cold-call). When Cyr called gamblers, he always tried to make them an offer they couldn't refuse. But when gamblers called Cyr, wanting something, then he got to play a little hard-to-get.

A smart host always wants to make it sound like whatever a player wants is iffy, like he might qualify, but then again he might not. Cyr likes his players to think that what they want means *work*—having to fight with his bosses for a bigger suite, more tickets to the show, better seats at the fight, higher room-service limits, and so forth. An inexperienced or scared or slow-witted host often falls into a trap where, when a player calls and asks for something like four tickets to the Tyson-Holyfield fight, he says, "No problem, Mr. F." He wants to make it look effortless, so Mr. F'll stick with him, knowing that anything he wants he gets.

But all the while Mr. F is thinking, "Hell, that was easy. I should've asked for *eight* tickets.

A host like Cyr says, "Jesus, Mr. F! *Four* tickets? You're killin' me. I mean, you're definitely worth it, but they're not easy to come by and they cost like four thousand each and that's sixteen K and you know Mr. G is also after me for four tickets and he's a five-million-dollar player. … But listen. It's ten o'clock now. Let me see what I can do. I'll call you back in an hour."

Of course, Cyr already has the tickets. They're sitting right there on his desk. Five of them, in fact (so Cyr can sit with the party), Section Five, Row A. He's actually shuffling them while he's stringing Mr. F along.

At eleven, Cyr calls back.

"Did ya get 'em? Did ya get 'em?" Mr. F is a bit too anxious, so Cyr decides to keep him on edge. "Listen, I'm gonna get 'em. I'm gonna take care of you. Have I ever let you down?"

And then, when he finally cops to having the tickets, he can say, "Hey, who's your fuckin' hero, baby?"

His job might be to give his players what they want, but between "No" and "Yes" there's a whole universe of "It depends on the whether."

Part Two
Harpoons

"Here's a little tip I would like to relate,
Many fish bites if you got good bait."
—Taj Mahal, "Fishin' Blues"

"And the people bowed and prayed
To the neon god they made."
—Paul Simon, "Sounds of Silence"

7

Rolling Dead Chips

All gamblers, big and small, look for excuses to be in action. The surface motivation for most is straightforward. Many play for the adrenaline buzz of placing money at risk. Others are in it solely for the competition, to match their bankroll against the casino's and may the better bettor win. Some play to drink and get loose and wild. Others put themselves out there to attract like-minded members of the opposite sex. Some just want to feel like sports and wheels.

It doesn't take much for most, but some need more.

In order to validate their gambling indulgences, casinogoers often seek to entitle themselves. Entitlement comes in various forms: learning perfect strategy at video poker or basic strategy and card counting at blackjack, or even just reading a how-to book in order to get (or to *think* they've gotten) to the point where they have an edge in the game. Less effort is required for gamblers to simply convince themselves that they're preternaturally lucky and that losing is a mere aberration in the long-term winning scheme of things.

Or they tell themselves that the comps are much too strong to pass up. This is where the hosts come into play. Hosts give gamblers any and every excuse in the book. After all, hosts have more different kinds of temptations at their disposal than Willy Wonka.

Ten-room penthouse palazzos? Right this way.

Gift certificates for $50,000 at the mall? Just hold out your hand.

Streisand on New Year's Eve? How's fifth-row center?

A hard-bodied young sex goddess to hang around with, both vertically and horizontally? Someone knows someone who knows one.

A little jaunt to Cabo? Cancun? Caymans? Costa Rica? Cairo? Calcutta? "Who's your fuckin' hero, baby?"

There are as many reasons for gambling as there are gamblers, and each has his own preferences for casino treats. But the one thing they all care about in common is the deal.

❖ ❖ ❖

The deal involves comps, credit lines, minimum and maximum bets, appearance fees, and discounts on losses. The former three would be recognizable to any casino boss who's lived during the past 2,000 years. The latter two are recent wrinkles on the high-roller scene.

Automatic discounts on losses originated in Las Vegas in the depressed pre-Mirage 1980s. Early in the decade, Caesars began offering 5% discounts—secretively, to be sure— to its international high rollers who paid off their markers within 30 or 60 days. It was a minor incentive, but it was, nonetheless, a perk that any gambler who heard about it and could do rudimentary arithmetic wanted for himself. As soon this new wrinkle on the deal spread through the gambler grapevine, big international players started demanding the same discount on their losses from all the premium casinos. The bosses had no choice but to provide a 5% discount to any player who qualified. This opened Pandora's box—and competition for high-stakes international play edged the discount ever upwards.

For a time, the industry standard on these rebates was 10% on all losses above $1 million. Then it went up to 15% on $2 million and 20% on $3 million or more. No discount on less than a million held up for a few years, until some player negotiated a rebate on a half-million and the rest of the casinos had to fall in line. From there, losses that qualified for a discount dropped to $250,000, then $100,000.

At some point in the brief history of discounts, the domestic hosts started making noises that it wasn't fair that only international players qualified. Cyr had shouting matches with the credit managers: "How stupid is this? You won't give Larry Flynt a discount on losses and he owns a thirty-eight-million-dollar building on Wilshire Boulevard that you could attach. Just the threat of it would hurt his business. Meanwhile, you're giving a Saudi prince ten percent off a half-mil if he pays in sixty days. How much more is it gonna cost you if you have to collect from *him*?"

In the beginning, aggressive hosts began rebating the losses of domestic players under the guise of airfare reimbursement. Of course, neither the host nor the credit manager relishes returning actual cash to a player, which he can then take to the tables for another shot at winning out. So "airfare" got refined. Instead of accepting a check for a $50,000 loss and giving back $2,500 cash in airfare reimbursement, the casino started calling it "marker reduction." When a player lost fifty, the host was authorized to collect $47,500.

It was just a matter of time before casinos ended this particular pretense and started calling the discount a discount. And once that happened, savvy domestic players again clamored to have their airfare reimbursed, on top of the loss rebate! Before Binion's Horseshoe was bought by Harrah's in early 2004, the legendary downtown Las Vegas joint was known to offer a discount as high as 20% on a loss as low as $100,000 if the player paid up in seven days. The joke among the Horseshoe hosts was, "Pretty soon we'll be giving discounts of a hundred percent of a player's losses."

Then another cash incentive entered the picture: show-up money, or what Cyr calls appearance fees. Initially, the amounts handed out were modest, but like discounts, the amounts quickly escalated to where it's now not uncommon for whales to ask for, and receive, $100,000, $150,000, even $200,000 in free play just to walk through the door.

❖ ❖ ❖

Walk-in money and discounts are poison-tipped harpoons in the harvesting of high rollers. The knife edge efficiently bleeds the bankroll of its blubber, while the poison has a powerful, though subtle, effect on a player's mindset. When the house provides a gambler with his first bets, it stimulates the love and the fever, which morphs into greed or fear by the time the sucker's playing with his own money.

In addition, a rebate keyed to a certain minimum loss often tempts a gambler to play higher. Mr. G knows that he'll get a 15% discount on a $100,000 loss. He's down $60,000 at the blackjack table. He figures that, although the $60,000 hurts, he might as well keep playing. If he loses another $25,000 to reach a total loss of $85,000, the next $15,000 is actually a free shot, because he'll only have to pay $85,000 if he tanks and blows the whole megillah. True, Mr. G might get lucky and battle back to breakeven (a win in his book: Getting unstuck is a true reprieve when you've been losing, especially losing big). But because of the discount, he won't stop at a $60,000 loss. He'll almost always play on.

Even so, many casino bosses and bean counters rue the day that the discount on losses was introduced. It's now a player entitlement that's almost impossible to rescind and many casinos have to swim pretty hard not to drown in these deep whale waters.

Put it all together. The casino has to give a guy money to come in. It has to reimburse his airfare, provide him with a limo, a villa or suite, food and beverage, a show, golf, and event tickets. It has to placate his lady with spa services and a shopping spree. And it has to give him a discount on his losses. (And if the player representative is a contractor instead of an employee, it has to pay his commission.)

The guy loses a million? After expenses, the million turns into $700,000. Not bad. But when the guy comes back and *wins* a million, the casino is upside down—and that doesn't include the tens of thousands in comps on the second trip. The joint now has to win $1.4 million or $1.5 million just to break even. The expense of buying casino business at the high end, many bosses believe, has gotten out of line.

In fact, an ill-structured combination of appearance fees and a hefty enough discount can actually negate the house advantage, so now the casino is in a situation where these whales have an advantage over them going in. If a professional video poker player making $25 bets on a $5 machine or a card counter getting away with $100 bets can hurt a casino by always playing with an edge, imagine what a $150,000-a-hand baccarat player with an advantage can do.

This problem is compounded by the fact that savvy players who keep an eye on the bouncing bankroll have figured out how to *maximize* opportunities created by discounting. Say Mr. H has a $1 million line of credit at the Hilton with a $25,000 appearance fee and a 15% discount on losses of $500,000 or more. Mr. H's goal is to win $475,000 (that plus the $25K bonus is a nice round figure, half his line) or lose $525,000 (that minus the bonus qualifies him for the discount). As soon as he loses the $525,000, there's no incentive for Mr. H to stay and play. He's already run through the free $25,000 and if he sticks around and tries to struggle back, he risks going below his rebate threshold, which means he'd have to win back more than $100,000 at that point to be in better shape than he'd be if he stopped and got back $75,000 for a net loss of $425,000. Mr. H is better off settling up for the $425,000 ($500,000 minus the 15% discount), then going to the Mirage, where he also has a $1 million credit line and a 15% discount on losses of a half-mil or more. There, he can start all over again, taking 100% of the wins, while only paying 85% of his losses.

Of course, it's in the Hilton's interest to keep Mr. H playing there, rather than have him pack up and move. So before the bosses let him walk out the door, they'll make him an offer that'll tempt him to stay: Settle up on the loss, reset the trip meter to zero, offer the 15% rebate on further losses, and maybe even fork over another $25K bonus. Amazingly, if Mr. H now wins back the original $500K, he still gets to keep the $75K rebate on that loss.

The predicament for the casino, of course, is that it can't go on indefinitely resetting the deal. The fact that the win/loss figure isn't looked at from a cumulative standpoint is what hurts the house. A player's expected loss (mathematically speaking) cannot overcome a deal that's segmented into too many sessions. There has to be a cumulative aspect or it's likely that the edge will swing over to the player's side permanently.

This gets technical, but briefly: Say the casino allows Mr. H to make a single bet at baccarat of $500,000. If he wins, he's paid the full half-mil. If he loses, however, he only has to pay $425,000. It doesn't take too many bets for Mr. H to start creaming the joint.

This is a serious conundrum for the casinos. Mandalay Resort Group (Mandalay Bay, Luxor, Excalibur, Monte Carlo, Circus Circus, among others) tried to institute a minimum requirement of 12 hours of play over the course of a visit to qualify for show-up money, airfare reimbursement, and rebate on losses, with a $10,000 minimum bet. This policy succeeded—in driving business to other properties that didn't have minimum bet or time stipulations. Competition for whales is so intense on the Las Vegas Strip that when a casino swims against the tide, it can easily tire itself out and pay an everlasting visit to Davy Jones' locker.

❖ ❖ ❖

Australian and Far East casinos, against which Vegas megaresorts also compete, have come up with a means for discounting losses without giving away the store.

In the Far East, casinos use a rebate technique known as "rolling dead chips." This method combines show-up money and a kickback on action. The chips the players get are "dead," meaning they have to be played through; they can't be cashed at the cage. And they "roll over," meaning players can continually buy more dead chips with cash or "live" chips.

For example, Mr. I negotiates a deal for a 10% bonus on $1 million. He goes to the cage, hands over the million, and receives $1.1 million in rolling dead chips. He plays his first hand of $10,000 and loses; the dealer sweeps away dead chips. He plays his second hand and wins; he's paid off with $10,000 in live chips (which can't be played, only cashed or rolled over). Ten hours later, Mr. I has played through all the dead chips and is left with $250,000 in live chips. He can take them to the cage and trade them in for a quarter-mil in cash. Or he can opt for $275,000 ($250,000 plus the 10% bonus of $25,000) in dead chips, with which he can go back to the tables and repeat the process. So the player can continually roll these chips (as long as he has any) and always get the same bonus. There's never a reason to leave the property—except when he's busted out.

Australia casinos use a different rebate formula, though it's no less precise than in Asia. Aussie casinos rebate, in cash, .65% of a player's total action, not just the losses. In addition, the player receives a tenth of a percent of his action in comps. Every bet is recorded and input into the marketing computer by a pit clerk. Win or lose, the player gets back a little more than a half-percent in cash, plus a tenth of a point in comps. If he puts $5 million into action at a baccarat table (two hundred $25,000 bets, for example), the casino gives him a $32,500 cash rebate and $5,000 in comps.

If it seems like the Aussie deal is better for the player

than the Las Vegas deal, take a closer look. The casinos didn't just pluck the .65% giveback figure out of thin air. At baccarat, the banker bet has a 1.06% house advantage. Even after the giveback, the casino maintains a .41% edge. Also, the player has to pay cash for all amenities over and above the 0.10% comp allowance. At a six-star hotel-casino such as the Crown Towers and Casino in Melbourne, the cost of room, food, beverage, and entertainment quickly gobbles up that 0.10%.

In addition, everything is mathematically precise. Except for the credit limit on which the bonus is based, there's nothing for the host and player to negotiate; the rebate and comps are wiggle-free.

Finally, the casino is providing plenty of incentives for the gambler to stay and play. For every $25,000 bet he puts into action, he receives $1,625 in return.

On the other side of the table, the player doesn't do too badly for himself. Though the casino maintains an edge with either the Aussie rebate or the rolling dead chips, it pays out the percentages win or lose. The bosses have to swallow hard to hand over $32,500 in cash and comps *any* time, but even more so when a player smokes them for, say, a half-million.

The discounting wrinkle is problematic no matter how it's handled.

On the other hand, if a casino doesn't offer 15% or 20%, the player can take his checkbook next door or across the street or down the block or to another continent. And all the hype about slots and slot players—how they're dominating casino floors and revenues—notwithstanding, the bosses know they can't bank on the bandits to pay off a billion-dollar building. Jimmy Newman used to stroll through the Hilton casino on a Saturday night when the joint was jumpin' and tell Cyr, "All this? Every seat at the tables and every stool at the machines occupied? It all means nothing. Mr. J, a whale from Singapore, is in the baccarat room winning a million." It's impossible for $5 and $25 bets at blackjack and craps and quarter and dollar slot play to square the books in the face of a seven-figure hit.

❖ ❖ ❖

Making things tougher, hosts know that they have to win a big player's money not once, but twice: First the casino has to beat him at the game, then it has to collect. So every aspect of the customer's profile has to be factored in before a decision can be made on how high a discount to extend.

The length of time a player plans to stay in action is one consideration. The shorter the play, the more volatility involved, which is of great concern to the bean counters. If a player wagers a million dollars by betting $1,000 on each of a thousand flips of a coin, chances are that the results will be smoothed over the duration of play and approximate the expected 50/50 distribution of heads to tails. A deviation in either direction tends to be minor (low volatility). But if you flip a coin 10 times at $100,000 per flip, the results can be wild. In this case, a nice little streak of eight or nine wins to one or two losses would mean that more than three-quarters of a million dollars will go from one side of the table to the other in a matter of minutes (high volatility). Of course, it's equally likely in this scenario—and even more likely in the casino where the house has the edge in the game—that the player will lose a tidy amount. But casinos don't like to take that chance. If the player wins and heads for the exit, it's goodbye money. Hit-and-run whales can whipsaw a casino.

Some of the premium casinos try to discourage hit-and-run play at any level. No discounts. No credit. The casino sees little earning potential in gamblers who come in just to flip a coin a few times.

Another important aspect of a player's profile is his tolerance to this volatility—an indication of a player's potential threat to the house. When examining a Central Credit file, Cyr always pays particular attention not only to a player's biggest loss, but also his biggest win. It's just as important for Cyr to know how much a gambler can take off his casino as it is for him to know how much the guy's ready to lose. The casino prefers gamblers who are satisfied with a small win, but are capable of taking a monster loss. As Cyr puts it, the best prospects are the ones "who eat like a bird and shit like a moose."

Mr. K has an appetite to risk a hundred large. He's ready and willing to lose it all if he gets behind. But if he's like most players, he has an unnatural bias against a big win. On the way down, he flies open like a ten-dollar suitcase in an attempt to get off his losses (shits like a moose). But on the way up, he's tighter than an accountant's asshole, not wanting to cross that disquieting line from winner to loser (eats like a bird). He'll lose six figures with aplomb. But if he gets ahead twenty grand, he'll rise from the table and float out of the casino on a cloud. This tendency is surprisingly ingrained in gamblers.

In a strange, but related, phenomenon, many players have an easier time living with their losses than they do with their wins. They can be philosophical about losing: "Hell, everyone loses." That's the way it's supposed to be; it's a rigged game. Precious few are wired to make a living beating the casino at gambling, so most naturally expect to lose.

But losers who suddenly find themselves winners? They often can't handle it, sometimes going completely off the deep end. They quickly convince themselves that they're gods and that they'll never lose again. They go on spending sprees—booze, jewelry, hookers, jewelry for the hookers, even jewelry for the wife. Winners often flame out faster than a shooting star. And when they inevitably lose again, their whole world crashes in around them.

In many ways, it's just plain easier to lose.

Wine, Women, and Song

Some big players don't care about show-up money and discounts. Some don't even know about them. They're in it for the comped vacations and luxuries, such as personal rides on company jets.

Gulfstream, a division of General Dynamics (since 1999), manufactures seven small jets, from the G100 to the G550. The G100 is a seven-passenger business aircraft with two Honeywell jet engines, a cruising speed of Mach .75, and a maximum range of 2,700 nautical miles (Boston to Dublin). The G550 accommodates 19 passengers, has two Rolls Royce engines, and a maximum range of 6,750 nautical miles (New York to Riyadh).

Most casino Gulfstreams, as well as the Hilton's Hawker, a product of Raytheon Aircraft, are good for picking up a whale and a small entourage from anywhere in North America. A high roller coming from Asia or Arabia would probably prefer a non-stop chartered 747. But maybe a Malaysian whale is in New York on other business and wants the G3 or Hawker to get to Vegas comfortably and privately. Or maybe a Hong Kong magnate vacations in Hawaii before summoning the private casino jet.

With the Hilton's fleet of aircraft, Cyr had a major advantage over hosts at jetless joints. Hilton's planes were just sitting in wait at Signature (the private-plane area of

McCarran Airport), so if someone wanted to fly in from Ottawa or Savannah or Guadalajara, the Hawker could be there in a hurry, a few hours max from phone call to pickup.

What about the casinos that don't own their own planes? Some simply charter a business jet when they need one. Others have a stake in NetJets and other private jet-membership or fractional-aircraft-ownership programs. Both are popular with casinos, since they don't have to pay for deadheads (empty one-way trips to pick up or drop off a gambler); they fit passenger pickups and dropoffs into NetJets' schedules, depending on where its planes are flying at a given time. Still, it might take six, eight, even twenty-four hours for a host relying on NetJets to have a player fetched, and by then the player's had all the time in the world to make more immediate arrangements with another casino.

Whether they fly in on a casino Gulfstream, a chartered 747, or a NetJet, whatever air arrangements they find most convenient and comfortable are available to the world's highest rollers. The rest of the premium players take what they can get. A lot has to do with how much a player knows he can ask for. To the four questions Cyr uses to size up a prospect—bankroll, average bet, largest loss, and biggest win— add a fifth: What's the least that must be done to get him in?

A super perkmeister like Cyr tries to get away with not bringing up the perks. If he can hook a fish without paying airfare, he's not about to offer it. But if he hears from a new player that his host at another casino never mentioned airfare, he can cough it up and look like a sport in the process.

For example, if Cyr is trying to seduce an MGM player into defecting, he can say, "What do they do about your airfare?"

More often than not, he'll hear, "Oh, MGM always pays it."

"Pays it? Waddaya mean?"

"Waddaya mean what do I mean? I give my host my ticket and he reimburses me."

"Aw, you're gettin' fucked."

"Huh?"

"What's the benefit of having your airfare reimbursed? Sure, it's money, but how much is your time worth? You gotta buy your own tickets. You gotta stand in security lines for three hours with all the cretins and get searched like some kind of criminal. And what if your plane's late? And what if they've run out of peanuts? And are you reimbursed for the cost of your drinks? I'll send the Hilton's Hawker to pick you up. No muss, no fuss. Just give me the date and time."

Of course, the opposite is also true. If Cyr's player first hears about airfare from the MGM host, he's gone. No big thing, though. Players are like water that you pour into a bucket with a hole in it. They continuously fall through. They burn themselves out. They're burned out by hosts and bosses. They find a better host. That's why hosts are always always *always* ravenous for more players to pour into the bucket.

❖ ❖ ❖

Then there's ground transportation. Unlike discounts and airfare, almost every premium player with a credit line qualifies for a limo ride to and from the airport.

On one occasion, Steve Cyr landed a half-dozen tickets to a heavyweight prizefight at the MGM Grand Garden Arena for himself and several of his best customers. No big deal; he'd done it many times before. Still, these were center-ring fifth-row—some of the best seats in the 12,000-seat house. But when he looked down to the *very* best seats in the arena, first-row center, he saw ... a Las Vegas Hilton limo driver. He was sitting with a high roller who holds a lucrative patent on an automobile accessory. Cyr had to shake his head and laugh: He'd been outjuiced by a chauffeur.

A smart limo driver takes advantage of his time with passengers to get to know them. And there's plenty of time: waiting for luggage at the baggage carousel, during the standard ride from the airport to the casino, taking the family into the desert to photograph wildflowers, dropping the wife at the mall, hanging out at a topless club. One of a driver's most valuable assets is his memory for names, faces, and details. When he's on his game he can easily dredge up what he remembers about his customers on a subsequent trip. This almost always translates into repeat business, bigger tips, and referrals.

That's not to say that a limo driver will become a high roller's new best friend between the airport and the casino. The good ones follow the unwritten rules of service personnel: You speak when you're spoken to. You're wise about how you respond.

When a limo driver is in his car, there's no boss standing over him, breathing down his neck, examining his performance under a microscope. He can pretty much go anywhere and do anything he pleases, as long as he takes care of business. It's just him, his passengers, and his mobile office. He gets to meet people, especially rich ones. Most of them, it turns out, tend to be relaxed, personable, and communicative in a limo.

And sometimes more.

Surprisingly, perhaps, in this day and age, some customers ask drivers to hook them up with drugs. Any limo driver who values his job won't allow drugs in the car: Cops have been known to target limo drivers in drug stings on occasion.

Not surprisingly, limo drivers are constantly fired on by customers about getting them girls. Some drivers have a few phone numbers in their glove compartments. Most drivers know the locations of the social or swing clubs sprouting up around the Vegas valley. These are typical Southwestern-style suburban houses with red-tile roofs, off-white stucco walls, windows that don't open, and spindly palm trees in the front yard where, atypically, swinging couples swap partners. Most of the clubs are legitimate; only couples (presumably married) and sometimes single women are admitted; a few charge a hefty admission fee to weed out the riff-raff. Others, however, accept single guys, and the cover charge is kicked back to the limo driver for delivering a passenger to the swing club for a night of consensual sex.

Even if a driver knows—and shares profits with—a few working girls, he might not be familiar enough with a passenger to risk getting popped for procurement, so he suggests the swing clubs, the legal brothels in Pahrump, or the Yellow Pages, where the listings of outcall sex providers, thinly disguised in the "Entertainers" section, occupy more than 100 pages.

No matter where the girls come from, limo drivers are often an unobtrusive part of the passenger-sex thing. Answering the inevitable question about how often his passengers have had sex in the back of his limo, one veteran driver, without hesitation, claims, "Five hundred times."

Do they close the privacy partition?

"Occasionally."

And what do you do when they don't?

"What else? Watch! Wouldn't you?"

Through the rear-view mirror?

"Sometimes. Other times I pull over, park the fucking limo, and turn around."

The passengers don't care?

"If they leave the privacy partition down, they don't. They usually don't even notice. One time, a customer called and told me to pick up one of his girlfriends and meet him at the airport. He was flying into Vegas on a two-hour layover and needed to kill some time. We drove up and back down the Strip, and all the while the guy was on top of the girlfriend—with the partition down. He looked up and saw me watching and said, 'Hey, man. How ya' doin'?'

"I said, "Pretty good. How you doin'?'

"He said, 'How's it look like I'm doin'?' and he went back to boinkin' his babe. Then I dropped him off at the airport to catch his plane."

Ever get in on the act?

"Another time, a guy asked me about getting him a girl.

I said what I usually say, 'Let your fingers do the walking.' The guy said, 'Well, I wanted a *personal* recommendation, but if I'm gonna look in the Yellow Pages, I'd better get three girls so I can have my choice.' When they showed up, the customer took the one he liked and gave the other two to me. And he paid for all three."

That, it turns out, was a decent toke. On average, limo drivers make $20 per trip in tips. Hundred-dollar handoffs from Georges aren't unusual, especially for the senior drivers, whom the hundred-dollar Georges request by name. These tokes aren't automatic; chauffeurs have to work up to black-check tips. The first time a guy might treat a driver like a peasant and toss him a five. If the driver's patient and professional and plays his cards right, the next trip it's $20. And in time, it's more. It's just a matter of being cool.

On an average Saturday night, a Strip megaresort will get 30 to 40 calls that are split among six or seven drivers. If the employee chauffeurs can't handle the demand, the casino contracts out with a limo company, such as Bell Trans. House drivers are typically sharper than contract drivers— you don't become a house driver unless you have plenty of experience and can prove that you know how to provide good service and promote good customer relations.

Limo drivers take some abuse. A lot of gamblers who get comped limo rides as a matter of course are in a position to have a bad day. They don't get the suite they were promised. They're served a mediocre meal. The hotel runs out of Cristal or Dom (or that's what the host told them, anyway) and they have to settle for Moët & Chandon. They get into it with the wife or girlfriend. They lose their money. When some guy in the back of the car has just been banged for $50,000, only $10,000 of which he could truly afford, the limo driver is nothing. Not even a blip on the radar screen. If anything, he's the booby prize—a free ride to the airport, out of town.

If a driver gets caught up in the middle of a passenger's

bad mood, his feelings will definitely get hurt. This is why the savvy driver knows how to stay out of harm's way in such situations. He won't expect a toke. He won't even think, *What about me?* And if he can't put such moments into perspective and accept that they come with the territory, he's not cut out to be a limo driver in Las Vegas. Or anywhere.

The good drivers treat everyone the same. Most can ignore wealth; the best can even ignore fame. The important thing about a passenger for the experienced driver is personality; that makes the job fun. Then comes tips, which make the job lucrative. If a guy is cool and tips well, that's limo-driver heaven. If a guy gets chauffeured around all day and stiffs the driver, he might be personable, but he's not cool. Similarly, if he's a dickhead and tosses the driver a hundred, he's not cool either. A dickhead's a dickhead, no matter how much he tokes.

One driver related the story of chauffeuring Pierce Brosnan—a guy with a healthy dose of both fame *and* fortune. It was eight o'clock on a Sunday morning and the dispatcher told him a player needed a ride to a Western clothing store. The driver was vocal about his displeasure over the situation. He wanted to be ferrying high rollers to the airport on a Sunday morning, quick trips and big tips. Brosnan was standing right behind him as he was sounding off. At first he didn't even recognize the actor, who was registered under an a.k.a.

The whole thing got off to a bad start, but Brosnan was cool. He didn't know the name of the clothing store he wanted to be taken to, but he knew it had a statue of a bucking bronco in front. They tried Sam's Town's Western Emporium. Sure enough, there was the statue. But the store didn't open till 10. Brosnan said, "C'mon, I'll buy you breakfast."

They sat in Sam's coffee shop and talked about how Brosnan was looking forward to playing James Bond. Meanwhile, every waitress in the restaurant made her way around to the table to salivate over the superstar. Finally, the store opened, and as Brosnan searched out a pair of Western boots, it was the salesgirls' turn to ogle.

When the driver dropped him back at the hotel, Brosnan tossed him a couple of twenties. It was the perfect example of personality and generosity on the part of the passenger, and the wisdom of treating everyone the same on the part of the driver.

A driver never knows where he'll end up on a shift. He'll make a ton of runs to and from the airport, standing at the entrance to the luggage carousel holding a sign. (And yes, people *still* come up and pretend to be the guy they're waiting for, then laugh about the old Bud Light commercial.)

Strip clubs are the second most popular destination after the airport.

A driver accompanied his passenger into a topless joint, where his guy started handing out honeybees (hundred-dollar bills) like he owned the printing press. The driver took him aside and said, "Hey, they'll dance for you for twenty dollars!" He was worried there wouldn't be anything left for him.

Another time, after dropping a passenger off at a strip club, the guy said, "Now go pick up my wife at the Fashion Show Mall and take her back to the hotel, but don't tell her where I am." When he picked up the wife, she immediately asked where her husband was.

"Uh, I don't know."

This told her all she needed to hear. "I know where he is, so don't bother denying it. He does the same thing at home. But I count how much money he leaves with and how much money he comes back with, and if he spends two grand at the titty bar, I spend two grand at the mall."

The driver laughed to himself as he pictured the husband drinking and getting lap dances, confident that his wife didn't have a clue.

Some passengers use the limos to go out to the brothels in Pahrump. Occasionally, a driver will take a gambler to

Los Angeles or San Diego. Maybe he can't get a flight. Maybe he lost all his money. On September 11 and 12, 2001, with no planes in the air after the terrorist attacks on the World Trade Center, limo drivers went as far as New York City; one limo company booked two trips to Manhattan for $10,000 apiece (the drivers were tipped $1,000 each).

Sometimes a random favor yields a steady customer. A driver on swing shift was dropping off his last passenger of the night in front of a megaresort. He was about to go off duty when he saw a guy at the cab line-up, staggering around with four scantily dressed girls in tow. It was four a.m. and there wasn't a taxi in sight. He thought to himself, "Shit, somebody's gotta take care of this situation." He piled the party into his limo, delivered them to where they were going, and along the way made friends with the guy, who turned out to be a big gambler. Now the player stays at the driver's hotel and he's good for a black check every little trip around town.

Sometimes a high roller who has suites at two different casinos will hand over the keys to the empty one for the driver's personal use. One veteran chauffeur was given a Mercedes 500 SL. (It was one of three cars owned by the high roller, the one he never drove.) For the senior drivers, $800, $1,000, even $1,200 worth of tokes in a day isn't unusual.

Then there are the stiffs. Hosts occasionally have to take a player aside and tell him, "Hey, take care of my guy here. Don't make me look bad." On occasion, Cyr has to toss the driver a toke out of his own pocket to make up for a stiff.

It's in the host's best interests to do business with limo drivers, who, at any given time, are apt to know more than the hosts about where the high rollers are. Drivers drop them off where they're playing and staying. Drivers also share information among themselves. And if a host is in good with a chauffeur, a hint about a high-roller's whereabouts can turn into a lucrative lead.

Occasionally, a limo driver even makes the transition and becomes a host.

❖ ❖ ❖

The top chefs in the world work in Las Vegas.

Everyone appreciates fine dining and anyone who can afford the tab can partake thereof at Bellagio's Picasso or the Mirage's Renoir, both five-star five-diamond restaurants. But for high rollers, Asians especially, there's more to it. It's also about tradition and ceremony and individualized attention.

Asian chefs often have pre-existing personal relationships with Asian whales. They know their preferences in tastes, pace of service, and presentation. The brother of the Asian chef who prepared the banquet for the changeover ceremony when the British handed Hong Kong to the Chinese in 1997 works at Caesars. When the brother came for a visit to Las Vegas, he liked the city and auditioned for a chef's job at the exclusive Mansion at MGM Grand. He whipped up an appetizer and a couple of entrées and was hired on the spot. Despite his culinary talents, however, he's still a secret to the outside world, because only guests who stay at the Mansion get to eat his food.

The pastry chef at the Mansion is a top gun from Austria. His signature dish is Mansion apple tart. The butlers heat it up in the villas' toaster ovens and put a dollop of vanilla ice cream on top.

Shanghai Lilly, the classic Cantonese restaurant at Mandalay Bay, has private dining rooms for high-roller parties. Each diner in the party is served by his and her own private waitperson. In the kitchen, the chefs use special high-powered woks imported from Hong Kong. Because the heat can be cranked way up under these woks, the food—especially fish that's as fresh as is physically possible in a desert city 250 miles from the ocean—cooks more quickly, which sears in more flavor. The Asian high rollers are said to be able to taste a smoky residue left by underpowered woks. The woks used at Shanghai Lilly cost $15,000 apiece.

One Asian chef, knowing that a particular Japanese whale is partial to an artistic presentation, carefully removes lobster meat from its shell and prepares it. He then reassembles the shell and has it electroplated with gold leaf. The gold-plated lobster shell is served with the entrée as decoration.

But $15,000 woks, gold-plated lobster shells, and seafood airlifted from Hawaii mere hours in advance of being served aren't enough. One Asian whale liked a Chinese take-out joint called, prosaically, Food Express, located in one of Vegas' hundreds of nondescript strip malls. When in town, the whale regularly took his group to eat there. The Hilton got wind of this and the next time the whale came to town, the Food Express chef was working at the Hilton.

Wine is another harpoon in the whale hunter's fine-dining arsenal. Valentino's restaurant at the Venetian has a private dining room in which high rollers are served special wine-tasting meals surrounded by the thousands of bottles in its exclusive wine collection. Aureole restaurant at Mandalay Bay has more than 40,000 bottles of wine, 10,000 of them stored in a 42-foot-tall stainless-steel-and-glass "wine-tower" cabinet; female attendants known as wine goddesses strap themselves into special harnesses and ascend the tower on motorized cables to retrieve selections. There are also six wine cellars. Several bottles cost $250,000. Mandalay Bay hosts have a field day with wine-loving whales.

❖ ❖ ❖

Steve Wynn once commented that the husband decides he wants to go to Las Vegas, but the wife chooses when to go, how to get there, where to stay, and what to do and see. This observation is a good illustration of the conventional wisdom that women control 70% of the money.

Meanwhile, every day, the front-line casino employees see at least one good example of an even stronger wisdom: that women control 100% of the pussy.

Limo drivers, along with bellmen, dealers, hosts, bosses, and cocktail runners, get to see big-fish behavior as it relates to the different schools they travel in. When male gamblers come with their buddies, they behave differently than when they come with their girlfriends. And when they come with their girlfriends, they behave differently than when they come with their wives. Casino employees have to be discreet and fast on their feet not to blow a customer's cover.

It's a tough detail, because when a guy shows up with a girl, a limo driver or dealer can't know for sure what their relationship is. She could be the wife, ex-wife, new girlfriend, old girlfriend, secretary, a stripper he just picked up, a hooker from back home. … The one thing they do know is that she's important enough at *this* time for him to take her on a high-roller weekend in Las Vegas.

A new woman with a veteran guest puts everyone on guard. The staff might get a little advance notice from the host, but they still have to be very careful. They rarely use the word Missus. Rather, it's "Good afternoon, Miss Helen." Or, "Hello Mr. L. And how's the lady tonight?" This is one old-school rule that's still rarely broken, and only by accident or ignorance when it is.

Even if a guy shows up with the same woman several times in a row, it doesn't explain much. For example, a limo driver chauffeured a player, Mr. M, and his lady around for a year. He knew Mr. M was married—he wore a wedding band—but he knew the lady only as Gina. One day Mr. M showed up with a different woman and introduced her as his wife. The driver had to bite his tongue not to exclaim, "*This* is your wife? So who's Gina?"

This same driver had a steady player who showed up with a different girl every trip. Finally, one of them turned out to be his wife. Again the driver had to choke back the urge to say, "Your *wife*? Who the hell figured you to be *married*?" And his next thought was, *Buddy, I could blackmail you for a million dollars. It's a lot less than what your wife would take you for if I told her what I know about you.* But that didn't happen. The limo driver liked his job.

Many casino service workers complain that players are no fun when they're with their wives. They have to behave themselves. They don't drink and party. They don't flirt with the dealers. They don't stay up all night. And they certainly don't gamble anywhere near as high as they'd like to, which also means they don't toss around as many tokes as usual. In fact, some dealers swear they can tell by the size of a player's bet if the woman at his side is the wife (small), the girlfriend (big), or someone he just picked up (huge).

Cyr occasionally used this change in attitude to his advantage. If Mr. N came in with his wife and Cyr knew that she didn't want him to spend all his time gambling—she either didn't like him risking their money or wanted him to spend time with her—it was an easy call. He comped everything, while suspending the gambler's credit line entirely, making sure he couldn't bet a dollar. Now Mrs. N was overjoyed, getting exactly what she wanted. Mr. N might be a bit miffed, but it was his own damn fault for bringing her in the first place. Cyr softened the blow by telling him that if he came in next time without his wife, he'd double his credit line. All that was left was to convince his boss that his guy would lose twice as much on the following trip.

One of the main attractions of Las Vegas for high rollers is its code of discretion. Las Vegas personnel have an instinct for guarding a big player's privacy. This results in confidence on the part of megarollers that their innermost secrets are safe in the desert. They can't wait to get out of their hometowns and start living their double lives, acting out their fantasies without fear of repercussions or reprisals.

It's not, by any means, 100% guaranteed. Perhaps a stiff ticks off a dealer, then brings the wife with him to her table next trip. Look out when he leaves to go take a leak—enough time for the dealer and the little lady to get a sisterhood thing going. In most cases, it's the little lady pumping the dealer

for information. The wife wants to know how much he bets
when she's not around. The pickup usually asks about money
too, while the girlfriend wants to know how often he brings
the wife instead of her. The player's entire world can change
in the time it takes to piss out all that booze.

It's a good reason to toke—for players with something
to hide.

❖ ❖ ❖

Hosts, limo drivers, high rollers, and girls all come together in topless clubs, of which Las Vegas has more than its
quota. Indeed, since 2002, the Sin City skin scene has ex-
ploded in both quantity and quality, including the debut of
several megajiggle joints.

The biggest of the bunch is Sapphire, which took over
the Sporting House, Cyr's old athletic stomping grounds.
Sapphire bills itself as the world's largest "adult entertainment complex." Sitting on a seven-acre lot across the street
from the back door of the Stardust, Sapphire features a 10,000-
square-foot main floor, a 400-seat showroom, a steakhouse,
private party rooms, and a roster of nearly 1,500 girls.

Where do all these girls come from? Las Vegas is a mecca
for strippers. The clubs in most other cities are open till only
2 a.m. or so and are full of tourists, construction workers,
and run-of-the-mill pervs, while the Vegas clientele consists
of high rollers, other gamblers, convention crowds, and all
the components of a major party scene.

Strippers don't work *for* strip clubs, they work *at* them.
Similar to the professional prostitutes at Nevada's legal brothels, the girls are independent contractors. The pros split their
fees with the brothel owners; strippers rent space at the club
by the night. Inflation in the rent figures has been enormous.
In the early '90s, the girls had to cough up $15 a night. By
1995, it'd gone up to $35, and these days it's about $70. At a
small club like Cheetah's, up to 200 girls work over a 24-

hour period. Multiplied by $70, that's a quick $14,000, cash, in the drawer. The men pay a $10 cover, for another $10,000 to $12,000 a day. Not to mention the profits from the over-priced alcohol. Added up, it easily outdistances the payroll, as the only true employees are the bartenders, bouncers, and bookkeepers.

Most hosts make the strip-club rounds, either with their own fish or to cast a line. The guy who looks like he's a regular—drinking, partying, having fun, blowing money? Sure as the silicone in those big bowl-shaped boobs, he's a gambler, and a potential customer.

Any host worth his salt is constantly in need of big boobs, small waists, and long legs to dress up a trade show, cocktail party, or dinner engagement, not to mention to strip at a bachelor blowout or just impress a potential player. "Eye candy, baby!" And plenty of hosts just like lap dances.

The scenario goes something like this. Host X walks in, sits down, and waits for a girl to approach him. He's done it a million times: "Hi, I'm X. I'm a host over at the Hats and Horns casino. Here's my card." He then proceeds to get several table dances, handing out $20 per tune. He spends $80 or $100 to hang out a little bit, long enough to pop the question: "Hey, do you do parties?"

They all say, "No"! Every last one of them. And they recite the line with such conviction that a polygraph couldn't determine whether or not it was true. Just like every *Playboy* Playmate who, when relating her experience of disrobing for the first time, insists—*insists*—that she was so shy she thought she was going to die (or at least barf).

But the fact is, not many of them will turn down a chance to make $250 for a two-hour appearance at a cocktail party. Of course, Host X knows he has to go through 50 strippers to find 10 who are reliable. So he's constantly on the prowl.

And strippers don't last long. They get jaded and burned out fast. Many are very young—18-, 19-, and 20-year-olds working in the all-nude joints (which don't serve alcohol) or

21 and a few years older in the topless clubs. They have to work long hours, sometimes all night. Their customers are almost exclusively men, but the normal guys are few and far between. Most are lecherous, macho, or just plain gross; many are drunks and weirdoes and fetishists. And the girls make enough money—$50,000 a year on average; the good ones pull down $100,000, all cash—to save up and get into something more clothed. Some do.

Most don't. Many of the latter group "graduate." Because when they're getting "old," in their mid- to late 20s, their hips aren't as slim, their tits aren't as firm, their asses aren't as round, their skin's not as smooth, and their eyes are too hard. In short, they look better lying down in the dark than standing up in the light. They figure, instead of going in and shaking their thang all night for $500, they can put out for an hour for the same $500.

Not all strippers become hookers, but many do. And a host who's willing to run the risk of falling afoul of the state regulators at Gaming Control to hook up his customers has a happy hunting ground at the clubs.

Host X: "Well, I know more than one high roller who'll give you a thousand bucks just to go to a party with him. All you have to do is hang on his arm."

Or, "Would you go to a prizefight, sit in ringside seats, and look hot for five hundred?"

Or, "You know, eight out of ten times, a Las Vegas hooker doesn't have to fuck anyone. Seriously, you wouldn't believe how many guys just want a girl to get naked and watch him pleasure himself."

Of the 20 hookers on Host X's list, 18 of them either are, or started out as, strippers. He claims he had to "research" 100 women to come up with 20 reliable ones. They'll show up drunk. They'll show up on crack. They'll show up messy. Or they won't show up at all.

It's hard to find good help.

The Furniture of Love

High-roller suites—penthouses, villas, bungalows, palazzos, mansions, sky palaces—or whatever highfalutin appellation architectural designers and interior decorators and casino marketers can dream up for these hypersteroidal sleepers—are the most unrestrained representation of the classic Las Vegas cliché that nothing succeeds like excess.

Copywriters gush about the "mysteries behind the secret walls of the party palaces of the kings and queens of the casino" with breathless banalities and hackneyed superlatives. "The largest and most luxurious hotel accommodations in the world." "Unrivaled in their degree of elegance and opulence." "The epitome of elitism and escapism." And of course, since this is Las Vegas, "the grandeur of ancient Rome," "the ultimate expression of Venetian perfection," "French Imperial splendor," even "the expansive yet understated urban chic of Manhattan."

Which is not to say that the suites and villas reserved for the gigarollers who qualify to stay in them, some of which you can't rent for any amount of money, are not magnificent. They are—whether or not you can appreciate, or even understand, the kind of design and workmanship and *collections* (more copywriterese: nothing so mundane as *furnishings*) that feather these nests.

Presumably, and this comes part and parcel with the

high-roller mystique, the world's wealthiest gamblers populate the cultured and sophisticated ranks of the Robin Leach
rich and famous: people who are classically educated, con-
versant with the fine arts, appreciative of historical signifi-
cance and technological innovation, knowledgeable about
value and price, and respectful of property.

Presumably, the high roller staying in these suites isn't
some bent-nose street thug from Hoboken who likes to
gamble away the millions he extorts from the Manhattan
garment district in a protection racket. He's not the Shoeless
Joe who turns a Social Security check into seven figures during a legendary run-up at a Caesars crap table, spends a
couple of nights in the Louis XIV Suite, and has no clue that
the priceless Ming Dynasty vase sitting on the credenza
didn't come off the close-out shelf at Wal-Mart. Nor is he the
gutsy video poker pro who takes a pot shot at a $100 ma-
chine and lasts long enough to wangle a few nights in one of
the smaller villas in the Mansion at the MGM Grand.

Rather, presumably, he's the kind who's aware enough
to relish decorative 22-karat white-gold stripping around an
antique $5,000 saddle seat, or even just observant enough to
notice this one stool among dozens. The kind who knows
that the wall-covering in the billiards room isn't just Home
Depot glue-on, but has gone through a weathering process
of dying, steaming, and cracking to give it the look of 100-
year-old red-leather upholstery. Who can recognize a million-dollar hand-embroidered rug from Izmir even if he
doesn't trip over it. Who can also figure out how to use the
touch-screen control panel to adjust the lights, raise the pro-
jector at the foot of the bed, lower the movie screen from the
ceiling, program the CD player, flick on the fireplace, open
and close the draperies, answer the phone, answer the door,
even summon the butler, all from the bedside console. And
whose pride swells when he realizes that he qualifies for the
15,500-square-foot Verona Villa at the Hilton, and not just
the 14,000-square-foot Palazzo Suite at the Rio.

(Designers and decorators actually discuss the challenge of differentiating high-roller suites from museums. Why bother? Anyone who stays in these palaces would probably be grateful for informational signs—okay, maybe just a hand-book—describing the history, cost, craftsmanship, and de-tails of the dozens of collection pieces throughout the suites. For that matter, why hasn't a $40,000-a-year bean counter, who knows how to vacuum every last nickel out of every last sucker, come up with the idea of charging for *tours* of the suites? Install a few stanchions, arrange for a guide and security guard, and visitors would pay good money just to traipse through them when they're not occupied.)

But even if the guests *are* the ideal occupants who can fathom and delight in the essence of opulence, is there any-one who can actually make total *use* of whale digs five times larger than a spacious middle-class house? Is there any nor-mal human being who wouldn't feel insignificant around 13 separately controlled shower heads in a stall lined with Span-ish marble in one of six bathrooms, all complete with steam rooms and saunas, Jacuzzi tubs, even fireplaces, along with towel warmers, floor heaters, and solid-gold swan-curved faucets? And those are just the bathrooms. Is there a person on Earth who can spend even a portion of his day in six bed-rooms, living room, dining room, office, three sitting rooms, media room, billiards room, party room, bar, and outdoor deck sporting swimming pool and spa, nine-hole putting green, telescope, and gas-fired barbecue grill—let alone avail himself of it all?

(A whale staying in one of the largest suites in town once complained to his host that he couldn't find his wife.)

These are, of course, rhetorical questions. For starters, many whales live in far more splendorous, opulent, and ex-pansive pleasure palaces than these mere hotel suites. A few miles west of the Strip, for example, there stands the 35,000-square-foot winter-vacation mansion of one of the princes of Brunei, who spends upwards of $60,000 a month on the overhead of the place, which includes a dozen year-round servants, housekeepers, landscapers, and security guards—all for the few weeks a year he stays there.

Also, whether you're a Boston blue-blood who went to Harvard, did your graduate work as a Rhodes Scholar at Oxford, and are now head curator for the New York Metropolitan Museum of Art or a T-shirted, Bermuda-shorted, cigar-chomping bail bondsman from Beaumont, Texas, who dropped out of junior high school and wouldn't know the difference between Dom Perignon and Martinelli's sparkling cider if you read both labels, it doesn't take long to become *accustomed* to these levels of luxury. At the end of the day, it's all just beds and furniture and fixtures. And beauty, it's been said, is in the eye of the beholder.

Finally, no matter who stays in them, these epitomes of elitism and escapism accomplish exactly what they're meant to: They control the mood of the gambler. They stroke his ego, stoke his passion, and poke him to risk his sky's-the-limit stakes downstairs at the tables.

❖ ❖ ❖

In the early surly days of Las Vegas, high-roller suites were basically unknown. Hotel rooms were a long way down the pecking order in the Las Vegas scheme of things. The first resort-casinos—El Rancho Vegas, Last Frontier, Flamingo, Desert Inn, Sands, Sahara—had barely 1,000 rooms among them. Tourists and passers-through might rent one for a night or two from the clerk behind a tiny front desk, but most rooms were controlled by the casino bosses, kept available for players and the boys, as well as the boys' buddies, the boys' families, the boys' girlfriends, and even a few juiced-in squares. The rooms were so low in priority that one old-timer remembers being comped at the Sands for his honeymoon—into a room with twin beds.

The hotels were built with a few suites. They had a sit-

ting area or an extra bedroom to appeal to superstar headliners like Frank Sinatra or VIP visitors like Senator Jack
Kennedy. But no one had yet thought of using them as bait
to lure the fish.

In those days, as far as the bosses were concerned, Las
Vegas hotel rooms were nothing more than places to sleep,
shower, and do it—all in as brief a period of time as possible. They were designed specifically *not* to be comfortable
and relaxing. The average room lacked a radio, TV, or clock,
and there was no room service. Case in point: Into the late
'80s, Circus Circus decorated its digs with orange shag carpeting, pink walls defaced by clown murals, red bedspreads
and towels, and extra-loud air-conditioners, all aimed at driving guests back into the madhouse casino.

The high rollers back then had $5,000 credit lines and
fired it up with $100 bets. Small change today, but in those
days the table maximums weren't much higher. For years,
the upper-limit bet at the Stardust was $200. At the Desert
Inn, Sands, Tropicana, and Flamingo, it was $500. (If you
wanted to play for higher stakes, there was only one place to
go: Binion's Horseshoe, where your first bet, even if it was a
quarter-million dollars, was your max bet.) Even Caesars,
which had a reputation as the high-roller capital of Las Vegas and therefore of the world and was the first casino to go
to a $1,000 maximum, required a full meeting of the opera-
tions honchos to approve a player's request to up the highest bet on a single number at roulette from $100 to $200.

On the other hand, every comp *but* fancy suites was
within the grasp of all but the lowliest pukes. When the boys
ran things, there were no electronic data files to check average bets or time played, no comp equivalencies, no lifetime-
loss records. If a boss knew your name and you bought in
for $2,500 and played for an hour or two making $50 bets,
you'd be all set up. The Big Five complimentaries—room,
food, booze, show, and girl—were yours for the asking. And
you requisitioned them right in the pit. In those days, the pit

and shift bosses doubled as the hosts. (It was when these same guys shed their boss responsibilities that the first dedicated casino marketing executives came into existence.) They'd write a comp ticket to take to the front desk where you'd get the key to a room. Or they'd bring a key right to your table.

The room itself was just that—standard-issue hotel accommodations. As long as there was a bed, a shower, and an air-conditioner, no one gave it a second thought.

❖ ❖ ❖

In the early '60s, the Flamingo underwent a change of ownership. A group of Miami hotel operators bought Bugsy's old joint and flew in a planeload of preferred guests from the Fountainbleau and other luxury South Florida hotels for the grand-reopening party. The junket had been born. Soon, planeloads of gamblers who qualified for free airfare, room, food, and beverage by putting up $5,000 to $10,000 to play with were arriving at the Flamingo, Dunes, Sands, and other premium Strip casinos on a twice-weekly basis. These cosmopolitan players were used to fancier places to sleep, and in 1962, when the Flamingo underwent its first expansion— a four-story "tower" complete with elevator—the entire first floor was given over to 16 high-roller suites, Las Vegas' first.

The suites were all one-bedrooms, but the big attractions were individual swimming pools in fenced backyards for privacy and, of all things, Japanese houseboys (which presaged butlers 35 years later). But because most junket gamblers came solo, without their wives or girlfriends, they were asked to *share* the suites, two to a room. The road from there to where we are now was long and winding, but the era of using bigger and better accommodations to cater to high rollers had been inaugurated.

As usual in Las Vegas, the other hotels followed suit(e). In the mid-'60s, the Stardust remodeled a two-story hotel wing and introduced bi-level suites with spiral staircases. Unlocking doors enlarged certain suites to two and even three bedrooms. The original MGM Grand (now Bally's) opened in 1972 with nearly 3,000 rooms (largest in the world at the time; today it's the 13th largest just in Las Vegas), with one floor of 1,000- to 2,000-square-foot penthouses and two floors of oversized connecting rooms that could pass for makeshift suites in a pinch.

Whale digs were introduced in the late '70s by Caesars Palace, which had by then assumed the mantle of Big Fishville, bringing in the heaviest hitters in the world. The 600-room Olympic Tower was built in 1979 for an unheard-of $50 million; the whole hotel-casino had been built, 13 years earlier, for half that cost (today, the same $50 million will finance a small casino expansion with, perhaps, a fast-food court). The Olympic Tower boasted 10 two-story two- to four-bedroom suites, complete with floor-to-ceiling picture windows, round beds, mirrors on the ceiling, sunken tubs, and wet bars—the height of high rollerdom at that time.

As late as the late '70s, Las Vegas casinos continued the 50-year custom of marketing exclusively, except for select high rollers, to a domestic clientele of tour and travel visitors. The earliest international travelers to Las Vegas were the Japanese, who began coming in after a bright young executive from Japan Air Lines put together the Asian penchant for gambling with big long-distance jetliners and came up with Tokyo-to-Las Vegas 747-sized planeloads. These weren't Asian whales, to be sure; the Japanese tour groups mostly played the slots, since they didn't have to speak English to do so. But they began to raise occupancy rates all along the Strip. Even then, there was no active marketing involved. One former Flamingo executive remembers meeting with JAL in San Francisco to thank them for their business—"I didn't even have to go all the way over there to Japan."

Around that time, the Las Vegas Convention and Visitors Authority began opening international marketing offices. They weren't the first—Hilton had a one-man branch office in Hong Kong in the early '70s to try to keep its baccarat room busy—but it signaled Las Vegas' intention to market to overseas travelers and big players in earnest. Meanwhile, Caesars, under the stewardship of Terry Lanni, began to develop and refine international marketing to superwealthy gamblers who expected a level of luxury and service otherwise on a par with New York, Paris, London, Hong Kong, and the like, utterly unknown in dumpy pre-Mirage Las Vegas.

Despite these efforts, up through the mid-'80s, Caesars' suites maintained the outdated look of overwrought boudoirs straight from a Hollywood soap opera, full of pastel walls, linoleum floors, Formica counters, and brass-plated fixtures. It didn't matter. Caesars retained its monopoly on the whale business. Anyone with a lot of money who came to Las Vegas, from anywhere in the world, went to Caesars. It was one of the most famous hotels on Earth. It had a reputation for unbridled, unmitigated, unparalleled opulence. It was the Casino of Casinos. It was a large part of the reason that Steve Wynn felt he had to spend $650 million (roughly $649 million more than he had) to build a joint next door.

❖ ❖ ❖

The opening of the Mirage in 1989 launched the biggest hotel-building boom in history—not just in Las Vegas, but in the world. The first hotel-casino to be built from scratch on the Strip in 17 years, the Mirage set a standard of overall quality, including its specific catering to high rollers, that was head and shoulders above Caesars, not to mention the lesser resorts around town. Not the least impressive of the Mirage's amenities were its more than 200 oversized rooms and suites, ranging from 600 to 1,500 square feet. It was expected that they would more than handle the high-end demand.

The fact that many pundits believed (and all the competitors hoped) that Steve Wynn was *meshuggah* to build the Mirage is one of the great quirks of the city's recent history. Wynn recognized in the mid-1980s that his city was in trouble. It wasn't properly serving the existing market, and couldn't hope to address the pent-up demand for gambling that Atlantic City had revealed. Either Las Vegas had to respond to evolving market conditions or some other city would.

Regardless, more than just a few analysts, observers, and second guessers were convinced that Wynn was committing financial suicide by building such a huge and expensive resort-casino. He would have to service more than a half-billion dollars in debt, junk-bond debt at high interest rates at that. Story after story appeared asserting that the Mirage was destined to be one of the most monumental failures in the history of civilization. It would never be started. It would never be completed. It would never open. It would never turn a profit.

But Wynn and his team knew what they were doing. They designed a magnificent property, even by today's inflated standards. They offered a whole new product in terms of theme, spectacle, entertainment, and luxury—the gamut of which has come to epitomize the New Las Vegas. The Mirage hired and trained the best employees in the business and actively marketed to big players. Thus, even though the financing *was* dicey (upon opening, the Mirage had expenses of $1 million a day and $25 million in working capital—in other words, three weeks worth of reserve funds), what Wynn calls the "big jury" returned its verdict: The Mirage netted $40 million ($1.29 million a day) in December 1989, its first full month of operation in what is traditionally the slowest month in the Las Vegas year, *in the casino alone.*

Neither the Mirage, nor Las Vegas, ever looked back.

For the competing casinos, the Mirage was a wake-up call. Once those doors opened, every casino operator in Las

Vegas had to re-evaluate his position. Most of the old-school bosses didn't know from villas, but all of a sudden, they realized, "Uh oh! We got competition. We gotta build a better mousetrap."

Six weeks after opening, the Mirage borrowed another $100 million (at much lower interest rates) and invested upwards of 30% on super-high-roller accommodations: six 3,500-square-foot lanais and eight 5,000-square-foot villas.

The story goes that shortly after opening the Mirage, Steve Wynn was curious about what effect the new resort was having on the company's million-dollar play. At Wynn's other property, the Golden Nugget downtown, they dealt to a dozen premium players who gambled as much as $50,000 per hand at baccarat. But the Mirage was designed to appeal to a super-select clientele that gambled at double or triple that.

Wynn called Al Faccinto, Jr., his international marketing boss, and asked for a list of all the people who'd signed up at the Mirage for lines of credit of a million dollars or more; he was expecting 40, maybe 50, names. Faccinto showed up at Wynn's office 20 minutes later, carrying a 40-page print-out that listed 500 names. Unbelievable! No one—not Faccinto, not Charlie Myerson, not even Wynn—had any conception of just how overwhelming the crush of high-end play was at the Mirage. That could have been the day that Wynn began planning to build Bellagio.

Luxor and MGM Grand upped the suite ante in 1993, but it wasn't until late 1994 that the competition to build lodging suitable for whales began to heat up in earnest.

❖ ❖ ❖

In 1967, Kirk Kerkorian paid $13 million to buy the Flamingo from Morris Lansburg, Sam Cohen, and their Miami-hotelier partners. In 1969, he opened the International at a cost of $60 million. In 1971, due to one of the rare missteps in

Kerkorian's long and wildly successful career, circumstances forced him to sell the International for $54 million to Conrad Hilton, who renamed it after himself. And in 1994, Hilton Corporation spent $45 million, only $9 million less than it paid for the whole original hotel-casino, to build three pent-house Sky Villas to enhance Hilton's prospects for the proper care and feeding of Asian, Arabian, and even American whales.

By 1994, Jimmy Newman, head honcho at the Hilton, had been marketing to international whales for nearly a decade. During that time, all he had in his lodging inventory were the nine Classic Suites on the 29th floor. Built in 1986, they were aging and small at 1,200 to 2,000 square feet. Newman desperately needed big villas to accommodate Asian high rollers, many of whom wanted to come in large groups. And he got them.

The largest of the 30th floor Sky Villas, the Verona, is 15,400 square feet; Hilton marketing claims it's the largest hotel suite in the world. The Verona features 30-foot-high neo-Michelangelo-style hand-painted ceilings, three bed-rooms, three and a half bathrooms, two hot tubs, two fire-places, a huge living room, cozy media room, a glassed-in observation area overlooking the Strip, a 2,000-pound marble dining-room table (it's not among the expensive trinkets that the Hilton fears will disappear), more tons of marble for the floors, pillars, columns, arches, pedestals, counters, and stat-ues, and gold gold gold—lamps, chairs, faucets, even gold-threaded pillowcases. At the touch of a remote, high-defini-tion TVs appear from hidden consoles at the feet of the beds. The $85,000 Bosendorfer grand piano had to be airlifted in during construction, before the roof was sealed.

One wing of the Verona Villa is built around an outdoor pool and garden; sliding glass doors from the master bed-room open onto the "back yard." There's a swimming pool and two hot tubs, plus a pond with koi (large goldfish that symbolize luck and longevity to Asians), barbecue grill, sumptuous turf with room for two removable tent pavilions, and a fountain.

One night a whale was wasted and Cyr and a butler literally had to help him into the sack in the Verona's master bedroom. He woke up the next morning in a huge room he didn't recognize, and couldn't remember how he'd gotten there. He called his butler and said, "What did you put in the champagne last night? I must be dreaming. I keep hearing the sound of a lawnmower outside."

The butler responded, "Well, sir, they're cutting your grass."

"I'm at the top of a tower, aren't I?"

"Yes sir, but you've got a big back yard. Hit the button on the console next to your bed to open the drapes"—and there was the landscaping crew tidying up the large lawn on the roof of the Hilton.

For more than six years, the Sky Villas couldn't be rented for any amount of money. Cyr once had the following conversation with Bill Gates, who wanted to stay in the Verona during the huge Comdex convention, at which he usually makes the keynote speech:

Gates: "How much to rent one of the Sky Villas?"

Cyr: "Sorry, Mr. G. They're not for rent."

Gates: "Really? Not even for twenty thousand, twenty-five thousand, a night?"

Cyr: "No, sir. The Villas are reserved for players who bet twenty-five thousand *a hand*."

These days, though, you can pay to stay in the Villas. The Verona runs $17,500 per night, but if you stay three nights, you get a $2,500-per-night price break, so it'll only set you back forty-five large for a long weekend.

Now that Newman had the Classic Suites and the Sky Villas, he found that there was too large a gap between them. A $100,000 player could go into a Classic Suite and a $1 million player into a Sky Villa, but neither was suitable for the $250,000-$750,000 player. In 1997, he transformed part of the

29th floor into three mini-villas in the 5,000- to 7,000-square-foot range at a total cost of $13 million.

The nearly $60 million Hilton invested in its six villas is only $22 million less than it shelled out to buy the entire 2,001-room Bally's Reno Hotel-Casino five years earlier.

❖   ❖   ❖

In 1998, Bellagio opened with a full complement of high-roller suites and villas; representative is a 6,000-square-foot three-bedroom suite with a private French garden, swimming pool, and Jacuzzi that goes for $6,000 per night retail.

That same year, the Rio completed a $55 million high-roller complex (the first in a separate building) known as the Palazzo Suites. Consisting of nine units from a modest one-bedroom 2,000-square-foot suite to a six-bedroom 14,000-square-foot supersuite (reportedly, all nine palazzos can also be connected to create one 18-bedroom mansion), no expense was spared in the effort to create the ultimate in luxurious peace and quiet.

Feng shui and geomancy experts were consulted to ensure optimal siting, positioning, and flow in, of, and around the building and suites. Six feet of insulation and soundproofing separate the floor of one and the ceiling of another; the walls, likewise, are eight inches thick and covered either in the highest-quality Venetian plaster or upholstered with silk-covered cotton batting, or both.

The Palazzo Suites opened on Christmas Day 1998. Ironically, Harrah's had bought the Rio for $880 million four months earlier and, shortly after merging the corporate cultures, it extricated the Rio from the gigaroller business. Now the Rio says it markets these suites to CEOs (read: non-gamblers), A-list celebrities (ditto), and elite invited guests (the thousands who can afford the Rio's maximum bet: a mere $15,000 a hand).

Finally, in 2003, Peter Morton, who owns the Hard Rock

Hotel and Casino lock, stock, and rock 'n' roll, built what he claims is the ultimate high-roller digs, the Penthouse, on the 11th floor of the hotel tower. It boasts the world's first bowling alley in a hotel suite, complete with racks for shoes and balls. Next to the alley is the billiards room and a marble bar. The 500-square-foot master bath contains a six-person hot tub equipped with two plasma TVs wired up to receive live feeds from the Joint, the Hard Rock's music venue that hosts some of the world's great rock and pop acts. With today's celebrity- and pornography-crazed audiences, Morton could probably install the video cameras in the suite and the TVs in the Joint— and fill the concert hall with people who just want to watch what's going on in that hot tub.

❖   ❖   ❖

It was with the debut of the six-acre 29-villa Mansion at MGM Grand in May 1999 that Las Vegas reached the pinnacle of exclusivity in accommodating its whales. The joke goes that in building the Mansion, money was no object: There was no budget, but they exceeded it anyway. Actually, the place cost more than $200 million to open (roughly the same amount spent by Coast Casinos three years earlier to open the Orleans Hotel-Casino down the street, with its 70,000-square-foot casino, 760 rooms, four restaurants, showroom, 12-screen movie theater, and 70-lane bowling alley).

The Mansion occupies a completely separate building from the 5,005-room MGM Grand mother hotel; it's built on property reclaimed from the unsuccessful MGM Grand Adventures amusement park. The well-heeled guests enter through a one-ton solid-bronze gate inlaid with Austrian custom-beveled glass, which accounted for a full percentage point of the Mansion's total cost. In the common area at the entrance they can smoke a cigar, sample exotic fruits from the welcome basket, or sip a glass of champagne. They can also examine 200-year-old French vases, antique Moroccan

PREVIOUS PAGE: Whale hunter Steve Cyr, at 40, is at the top of his game.

RIGHT: A three-year-old Cyr is already at ease on the phone. Cyr relied on telemarketing techniques in his ascension to superhost. CENTER: A young Steve helps out on his grandparents' Kansas farm. BOTTOM LEFT: Cyr got his start in the hospitality business at his parents' HoJo Motel in Salina, Kansas. BOTTOM RIGHT: Jean and Carroll Cyr (with Steve's daughter Savanna), who instilled a host's work ethic in son Steve.

Some of the Hilton Orangutans (1999)—(Left to Right) Robert Coury, Tina Jones (seated), John Straus, Steve Cyr, Douglas Stewart, Chris Gallegos (seated), and Ralph Kline.

Dan London at a speedway test drive. As a "branch guy," London worked his leads from outside the casino.

Latter-Day Saint and casino marketer Doug Bean had no trouble reconciling his religion with his racket.

One of Cyr's first host hires, Ray McIntosh had spent 20 years as a crap dealer.

Hosting at the highest level has its perks. TOP: River-rafting on a Hilton-sponsored trip to Costa Rica with Fast Eddie Duvall. CENTER: At Super Bowl XXXVII with wife Tanya and *Cigar Aficionado* gambling writer Michael Kaplan. BELOW: Sometimes it's Cyr that gets hosted, as he did in this trip into the Indy pit with car owner Fred Treadway.

Barron Hilton gives *Hustler* publisher Larry Flynt a trophy for being "The World's Greatest Blackjack Player."

Cyr hosted Michael Jordan at the Hilton—and Jordan hosted Cyr at his Senior Flight School basketball clinic.

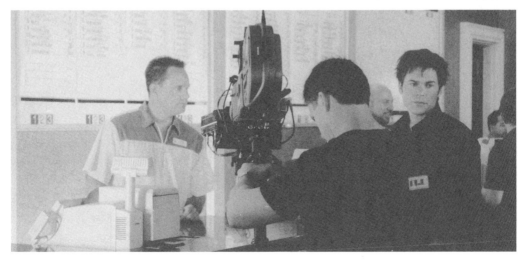

Cyr studies lines for his cameo appearance in CBS' "dr. vegas." Series star Rob Lowe is seen at right.

Steve Cyr's whaling harpoons include stretch limos, private jets, and a custom party bus driven by a guy named Johnny Fever. The center photo is the sleeping area on high-roller Ramon Desage's private 727.

High-roller suites are the most unrestrained representation of the classic Las Vegas cliché of excess. Pictured here are the Sky Villas on the 30th floor of the Las Vegas Hilton.

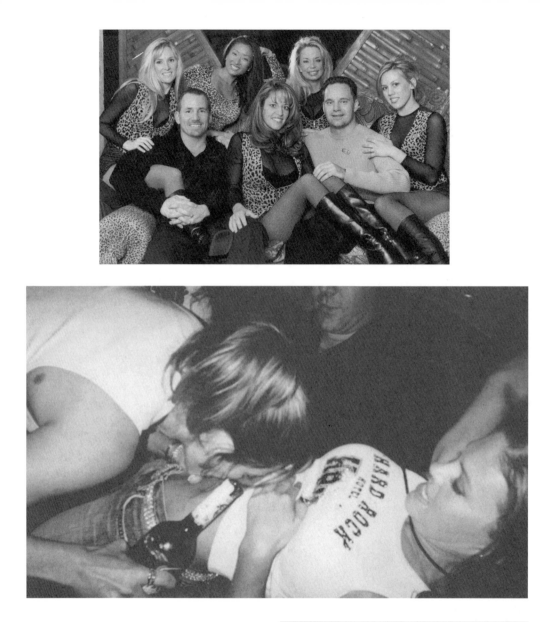

Wild parties populated by beautiful women are a staple of the high-roller social scene. TOP: Hard Rock cocktail waitresses add to the atmosphere. CENTER: Risqué party games include tequila "body shots." RIGHT: Pajama parties are a Steve Cyr specialty.

OPPOSITE: The "Steve Cyr Show" has been splashed across the national media.

THE WORLD'S FASTEST GROWING MEN'S MAGAZINE!

FHM

FOR HIM MAGAZINE

THE MONEY ISSUE!

MONEY MACHINE

BY ED MCGRAW PHOTOGRAPHY BY ROGER ERICKSON

'I WANT LOSERS!'

Vegas host Steve Cyr does whatever it takes to lure high rollers into his casino. Then he plays them to...

cigar aficionado

THE GOOD LIFE MAGAZINE FOR MEN

LEBRON JAMES:
HIGH SCHOOL
MULTI...

THE whale HUNTER

BY MICHAEL KAPLAN
PHOTOGRAPHS BY GARY MOSS

Steve Cyr has 72 hours in which to make $300,000. If he succeeds, it will require many sessions of high altitude gambling, endless schmoozing, world-class coddling, a bit of lying, a few dozen Super Bowl tickets, and the kind of bad luck that brings even the most resilient high rollers to their knees.

Though Cyr's fortunes hinge on high-stakes action, he himself is not a gambler. Well, not exactly. He is a whale hunter, a schnizzer for a person who wrangles the industry's biggest players and sets them up to risk millions of dollars at games in which the long-term odds are hopelessly tilted against them. For this particular weekend, which coincides with the 2003 Super Bowl, Cyr has flown in 16 big players—whales in casino parlance—their 25 guests, and credit lines that total $3 million to the Barona Valley Ranch Resort and Casino, a posh gambling complex that opened near San Diego last December. If they all go through their money (far from an impossibility, but an admitted long shot), Cyr, who consults for eight other casinos in Las Vegas and the Caribbean, will go home with a juicy cut of their losses. "And if they all win," says the strapping and hyperactive 39-year-old Cyr, "then I go home with nothing." The subject of a forthcoming book called Whale Hunt in the Desert by Deke Castleman hesitates for a beat and smirks. "But you know that's not going to happen. It'd be impossible."

You can't throw something like this together overnight. In November, when gamblers were still talking about the World Series, Cyr, who cut his teeth by telemarketing vitamins, was already in sales mode. From his home office in Vegas, he called 60 of his best players...

THE BEST OF OUR CITY

LAS VEGAS LIFE

THE VEGAS 100

Time for a Sit Down with Sopranos Star Steve Schirripa, Boss of Our Annual List

DECEMBER 2002

BEST CASINO HOST

Ask any casino executive for an opinion on Steve Cyr... in the ass."

But he's an effective pain in the ass, which is why those... doorstep—that is, assuming he's bringing in a high-roller, no... people who gamble," Cyr says. "Real gamblers. Risk takers...

The 34-year-old has worked in the past for Caesars... hosting business (called H-SIX) for wealthy clients that inc... for players," says Cyr, who'll never be accused of lacking... take them on trips, get them cars, concert tickets, Super... on. I'm that good."

As a host, it's Cyr's job to round up loose pocketed... $10,000 neighborhood, and then he shops them to loc... ties to meet players. I'm a hustler ... I'll wait outside y... the cushiest deals, comps, airfare, you name it, I g... depends on various factors, including how much a w... on a million-dollar bettor. "I can affect the casino's b... it's all about the host. I'm the one getting the player...

Or taking them out Cyr has been eighty-sixed... and relocate him to another property—a maneuver... ting bounced. "They're afraid of me ... The best h...

These days, Cyr is expanding his shopping m... high-rollers. "There are a lot of whales [in Las Ve... That's going to be my niche soon. I'm looking t...

We bet he finds them. Cyr can be reached...

BEST CASINO HOST
Steve Cyr

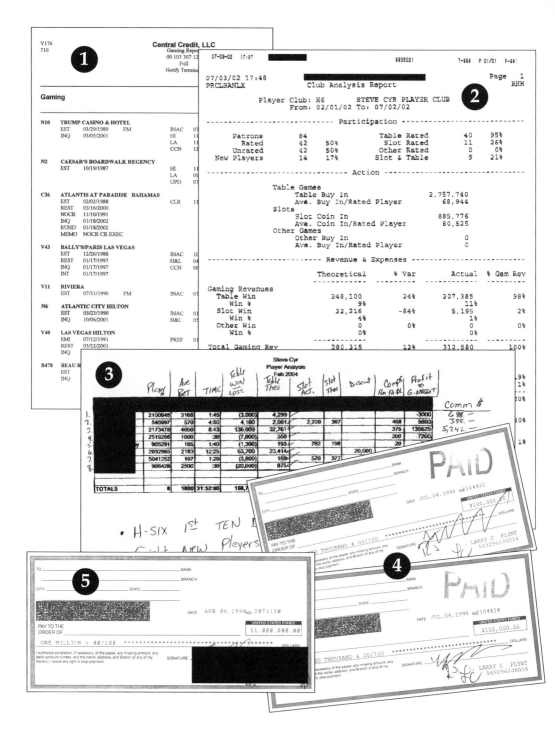

In the end, it's all about the numbers. (1) Central Credit reports tell a host who's got money to lose. (2) Casinos compare the generated "theos" (theoretical) with actual losses. (3) Contract hosts such as Steve Cyr calculate the bottom line, which determines their commissions. (4) A paper trail runs through markers—redeemed and outstanding. Larry Flynt won enough to retire his two markers for $100,000 each. (5) Another player has 60 days to pay off his million-dollar marker.

"Golden Boys" Tim Poster and Tom Breitling used dot-com millions to buy downtown's Golden Nugget. Their plans to bring back Las Vegas' glory days include Steve Cyr's hosting magic.

Family man: Nick, Savanna, Steve, Tanya, and Chelcee

Cyr's tricked-out 2000 Trans Am wasn't bought with superhost commissions—it was a "tip" from a couple of his biggest players.

lamps, and abstracts by name artists, while listening to Mozart. Discerning guests might even notice the subtle aroma of bitter orange wafting through the air.

The concierge is available to: arrange for restaurant reservations, show tickets, in-room massages, spa treatments, chartered helicopters, Play Station games, private jet transportation, referrals for buying displayed Casablanca lamps; order sushi and champagne to accompany a private viewing of the latest MGM flick in the Screening Room; cater a barbecue party in the formal garden; get security to sweep the Meeting Room for bugs before a corporate confab; locate an employee who speaks Bahasa Indonesia or Basque; or attend to any of the hundreds of requests that VIP Services handles daily.

Each of eight garden villas has two to four bedrooms (two villas can be combined for a six-bedroom megavilla), a private garden, and an indoor pool. Asian guests are placed in the villas with fountains decorated with water lilies and stocked with koi. Separate service entrances admit the villa butler and housekeeper, and chefs keep the pantries full.

The master bath in the two-bedroom villa sports top-of-the-line marble and inlaid tile, along with Jacuzzi tub, his-and-her lavatories and steam showers, heated floors, BVLGARI toiletries, a large TV for viewing while bathing, and a small TV to watch while sitting on the commode.

The Mansion has 150 full-time employees, with a substaff of a few dozen butlers who speak upwards of 20 languages among them. Every member of the staff must sign a confidentiality agreement, ensuring that no one says nothin' 'bout nobody. The Mansion is an extremely secure enclave in the midst of the largest hotel in the world and there's plenty of privacy from the hoi polloi, but not from the Mansion staff. They get to see intimate personal details of these people's lives, and sharing any of it could cost them their jobs.

(Some non-MGM Grand hosts scoff at the confidentiality agreement. Cyr, for one, claims that the MGM has the most moles per square foot of any casino in Las Vegas. He says he's stolen more players from the MGM than all the other properties combined. It's not, as the slogan has it, the City of Entertainment. Rather, it's the Sieve of Entertainment. A C-note, according to Cyr, goes a long way at the MGM Grand.)

Some guests arrive with their own contingent of servants, who wait on them hand and foot in a manner they're accustomed to. Others are easygoing or don't want to be waited on at all. Many bring their children.

When the guests check out of the largest of the villas, the crew that descends consists of four to six villa attendants who make up and refresh the rooms; a floral team that replenishes the fresh flowers; a maintenance team that conducts routine inspections of the lighting, air-conditioning, electronics, and facilities; a landscape team that checks on the ponds, fountains, and greenery; and a water-quality team that treats the private pools.

Some of the villas are available to cash customers. A one-bedroom goes for $5,000 a night, while a 6,000-square-foot two-bedroom runs $6,000 per, and one of the larger suites merits 12 large. In addition, guests can pay retail for in-suite extras, such as $50 facials, $135 massages, $500-per-person private dinner parties complete with personal chef (10-person minimum), $1,000 private fashion shows, and $1,500 for a classical-music trio.

Primarily, however, the Mansion is reserved for the highest of high rollers, the most blubbersome of cetaceans, who can afford pretty much anything they want in this world, but can only find some things, such as home-away-from-home accommodations like these, in Las Vegas.

❖ ❖ ❖

MGM Grand has 29 megasuites in the Mansion. Bellagio has nine supervillas. The Rio has nine Palazzo Suites. The

Hilton has three Sky Villas and three mini-villas. The Mirage has eight villas. Combined, that's 61 sleepers for whales. Caesars, the Venetian, Mandalay Bay, the Hard Rock, the Palms, and others add high-roller accommodations to the mix. Ordinarily, this would be plenty of rooms to go around.

Bellagio's villas, for example, have an average occupancy of 50% to 60%. They're not like normal rooms where the hotel books to a tight marketplace. They require an enormous amount of maintenance. They're often reconfigured according to guests' tastes. The default setting is on empty, because exactly when a whale might swim in is often unknown. And when one does show up, there's no telling how long he might want to stay.

A few times a year, though, a majority of a casino's best players all want to come at the same time. Four score and seven whales call up, every one expecting the best accommodations in town. On the 15 or so nights a year that the 60 or so top accommodations in Las Vegas are at a premium, such as over Chinese New Year, a player must have a $5 million credit line even to be considered for one and those host-against-host suite meetings become dog-eat-dog.

But the other 350 nights—especially since the Asian deflation, 9/11, and the dot-bomb—the criteria drop like a rock. On a Wednesday toward the end of July in the middle of a record-breaking heat wave where the thermometer has topped 115 degrees, and hasn't dropped below 90, for two weeks straight, an aggressive host might wangle a smaller villa for a $50,000 player. With flexible travel plans and a ballsy host, a minor high roller can stay in multi-million-dollar digs. Whereas just a few years ago, the same $500 bettor might not have even qualified for a tour of the place, now he has the run of it. Furthermore, he knows that if a guy like him is staying in a Sky Villa or Palazzo Suite, the joint must be desperate. So he can eat like a moose and shit like a bird— and get away with it.

❖ ❖ ❖

All the attention to the luxurious surfaces—the exquisite detail, the total immersion of the senses, the perfect control of the environment, the immediate gratification of every caprice—built into hotel suites can be considered the climactic conclusion of the casino's agenda: the stimulation of the primal appetites. In the same way that the stark austerity of the typical '50s Las Vegas hotel room drove the low roller into the arms of a $5 dealer or the arm of a 25¢ slot machine, so the sheer opulence of the casino villas is meant to drive the high roller to make his year-at-Harvard-sized bets at the tables or put in his bachelor's-degree-worth of hours at the $25 and $100 machines. His host set him up in the $15 million Verona Villa, so now it's up to him to earn it—by playing.

And when he finds a suite that suits his fancy, he craves the housing as much as he craves the gambling. After all, what would his mistress say if he were downgraded? It just wouldn't *do*. That reality is yet another harpoon the casino has in its whale-hunt armory.

And then there's the action *inside* the villas and palazzos and megasuites. Gambling is only one of the appetites stimulated by a hotel-casino room, whether it has pink walls and orange shag carpeting or Egyptian linens hand-warmed by gloved butlers. A bed, especially in sexy Las Vegas, is more than just a place to snore. A lot more.

Have studies been conducted on people's preferred locations for carnal relations? If so, casino-hotel rooms must be at the top of the list.

Which leads, inevitably, to the topic of who's doing what to whom when it's time to leave all the distractions downstairs and get horizontal.

10

Condom City

Hookers, hosts, and high rollers. The intricacies and intimacies among the three are the second worst-kept secret in the casino business (the first is the house advantage). Of course, the connection is strictly verboten, and that's verbatim. Prostitution is illegal in Clark County and to ply their trade, call girls run a gauntlet that extends from the vice detective to the casino executive.

On the other hand, the fact is, and always has been, that gambling and sex go together like nectar and ambrosia. After all, the tension created by gambling is not dissimilar, in both the psychic and the physical sense, to the pressure that sex imposes. Making a bet is to pursuing sexual relations as winning that bet is to conquest and satisfaction and as losing it is to rejection and frustration. It's no coincidence that gamblers want sex, that casinos drip with licentious lasciviousness, and that Las Vegas boasts the most hotel-room beds of any city in the world.

A gambler needs sex—the suggestion of it, with scantily clad women parading around casino floors and showroom stages (and, lately, scantily clad men with stage shows of their own); the mysterious myth of its ready availability with gorgeous and expensive professionals; and the hope of its eventual consummation, achieving the relief of release whether he wins or loses.

By the same token, sex needs gamblers. Gamblers have cash, and winnings are meant to be spent on frivolities—like, well, rent-a-pussy. Arguably, nowhere on Earth does a hard-working upstanding discriminating professional servicewoman have more opportunity to hit the jackpot than she does in Skin City.

❖ ❖ ❖

The selling of sex is against the law in Clark County, where Las Vegas is; along with the counties of Washoe, where Reno is; Douglas, where Tahoe is; and Lincoln, where fifth-generation Mormon farmers and ranchers are; as well as Nevada's capital, Carson City, where Big Brother is. Two counties in Nevada, Storey and Lyon, have *legalized* prostitution. Here, the county commissioners have actually declared sex just another area of commerce, little different than the selling of hamburgers or housewares. In Nevada's 10 other counties—including Nye, which has the brothels closest to Las Vegas, 60 miles west—prostitution isn't illegal, though it isn't fully legal either.

It's neither legal nor illegal? How can that be?

Commercial copulation was a frontier tradition throughout the American West, but it's lasted the longest in Nevada. The town fathers of 19th century mining and railroad communities, a bit more down to earth and permissive than today's politically correct and morally staunch (though often ethically compromised or personally corrupt) bureaucrats tend to be, recognized the utility of maintaining a house of available women where miners could get their rocks off, railroad workers could have Dinah blow their horns, buckaroos could give the cattle and sheep a break, and travelers could deposit their dusty loads. These practical-minded pioneers knew that their towns needed a place to service the single men, so they'd at least stay away from the married women and schoolgirls.

Meanwhile, discreet madams kept their daughters of joy off the streets and managed to prevent them from harassing, scandalizing, or blackmailing the bankers and lawyers, reporters and editors, politicians and civil servants, married men, and even ministers who availed themselves of the house's prurient product.

The red-light situation was a matter for townspeople to manage; occasionally, if they couldn't agree, it was handled at the county level. Except for a single statute in the state books, passed in 1971, proscribing prostitution in counties with populations of more than 250,000, Nevada legislators have left it to the local governments. Seven generations of state lawmakers preferred to avoid wading into the moral swamp and political minefield of the commodification of sex. Thus, upwards of 70 convenings of the legislature in the libertine state of Nevada danced around the issue of sexual commerce; they neither legalized it nor outlawed it altogether. It simply remained acceptable, based on mostly unwritten rules that over the years were locally codified: Brothels aren't allowed within 500 feet of a school or church (one town moved the school); they're not permitted to advertise; the girls must be checked weekly by a doctor; no one under 21 is admitted—that type of thing.

The most famous red-light district in Nevada history, known as Block 16, occupied frontage along Ogden Street in downtown Las Vegas (where today stands a Binion's Horseshoe parking garage). When gambling was legalized in Nevada in 1931, the casinos on Fremont Street created new demand for the services provided on the Block. For a few wide-open years, travelers on the Los Angeles-Salt Lake railroad took advantage of the Las Vegas whistle stop, as the engines were serviced with coal and water, to refuel themselves. From the train, they stopped off at the Northern, Silver, Tango, and Las Vegas clubs for a whiskey and some faro or roulette, then perhaps made their way over to Ogden for a quickie.

In the early 1940s, the Las Vegas Bombing and Gunnery

Range was established. (It's now the huge Nellis Air Force Range, at three million acres the size of Connecticut, which contains the Nuclear Test Site, the infamous Area 51, and the proposed Yucca Mountain nuclear-waste repository.) Because the Gunnery school was training thousands of fighter pilots, bombardiers, and gunners for World War II, the feds insisted that Block 16 be closed. The girls, quite naturally, migrated from the "Line" into the joints, which put the casino managers into something of a quandary.

The old-school bosses knew they had to have a ready supply of curb-service pussy to dish off to the horn dogs, so they recruited, registered, and regulated the girls. They kept a stable of reliable hookers and let the hostesses, waitresses, and showgirls double as darlings of the desert if they so chose.

But they also knew they had to keep it covert and off the radar screens of the legions of straights who filled the casinos. So they saw to it that the front-line hotel employees, such as bellmen, bartenders, floormen, and limo drivers, knew how to dispatch love laborers to service the hard-ons.

Over the years, with the proliferation of megaresorts, the explosion of casino jobs, the evolution of a corporate mentality, and the continual pressure on overt prostitution, fewer and fewer casino employees kept their fingers in the pay-for-lay pie. In fact, when he opened the Mirage in 1989, Steve Wynn hired women bellmen for the first time in Las Vegas, in what some observers believed was a subtle attempt to discourage the traditional relationship between the bell desk and the B-girls. It might've even worked: Las Vegas vice detectives considered it a coup when they infiltrated a prostitution ring managed by bellmen at the Aladdin, Desert Inn, and Caesars in 1996. Any casino employee caught pandering, pimping, or in any way providing prostitution is not only termed, but also blackballed from the industry by having his or her sheriff's work permit revoked.

Of course, keeping prostitution out of the public eye is all pretend, a surreal disconnect, as if anyone really believes that the state legislators, gaming regulators, or corporate administrators don't realize that they're all—every last one of them—in the debauchery business together.

Host X claims that when he worked at a casino without high-roller suites, his boss' boss' boss, the president of the company, once told him, "Just make sure the guy's serviced. Who cares if he's not impressed by our accommodations? Get him good and laid in one and he'll think it's the greatest room on Earth."

❖ ❖ ❖

These days, the mass-market sex-for-hire business has evolved apart from the casinos. Sex is readily available to Las Vegas visitors via a variety of non-casino connections.

Common streetwalkers are rare. They're out there, but usually in the seedy parts of town.

Freelance pros hang around casino bars, usually the ones near the high-roller pits. You can't tell them by their dress—they need to appear obvious enough to be approachable, but not so blatant as to attract the attention of surveillance and security. The dead giveaway is that they're usually alone. How often does an attractive young woman go out to a bar by herself? She's either with another girl or two, a guy, or a group—unless she's soliciting. In Latin, it's called *solo ergo pro*.

"Exotic dancers" and "entertainers" are on call with escort services that advertise in the girlie rags found in newspaper vending boxes and distributed by pamphleteers outside casinos, as well as in the Yellow Pages and on the Web. The Internet is huge, of course, for girls. Plenty of Host X's customers pre-book sex at sites such as lasvegasescorts.com and vegasadultdirectory.com. They can see photographs of a few girls for free or they can subscribe and see thousands of them. They can click on blonde, brunette, redhead, exotic, mature, barely legal, and the like. And they can reserve them right there online or call a toll-free phone number.

If they call, at the other end of the advertised phone number an order taker (one of 100 manning phones at the largest
services) determines the caller's preferences, then pages
Candi or Sandi or Randi or Mandi or Dandi, or any one of an
estimated 15,000 girls plying this trade in Las Vegas, and
sends her to the room. A "dance" lasts 30 minutes and runs
around $150. In general, the dancer has to hand over the en-
tire fee to the booking company; thus, she has to negotiate
anything extra for herself as a "tip." And to take in, she has
to put out.

Though they work for a service and are ostensibly scru-
tinized, these girls are on their own and do a volume business, so the dangers of diseases and felonies are real. Both
john and jane are immeasurably safer in the legal brothels in
Pahrump, across the Nye County line a quick hour's drive
from Las Vegas. These places provide one-stop shopping for
booze and parties. Perhaps the fanciest brothel in the state,
Sheri's Ranch, has an outdoor pool area complete with wa-
terfall, lounge chairs, volleyball court, and often sunbathing
pros, along with Jacuzzi rooms, a bubble-bath room with a
king-size tub, an S&M dungeon, even a half-dozen themed
cottages—Africa, Arthurian, Roman, the Sixties. These girls
are examined, tested, analyzed, and approved on a weekly
basis. The house minimum for visiting with a pro in her room
is $150, while the sky's the limit for an all-night orgy. And
it's all legal.

Working at a brothel like Sheri's is a dream for prostitutes
around the country, the third rung from the top of the shady-
lady ladder. The second rung is occupied by the casino call
girl. A gambler who plays, drinks, and sleeps in a hotel and
isn't afraid to ask around can usually find the one employee
out of hundreds who can hook him up with a referral.

But the call girl who's most juiced-in to the jack-off jackpot is the one whose pager number is in the Rolodexes of the
casino executives who market to the highest rollers and biggest players—namely, the hosts.

❖ ❖ ❖

Hosts and hookers provide the same basic service. In a physical sense, the hooker's service is the natural end result of those the host supplies.

In a metaphorical sense, the host is the snake in the Garden of Eden. His job is to talk Adam into taking a bite from the forbidden fruit from the Tree of Good and Bad Bets. The wily host-snake knows that the means to this end is naive Eve. But wait a minute. Who knows what the historical Adam was really like? He might've been a dickhead. He might've been obese and ill-kempt and smelly—never soaping down in the warm and gentle rains of Eden, changing his fig leaf only once a year (and this was long before circumcision came along in the time of Abraham), and turning mean after one too many fermented-cherry juices. Or perhaps he was suffering a little phantom pain from his amputated rib. Still, both the snake and the cheesecake had to suck up to Adam like he was the only man on Earth or something.

The slithering casino host has to fly his guy in, pick him up in a limo, set him up in a suite, and arrange for the finest meals. During his stay, the host has to play golf with him, laugh at his jokes, and become his best buddy. He doesn't have to have sex with him (though more than one *woman* host has been known to trade her own sexual services for money, merchandise, and other favors), but Host X says he refers strippers and/or hookers to seven out of ten of his VIPs. All in the service of getting his sucker to eat the apple at the gambling tables.

Eve, for her part, doesn't have to do much seducing. All she has to do is show up, with the biggest breasts and tuckedest tummy and whitest teeth that money can buy, a sparkle in her eyes, and a willingness to do the nasty.

The best hosts have a stable of "players," whose pager numbers they can confidently give to their "players." (When Cyr refers to "players," he means high-rolling gamblers. But when a working girl refers to "players," she means women who sell sex for money and sometimes men who pay money for sex.) Of course, to preserve the ostensible straight-and-narrow image of the casino business, any host who gets caught hooking up girl players with guy players can lose his work permit, which means being booted off the gravy train at the very next station. More disconnect: For a host to even have his name associated with such a thing—in a book, for example—is dangerous. The words "Steve Cyr" and "call girl" can never, under any circumstances, appear in the same sentence. Cyr, in fact, insists he doesn't need hookers to be a successful host. Besides, his fish are so big that they bring their own talent with them. Still, a host without hookers is like a writer without sources.

Some hosts like to avail themselves of the services of their consorts. After all, these women are young, hard-bodied, willing, aggressive, and fun, and they like sex and action and money. Only the slickest hosts, however, get their pussy comped (Host X, for example, has spent "hundreds of thousands of dollars" on his own girls) and then only on special occasions. That's not to say it's always a cash transaction. A host is in a position to do favors. He can issue comps for the girls. He has players who own car dealerships and mortgage companies. He can occasionally recommend a girl for a straight job in casino marketing. He can do a lot of things—and in return, he collects a little body tax.

X describes a host of his acquaintance who has to test the merchandise so that he can be sure his players get top-of-the-line servicing. No test, no referrals, and he can and does blackball the girl with the other hosts and bellmen. Since he can throw plenty of big business their way, many of the girls give him a free trial. Predictably, he regularly needs to *retest* the product to ensure continued quality control.

A few hosts even demand a kickback from the players who service his players. A hook-up fee. The typical commission is 10% to 15%; greedy hosts have been known to ask for

20% or 25%. It's reckless, but some hosts go so far as to middle the transaction. The gambler gives him the money, then he gives the hooker her share. This can lead to overquoting the gambler and underpaying the hooker, which generally means it's time for both parties to find themselves a new host.

Careful hosts, however, will make an introduction, then quickly distance themselves from the transaction. They establish rules, which must be followed to the letter. Rule number one: If the girl ever mentions the host's name to anyone, like in "Mission: Impossible," the director disavows any knowledge whatsoever of her actions. The same goes for the gambler. He met the lady at a bar, a restaurant, a nightclub, a Parents Without Partners meeting. All a smart host wants to do is give a guy a phone number. That's it. He doesn't know a thing. He can plead complete and total ignorance in the event he winds up in the grease. He never does.

Well, almost never. On October 8, 2002, the Belterra Casino in southern Indiana was fined $2.26 million and shut down for 66 hours by the Indiana Gaming Commission over allegations that the casino arranged for eight to twelve female escorts to entertain 48 players at a casino-sponsored golf outing in June 2001. This in itself isn't unusual: At the Jimmy Newman Golf Tournament, the Hilton hired girls in skimpy clothes to ride around in the carts. And at the 17th hole, they had a refreshment tent with girls at a "rub-your-balls" booth (they'd stick a couple of golf balls between their boobs, then give the player a hug).

At Belterra, two female hosts complained to the human-resources department that the casino's director of security instructed them to "kiss and pat" male gamblers. For breaking the casino code of silence, one was demoted and the other fired. Lawsuits ensued. The company CEO resigned.

In addition, in spring 2004, six Atlantic City hosts were busted for their involvement in what police called a "highly organized prostitution ring," involving, mostly, Asian hookers out of Philadelphia. Such incidents demonstrate the kind of trouble a casino and its people can get into over testosterone.

Those, however, are the rarest of occasions. More than 500 player reps work in Las Vegas and for as long as anyone can remember, only a handful have ever been involved in a scandal with a scarlet woman.

That's saying something. On the supply side, a (girl) player claimed that at one time, her name and number were in the Rolodexes of *every* host working at one major casino-hotel property and of various hosts at other megaresorts around town. And on the demand side, there's Host X's seven out of ten high rollers asking about girls.

Even the three out of ten who aren't interested are never too far removed. A high roller was parked on the 50-yard line at the 2001 Super Bowl when his host, sitting on one side of him, asked if he'd like to attend a Penthouse Pet Party back at the casino.

Upon further questioning, the host promised the gambler "a girl for the weekend."

"A Penthouse Pet?" the high roller asked.

"Well, if not a real one, then one who oughta be," the host whispered with a wink.

The high roller politely declined. Sitting on the other side of him was his wife.

❖   ❖   ❖

While the sex screws have been tightened in the New Las Vegas, in the old-school days, things were a bit looser. The following incident probably couldn't occur today, but 20 years ago, it was commonplace.

A downtown Las Vegas casino had just spent $4 million on four suites—two stories each with floor-to-ceiling windows, black-marble bathtubs large enough to accommodate four comfortably, and mirrors everywhere—a hedonist's delight. One of the hosts decided to pull out all the stops in an effort to lure some big ocean-going mammals to break in the new suites. With the emphasis on all the stops.

He tracked down Mr. A, a blackjack high roller with numerous $250,000 credit lines around town. Getting Mr. A on the phone, the host went into rapturous detail about the new digs. Mr. A was unmoved. He'd stayed in more neo-brothel-style casino suites than he cared to remember. The swimming-pool-sized marble tubs were a nice touch, but not enough for him to put up with downmarket downtown for a whole weekend.

Then the host played his trump card. He said, "By the way, the room is decorated in ebony and ivory. The real thing."

Being a highly cultured man, Mr. A knew that ebony is an expensive hardwood and ivory is illegal to import, due to the dwindling populations of African elephants and Alaskan walruses. He was mildly intrigued.

"We use them as bookends," the host continued.

"Bookends?" Mr. A was perplexed. "Are they a gift or something?"

"Yes, in a way. Ebony is Jamaican, five-foot-ten with honey-brown skin and the bluest eyes you've ever seen. Ivory is five-two, with blond hair down to her butt, emerald-green eyes, and a smokin' little body. They're both dancers on the Strip. And they're yours for as long as you want to stay in the suite."

The host had hooked his whale.

Mr. A wound up visiting this casino on many trips, while getting his fill of Ebony and Ivory every time—*and* winning about $200,000 in the process. Little did the host know that Mr. A, also known as Ian Andersen, was a professional high-stakes blackjack player and author of a best-selling book on how to turn the tables on casinos. Subsequently, Ian hired Ebony and Ivory to hang with him at the blackjack tables, where they distracted pit bosses from scrutinizing his play, and in numerous oversized bathtubs around town, where they ... fade to black.

❖ ❖ ❖

Some super-elite sex players hit Vegas on those occasions when the "beauty-party" road shows roll into town. These are gatherings of the rich and gorgeous, put on by adult-industry event planners, porn video-production companies, or the girls' managers. They're often held in casino penthouses or villas, in conjunction with an XXX-rated trade show. The girls are beauty-pageant finalists, ex-Playmates and ex-Pets, top lingerie models, porn stars, and TV and movie bit players. The men are horn-dog gamblers who know a host who knows the sponsor who puts on the party.

The sponsors of the beauty parties feed off gamblers, same as hosts. They know that a guy who bets $5,000 to $10,000 a hand will pay $5,000 to $10,000 to get laid. And for that kind of money, the sponsors can get *Playboy*- and Miss USA-caliber talent.

The sponsors put together a group of traveling beauties, then call a few select superhosts in Las Vegas. It's utterly hush-hush, personal invite only. Host X, for example, is on a sponsor's list. Now he gets to call up a handful of his best players and say, "Hey, ever wanted to have a shot at a Penthouse Pet? There'll be a few at this party."

Playmates of the Year, Miss Universes, and well-known porn stars are the most expensive, charging roughly $15,000 just to walk through the door. Flash-in-the-pan actresses currently appearing in some TV show or movie get $4,000 to $5,000 to appear at a party in Vegas where select high rollers are trying to make a connection with them.

If there's mutual interest between a gambler and a girl, the sponsor charges him $10,000 (or some appropriate amount) for the introduction, then dukes off half to her. After that, the gambler pays direct for whatever the girl is selling—escorting, dating, sex. Maybe she spends an hour with him for $1,500. Maybe two for $2,500. Maybe she accompanies him while he gambles; when a guy's making $5,000 bets, with some discreet chip-hustling, she can bag a nice little haul on the side. Maybe they spend the night together for $20,000. And maybe he turns out to be the man of her dreams and it's a true-love connection. It's happened.

The hosts are on their own at these affairs. Again, if they're smart, they tell their players the whens, wheres, and how muches, then stay away. Some like to go to meet the other hosts' big players and some are just looking to get *very* lucky. The casino, meanwhile, has nothing to do with it, except renting the room at retail to the party planners. And Gaming Control tends not to get involved unless there's a complaint from someone or the closed-door activities spill into public areas and something unseemly gets captured on videotape.

Occasionally, a casino does hold a beauty party of its own. Every year the Rio, for example, sponsors a Miss Rio Beauty Pageant, then hosts a private get-together for the beauties and its high rollers who want to mingle with them. The annual Miss Hawaiian Tropic Finals, likewise, are held at the Tropicana. These are strictly eat-what-you-kill-type deals. If you want to try to pick up on one of the girls, take your shot. But you're certainly not entitled to anything and your chances aren't even very good. Still, whenever a beautiful girl and a wealthy guy get together, anything can happen.

All the casino's doing is having a party. All up and down the ranks, everyone does his best imitation of Sergeant Schultz from "Hogan's Heroes": "I see nuhthink. I hear nuhthink. I know nuhthink."

❖ ❖ ❖

Desirée married young and she and her husband needed money. So at 19 she began working at a jiggle joint in Colorado. She was much more afraid of the actual *dancing* than of taking off her clothes. She simply had no rhythm; she couldn't carry a beat in a bag. Her first night, she looked so scared that the manager booked bets as to whether she'd ever return.

She hung in with the dancing (though she bailed on the marriage) and by the time she was 21, she was the top earner in the club. That's when she made the pilgrimage to stripper mecca.

In Las Vegas, Desirée was working at Olympic Garden when a host, out trawling for trollops, approached her and asked if she ever did "extracurriculars." She was 22 and had been dancing for three years, but she didn't know what he was talking about. Still, she told him yes and gave him her number.

The next thing she knew she was in a hotel room with a guy who was fat, smelly, and just plain gross. There was champagne in the room and, knowing she'd have to get drunk to go through with it, she downed a whole bottle. Though she negotiated the fee, $500, up front, she made the classic beginner's mistake of not collecting beforehand. She managed the sex, but afterwards, she had to jump up and run to the bathroom where she puked her guts out. The whole sordid affair—champagne, gross john, sex for money, and not yet having gotten paid—put her head in the toilet.

Desirée cleaned up, came out of the bathroom, and said, "It's time for me to go."

The guy said, "Okay, but can you drop me off at Caesars?"

He knew he hadn't paid her. *She* knew he hadn't paid her. So she drove him to Caesars and just before dropping him off, she finally collected her courage and said, "You need to go ahead and take care of me."

And he said, "I'm only gonna give you two hundred, because you got sick."

From that experience, Desirée set up four ground rules for herself. Always get paid *before* the party. Never take a job with a john who's fat. Never take a job with a john who's smelly. And never take a job with a john who's gross.

Then she had to consider a bit more deeply what she

was doing. Her marriage had been a disaster and her most recent boyfriend was a loser. She figured she'd screwed enough assholes for free, so she might as well get paid.

Desirée is now 36. She stands only five-foot two, but always wears four-inch heels so she can measure up to the big boys. She weighs 114, some of it contained in the 36D bra she's worn since the surgery. Seven years ago, she told a couple of her regular customers that she wanted a new pair—after dancing for so many years topless, without support, they'd begun sagging. After all, she was the ripe old age of 29. She insisted that she needed $7,000 to cover the cost of the plastic surgery and two months of not working.

The guys sponsored a golf tournament for 12 of their buddies the week before the operation, making sure Desirée got enough money to pay for her new knockers. Of the 12, six put up a grand apiece for a half-hour of 69 (the kind of gig that Desirée calls a "ho-down"). It was an easy and lucrative assignment and she paid the plastic surgeon with hundred-dollar bills.

Desirée doesn't always have to have sex to earn her keep. She also performs hostess and escort duties. One high-powered salesman occasionally hires her and a friend or two to dress up business cocktail parties in his hotel suites. He pays them $1,000 each for three hours of meeting and greeting his clients. They don't even have to serve drinks. All they have to do is mingle, making sure his guests are comfortable and have pretty girls to talk to. They're his ice-breakers. For these affairs, she wears mini-skirts and tailored business jackets over low-cut blouses showing eight inches of cleavage. It may or may not have anything to do with the presence of Desirée and Sway or Susie, but the high roller usually closes whatever deal he's got cooking during the cocktail party.

Whether she has sex or not, Desirée always tries to get her guy to gamble, especially if he's come through a host. And it's not that difficult. Usually, all she has to say is, "Hey, let's go down and play for a while. I'll hang out with you."

It's a great deal for the host, whose guy is gambling. The high roller likes it too. Often, he'll give her money to play with when he buys in. Or if he's winning, he might toss chips to his good-luck charm. If he's losing, she plies him with booze and distracts him with her estimable charms. The guy's having so much fun, he doesn't care about the money, or that's the theory, anyway. And if she gets him drunk, she can hustle his chips.

Of course, she has to be slick. The casino is constantly on the lookout for chip hustlers, especially at the high-limit tables. Floormen watch for freelancers who stalk the pit, then all of a sudden glom onto a guy they don't appear to know. The girls are bold. "Hey, can you bet for me?" If security catches a girl dropping a drunk high roller's greens or blacks into her purse, she'll be 86ed in a New York-New York minute. And it's a cinch that the bored tech in the surveillance room will have all the cameras in the area trained on those 36Ds. However, if a guy walks in with a girl and they sit down together, floormen know the deal. And Desirée is an old hand at it. She's been hustling checks from marks for nearly 15 years.

Lots of high rollers, she's found, are terrible tippers. They're on the casino dole and think everything's taken care of. They're betting $5,000 a hand, pulling in 50 grand on a hot streak, and they might throw out an occasional $25 chip for the dealers. Plenty of times Desirée's seen a guy with a huge stack of $500 chips in front of him who won't toss the cocktail waitress a buck. In such cases, she often tokes the drink runner a $25 chip or two of her own. It's a good investment: The longer the waitress keeps her guy lubricated, the more money she'll make off him.

At the ripe old age of 36, with a decade and a half under her belt, so to speak, Desirée's settled down to a handful of regular customers, along with their referrals, and the occasional outcall from her favorite host or two. She's had her share of sugar daddies along the way. One client put her on retainer, sending her $500 a month for a whole year, just to go to dinner with him when he was in Vegas. She never did him; didn't even kiss him goodnight. Six grand for dressing up and dining out a dozen times.

This isn't unusual money for top call girls. Desirée's friend Dolly, for example, is so good-looking—and fun; she loves to have sex—that though she officially charges $1,000, she usually winds up getting $2,000 or $3,000 by the end of the job. And Rose, another veteran, has to perform, perhaps, six times a month—for one guy who pays her $5,000 and two guys who pay her $2,000 to be at their beck and call. She makes $120,000 a year. On her 1040 form, she calls herself an entertainer, claims $48,000 in annual income, and deducts all her clothing, beauty, and travel expenses.

Desirée has been at it so long, she's become something of a mother hen. For one, hosts are always on the prowl for new girls. Many of their regular customers like variety. When Host X, for example, lands a hot one, he'll call around and say, "Hey, I've got an up-and-comer you need to check out," which never fails to get at least a couple of big players into his casino. When he turns out someone new, a stripper, say, he always sends her to Desirée, to what he calls Puta University, where she hammers home several hard and fast rules.

First, collect the money up front. It's too easy for a trick to try to weasel out of paying after the fact. Newbies are always scared to ask for payment before the services are rendered. "Let's take care of the money first," she teaches them to say, "and then we can have fun."

Second, always bring condoms. Ninety percent of call girls, Desirée estimates, don't carry protection. Partly, they figure that if they don't bring condoms and the guy doesn't have one, they won't have to have too much serious sex. With luck they can get paid for a handjob. A lot of the girls will perform oral sex without a condom. Desirée brings them, so she never has to do anything without them.

Third, if a girl ever feels uncomfortable, she should leave. Grab her clothes, throw (some of) the money back at the guy if she has to, and get the hell out of there, before something ugly happens.

And fourth, no drugs. A lot of the girls like pot and coke and crank, even crack and junk. And a lot of the guys want the girls to get them drugs or do their own drugs with them. Desirée used to on occasion, but no longer. She tells the girls they'll feel like a babysitter for strung-out people who stay up all night—and want company. Of course, after all that coke or speed or whatever, they can't get it up. But they want the girl to keep trying and eventually they overstay their welcome. Also, when a customer, especially a high roller, is spending money on blow, he's not spending money on the girl or the gambling. The casinos hate drugs. So does the law. She teaches her girls to just say no.

Sometimes a guy'll come along and totally rock her world. Some of the players who pay her for her body skills have all the attributes in their own right. They're wealthy, good looking, well-groomed, sophisticated, generous, and great in bed. They take her shopping and buy her expensive gifts—clothes and jewelry, mostly. They take her to fine hotels and five-star restaurants and on jaunts around the world.

Finally, she still believes in love. She admits to going through a phase when she thought that men were a way to pay the bills and sock away some savings and that was it. But she's outgrown that and wants to get remarried. Of course, she's a lot more realistic about men now than the first time she had a husband: She has no expectations that any man will ever be faithful. She knows that some men out there can be, but she's not counting on it from *her* man.

She makes $100,000 a year now, and that's working only six or eight times a month, once or twice a weekend. She has a house, a Mercedes, and an automatic investment plan. She pays taxes. She figures she'll be out of the player scene in a couple of years. She hasn't decided what she'll do next—

probably some kind of business—but she's sure there's life after hooking.

❖ ❖ ❖

Desirée might make it. Hard work, maturity, her strict rule against drugs and gambling, and a savings plan are all working in her favor. It's taken nearly half her life to get to where she is, but she played her cards right, climbed the career ladder, and wound up frolicking with the whales in the desert.

Trixie, another Las Vegas player, not only didn't have to work nearly as hard, but she actually did hit the proverbial jackpot. A host set her up with Mr. N, a whale who owns a national chain of stores and is worth a billion or so. He saw something in Trixie that intrigued him, so he made her an offer that most sex sellers, in their insecurity and greed, would refuse. He gave her a choice: Take a couple thousand for services rendered in the usual fashion, or provide the coitus gratis and partner up with him at the tables. She didn't hesitate. He cut her in for a percentage of his winnings, then proceeded to kill the casino for $500,000 that night. Her share? Fifty grand.

She took the money, drove to a car dealership, and bought a top-of-the-line Lexus for cash (and had $1,500 left over for insurance and gas).

The next weekend, Trixie and Mr. N got lucky again. He took down $800,000. After he handed over her share, she stopped off at the local realtor's office and made a 20% down payment on a house.

Over the next six-month period, he won $3 million.

Trixie and Mr. N continued their deal every time he came to Las Vegas: free sex and partners in the gambling. After a while (and a highly publicized divorce on his part), they formalized the arrangement—and got married.

Part Three
Whales

"It is some systematized exhibition of the whale
in his broad genera that I would now fain put before
you. Yet it is no easy task. The classifications of the
constituents of a chaos, nothing less is here essayed."
— Herman Melville, *Moby Dick*

"Do I not destroy an enemy
if I make of him a friend?"
—Abraham Lincoln

"A Friend of the Devil
is a Friend of Mine"

It could be that Steve Cyr and his fellow casino marketing executives are merely event planners who happen to have
the world's most plentiful, elaborate, and seductive party
favors at their disposal. It could also be that they exploit the
basest proclivities—greed, lust, gluttony, envy—of the most
decadent element of society. It could be that they're simply
giving people what they want, a legal and acceptable, though
perhaps morally ambiguous, run for their money. It could
also be that they're vampires, sucking life's essence out of
weak and susceptible souls.

From the point of view of the player, it all boils down to
the bottom line, the result of the game. Win or lose. Good or
bad. When the gambler wins, he considers Steve Cyr a be-
nevolent and generous host.

When he loses, Cyr's the snake in the Genesis Garden.
Mephistopheles pandering to Faust. A saturnalia supersales-
man in Sodom. A godless beguiler in Gomorrah. A high priest
during the unholy last gasp of the Roman Empire. In short, a
bad influence.

From Cyr's point of view, the dynamic is a little more
complex. The host caters to his players. He eats with them,
drinks with them, parties with them, takes trips with them,
and hangs with them in the casino—all the while repeating
to himself, "Lose baby lose baby lose baby lose." His raises

in salary, his performance bonuses, his perks, his juice—everything emanates from the losses of his players.

And in the end, after all the glad-handing and ass-kissing and comp-granting, amidst all the memories of all the phone calls, limo rides, and Saturday nights, is the one thing that stands out in a host's mind about his every customer: "I beat him out of a million last year." Not the casino beat him out of a million. Not the dealers or the bosses or the marketing department beat him out of a million. Not even *we* beat him out of a million. But STEEEEVE CYYYYR—personally, individually, single-handedly—beat him out of a million.

This sometimes puts him in awkward, seemingly contradictory, positions.

❖ ❖ ❖

Take Denny Mason. Denny was a friend of Steve's, a basketball buddy, long before Cyr knew that such a thing as casino marketing executives existed. Mason helped Cyr early on by recommending him to a telemarketing friend, which greatly furthered Cyr's hosting career, albeit inadvertently. He was the first player Cyr signed up for a credit line at the Hilton. That first night, when Mason moseyed down to the Hilton, applied for credit, and signed out $10,000, Cyr walked him over to a slot machine, sat him down, and watched him promptly lose $2,500—an expensive laydown as a favor for a sidekick.

The first time Denny came in and lost $50,000, it seemed like so much money that Cyr was a little freaked out. After all, Denny wasn't a pretend friend; he was the real deal. Still, Cyr didn't have many other big players yet, so initially, it was a one-way street. Mason played and lost; Cyr doled out comps worth pennies, if that much, on the gambling dollar. Denny's bankroll provided bricks and mortar for Cyr's career edifice.

A month or so after Cyr signed up Mason at the Hilton,

the host arranged his first high-roller jaunt out of town. He and Johnny Oakes took Denny Mason, Denny's friend Doug, and a few other gamblers to Barron Hilton's private 515,000-acre ranch, which straddles northwestern Nevada and east-central California, to go fishing, shooting, riding, and whoring. All they had to do was play a little the night before and stay over at the Hilton, so they could be up early in the morning to catch one of the casino jets to the ranch.

Denny and Doug lost a bundle that night, and Cyr looked like a hero to his bosses, though he was anything but a sight for sore gamblers' eyes—especially since Denny and Doug had the worst hangovers of their lives after taking a 6 a.m. wake-up call to catch the jet. They flew for 40 minutes, then stepped off the plane onto a dirt runway. There, a ranch hand was waitin' to take 'em four-wheelin' down to the crick where they could go fishin' for crappie and target plinkin' with the forty-four magnum and skeet shootin' with the twelve-gauge. Just what a couple of boiler-room operators from Las Vegas—big losers the night before, sleep deprived, and heads pounding—wanted to hear at 7:30 in the morning with the sun in their eyes.

Cyr had never been to the Hilton Ranch either, but he'd heard stories from the older hosts and bosses about all-night poker games, girls in every corner, and a mysterious place up the road called the Red Dog. In fact, Guy Hudson called in Cyr the night before the trip and said, "When Oakes goes up to the ranch, he loves to spend time at the Red Dog. Don't feel like you have to go if you don't want to. And your players certainly don't have to go—especially the older ones."

"What the fuck are you talking about, Guy?"

"I'm talking about the Red Dog, the legal whorehouse near the ranch. If you want to go, go, but don't you dare expense it on your account. You pay out of your own pocket ..." and yadda yadda, a 10-minute lecture on bordello protocol.

Right on cue, Oakes strolled into the office and said, "Hey,

Hudson, I thought I told you not to tell the kid about the whorehouse!"

"He's one of us now," Hudson responded. "He's going to the ranch, so he's got to know about the Red Dog." The cat(house) was out of the bag.

When they got to the ranch, Oakes instructed Cyr to keep the players up till 1 a.m., then wait for him outside in the Suburban. It was cold in the high desert after midnight in March. Cyr, Denny, Doug, and an older player waited in the Chevy for Oakes to show up with the keys. While they sat shivering, the guys talked about how much money they had on them and what they were gonna do—and not do. The older one was nervous. "I'm just getting a blowjob," he said. "I don't wanna catch anything."

Cyr reassured him that everything would be all right, as if he knew what he was talking about.

Finally, the host went into the house to find Johnny Oakes, who was dead asleep, sawing off logs to beat the band. When Cyr woke him up, Oakes growled, "There's no Red Dog, you dumb shit! Hudson and I were dickin' with you. Go to bed." It was one of Cyr's many initiations into hosthood.

Mason's conservative when he's sober. He might tell Cyr, "Don't give me more than ten thousand tonight." But in the heat of the action when he's lit up from alcohol and down the ten grand, he wants more. Cyr says no and stands firm, regardless of the begging and pleading and threatening. He knows his friend is too competitive. He knows Mason never wants to call a bad night over and take his losses and walk away. Cyr won't let him chase his losses, which is a gambler's worst mistake. He's probably helping Denny, but in the back of his mind, he also hears that little voice that comes between a host and even his favorite customer: Lock it up, baby!

Sometimes it works the other way around: Cyr forces Denny to lock up *his* wins. Like the time Cyr took Mason and some big players to Atlantis, on Paradise Island in the

Bahamas. The two were drunk and beating the crap out of a crap table at 3:30 a.m. The casino was closing at four and the floorman said, "Mr. M, we're shutting her down in fifteen minutes."

The normally easy-going and low-key Mason wasn't having it. "Tell you what. Every time I roll a number, I'm gonna give the dealers each a hundred-dollar toke. So they'll stay open. Right?" The dealers glanced at the floorman, then back at the posturing American. "Right?" Mason asked again. "Sure," the floorman muttered. But Mason wasn't mollified. He pointed an index finger at the floorman and said, "And I'm gonna give you a lesson on how to run a casino."

Stone drunk, obnoxious, and stuck $40,000 for the night, Denny proceeded to go on a monster run. He hit point after point, number after number. Each time, he tossed the dealers a black check each, then paused to give the floorman a slurred little lecture on customer relations.

By about 5 a.m., Mason was up $55,000—a $95,000 turnaround. "Well, buddy," he croaked to Cyr, "I'm now gonna go piss away all this beer, then come back and piss away all these chips." Cyr knew he meant it.

While Mason staggered off to the bathroom, Cyr grabbed his stack and told the floorman to close the game as quickly as possible. He then went to the cage and told the cashier to suspend Denny's credit line. Meanwhile, the lights went off and everyone disappeared.

Mason stumbled out of the bathroom into a dark and deserted casino. He thought he'd passed out in the john. He assumed he'd already lost back his chips. The game was over, so he blundered up to his room and fell into bed.

Later that morning, Cyr called him to get up and get ready; they were leaving the Bahamas that afternoon. Mason said, "I have to write a check and settle up. Give me my figure. How much do I owe?"

"Come to my room."

While Mason looked on, Cyr opened up his room safe

and pulled out the $55,000 in checks. Mason couldn't believe his bloodshot eyes. He hugged Cyr, tossed him a handful of blacks, and together they went down to the cage, cashed out, and flew home.

The morning after the night before, no matter how furious the row over credit and wins and losses, there's never hard feelings. A lot of karma runs between Denny and Steve. But theirs is the rarest of the gambler-host dynamic.

❖ ❖ ❖

Gus Johnson is another big-time gambler with whom Steve Cyr has had a complex—and ultimately costly, for Gus—relationship.

Johnson is an entrepreneur. In the late '80s, still in his mid-twenties, he'd already built up a couple of lucrative businesses. By the time he was 35, he was the head of a billion-dollar dot-com, pursuing his dream of becoming a billionaire himself by the age of 40. That's when he picked up the phone one day and heard:

"Mr. J, buddy! STEEEEVE CYYYYR from the Las Vegas Hilton. Mr. O told me to call you. He said you and a few of your girlfriends might like to get picked up in the Hawker so you can take a look at the Sky Villas we've got up on the thirtieth floor. You have to see these digs to believe 'em. Waddaya say?"

"Well, can I *stay* in a Sky Villa?"

"That depends."

"On what?"

"The whether."

"The weather?"

"Yeah, whether or not I decide to put you up there, because I've got the power, baby! All you have to do is play a little …"

Gus wasn't a gambler; he'd been to Las Vegas only two or three times in his life. But he agreed to try it, just to stay in a Villa. And, of course, to impress the girls he was bringing with him.

He showed up that weekend and had dinner with Cyr. The host didn't give Johnson a Sky Villa on that first trip (or the next two), running a little carrot-and-stick game initially. He put him, instead, in the Mediterranean mini-villa, which was nice enough. After checking in, Cyr took him up a floor, showed him all three Sky Villas, then sat him down for crab cocktails and champagne in the glassed-in observation nook of the Verona, largest of the Villas. The bait was out and Johnson wanted it, but now the superhost had to set the hook. "Gus, this is our first date. I can't go all the way with you. You won't respect me in the morning if I do. Besides, you gotta earn it, baby."

Gus grumbled, but gambled. And for the rest of that first trip, he kept asking, "Am I there yet?"

On the second trip: "Am I there?"

On the third trip, "C'mon! I have to be there by now!"

Finally he was and Cyr gave him the Villa.

Meanwhile, however, a bad thing was happening at the blackjack tables: Gus was winning.

Of course, he didn't realize it was bad at the time. In fact, he felt like a king. He thought, *This is unbelievable. They pay me to come and stay in these fabulous suites and eat gourmet meals!*

He started by testing the waters, $1,000 a hand. Betting $1,000 a go on a $250,000 credit line is like making $4 bets with $1,000 in your pocket. Conservative. Controlled. Just for fun. When he got on a streak, he'd crank it up to $3,000, $4,000, $5,000. But that was all.

He kept winning. Over the next several trips, he couldn't lose and within six months, he was ahead almost a million. Jim Bradshaw didn't sweat it. He knew it would come back. A bleeder boss wouldn't have had the patience to wait him out. After the million, he would've told Cyr, "We don't want him anymore. His comps are high. He brings too many hangers-on. He gets a Sky Villa every weekend. His credit line is

only two-hundred fifty. He'll have to lose the whole quarter-mil four weeks in a row for us just to get even." But
Bradshaw wasn't a bleeder. After years in the business, he
was a rock.

Meanwhile, the girls were flocking to Gus. In L.A., he
met them at business meetings, nightclubs, the Playboy Mansion. He'd start talking to them about Vegas. They all liked
going to Sin City. He'd say, "Hey, me and a few friends are
going over this weekend. Wanna come along?"

Then he'd fetch them in a limo, which delivered them to
the private-plane area of the Van Nuys airport, where they'd
be whisked away in Gus' private DC-9, outfitted like a flying high-roller suite, with a bedroom, living room, office,
bar, and galley. At McCarran, the Hilton picked up the party
in a red limo and deposited them in a Sky Villa, where Steve
Cyr greeted them, saying to the girls, "Hey, you wanna go
shopping? Here's a thousand-dollar gift certificate to the
Fashion Show Mall. Have a good time. Meet us back here at
nine for dinner."

After dinner, the girls played blackjack with Gus, using
his money, of course. If they got lucky (or hustled some chips
into their purses), they could go home with a couple thousand on top of everything else. For his part, Gus liked sitting
at the high-limit tables surrounded by Playboy bunnies. And
he liked frolicking with them in the Sky Villa. For these young
women, each new moment was a surprise. It all built on itself and when it was time to pay off, Gus easily got what he
wanted.

He rarely took a girl to Las Vegas a second time. He struc-
tured it so the girls knew it was a one-time deal. So what?
They'd had their fun and won or palmed a tidy little score in
the process. Why not share some of the wealth with their
girlfriends back in L.A.? They'd tell Gus, "Hey, I've got a
friend you should meet who wants to go to Vegas."

This continued non-stop for two years, nearly 100 weekends *in a row*. Gus lived 10 minutes from the Van Nuys air-

port. Every Friday for two years, he took the DC-9 on the 45-minute flight to Vegas. Every Sunday evening for two years, he took it back.

Friends of friends tagged along each weekend and finally, Gus fooled around and fell in love. Pamela was the first and only girl he brought back a second time. And by the time he'd won the million, he'd taken to taking her with him on every jaunt to Vegas. (Pamela liked girls too. So when he brought her, she'd bring a gaggle for herself. There was plenty of room for a party of 10 to sleep in the Sky Villas. In fact, the record was 34—31 girls, two other guys, and Gus.)

It was an idyllic time for the high roller. He worked hard all week and looked forward to the weekends. Still a huge winner and always flush with mad money, he plunked down racks of chips at the cage and stuffed bundles of hundred-dollar bills into every pocket. Sometimes he didn't have room to put all the bundles away, like the time he cashed out for $165,000 and didn't think to bring anything to carry it in. He asked the cashier for something and she came up with a paper grocery bag, in which he lugged thirty-three $5,000 stacks of hundred-dollar bills around the casino.

Gus learned that when you're walking around Las Vegas with hundreds of $100 bills on you, everybody gets one. Suddenly, you're a hundred-dollar George. All the waitresses get a hundred. A bus boy brings you a clean fork: Here's a hundred. The valet gets a hundred too, even if you're driving around in Cyr's car and the attendant merely opens the passenger door for you. The limo driver gets a hundred. A housekeeper comes to the room to turn down your bed? Here's a hundred. You stop at the snack bar and wonder if you should toke the cashier a hundred for taking your comp ticket and handing you a $2 hot dog.

Gus also liked the way it felt to get his ass kissed. An African-American, he began to experience what so many other people of minority races and ethnicities have long known: that Las Vegas is a sort of everyman's country club.

Blacks, Arabs, Chinese, Jews—all those who were traditionally outcast, excluded from high society—could go to the
casinos and have the red carpet rolled out for them, as long
as they had money.

How does a minority guy with money—who's barred
from the country club, who when he goes to the opera, en-
counters the high-brow social-register third-generation blue-
blood who wants to know, "Hey, who let that low-life in
here?"—get treated with respect? How does he get to show
the doctor, the lawyer, the accountant that he's got just as
much on the ball as they do, maybe more? Simple. He steps
up to a crap table and buys in for $10,000. Now he's the man.
He's "Yes Mr. J, no Mr. J, anything more I can do for you,
Mr. J?"

Then they start liking to be chased. They've probably
never been particularly popular. They're fat guys who own
bars. They're old guys who own shoe stores. They're work-
ing-class guys who run construction companies. They're
truck drivers who have a dozen other truck drivers working
for them. They've got wealth, but they're not in the lime-
light. They don't get much respect.

All of a sudden, there's a young host in a $500 suit ply-
ing them with Cristal, walking them through the Villas, telling them, "Hey, Mr. J! You're the man. You and your lady
and your friends are *wanted* here."

Las Vegas was where Gus went to be a VIP.

Then, one fateful night in L.A., Pamela told Gus goodbye.
He was devastated and ran off to Vegas to lick his wounds.
Upset, angry, and exhausted, he shouldn't have gambled but
he did. The love turned to fever, then the crushing weight of
fear, as he watched pile after pile of chips return to the cus-
todial side of the table. He also experienced, for the first time,
the feeling of desperation to get it all back. Gus Johnson
started chasing his losses—and it was all downhill from there.

That first weekend, he started out gambling his usual
game, with $1,000 to $5,000 bets. But by Saturday evening,

he was down $150,000, so he cranked it up to $10,000 a hand. At first, it worked. He hit a streak and in 15 minutes he was even, then ahead a little. But it didn't last. In the next 15 minutes he was down again, this time $200,000.

He called Cyr. "I want to raise my limit to twenty-five thousand."

The seemingly simple request turned into a two-hour slugfest. It went back and forth—Gus begging, Cyr refusing—from midnight till 2 a.m., from the tables to the bathroom back to the tables over to the bar and up to the Villa. But Gus prevailed, insisting on his own doom, and finally Cyr relented. He consulted with the on-duty credit manager. He came back and told Gus, "Okay, you can have a twenty-five-grand max, but your minimum bet has to be ten thousand."

Gus didn't realize what he was getting into, so he agreed. And kept losing. At one point in the midst of the debacle, Cyr followed Gus into the bathroom. "Gus, you're my friend. I wouldn't tell you this on the floor with my bosses looking, but you're steaming."

"What do you mean?"

"What do I mean? What's been your minimum bet for six months?"

"Five hundred."

"Exactly. You'd hit a cold streak and you could drop back down to one unit. But now you're betting a minimum of *twenty* units. This is a bad deal for you."

"You're wrong," Gus insisted. "Twenty-five a hand can get me out."

"I love you, buddy, but *you're* wrong. Twenty-five a hand can get you buried."

By the end of the weekend, he'd lost back the entire seven-figure sum he'd so carefully and conservatively amassed over the past year.

But he hadn't learned his lesson yet. Firmly gripped by the fear, Gus kept chasing and losing. Down $2 million. Down $3 million. Down $4 million. Down $5 million. Down $6 million in three months. In one shift, he dropped $1.3 million in about six hours. There he was, losing $10,000 to $25,000 a hand, hand after hand, and getting so little sympathy from one dealer that he finally lost his patience, though in a weird and perverse way. "Let's see how *you* like losing this kind of money!" he yelled and proceeded to lay down $1,000 bets *for her* on every hand. Of course, in six hours, he won a fair number of hands, enough that the dealers made $55,000 off him that night (dealers don't have to put winning tips back into play), although he still wound up a big loser.

It never seemed like real money, neither on the way up nor the way down. He'd made so much money in his life—how much does one guy ultimately need?—that it stopped meaning anything. It was just numbers on the screen. He'd electronically transfer a number into the Hilton cage, then get thousand-dollar chips at the table—more play money. When he was losing, he never touched actual cash. If he'd been shoving out $10,000 in hundred-dollar bills every hand, he probably wouldn't have lost anywhere near what he did.

Finally, a loser to the tune of $6 million, Gus quit. He wasn't busted out by any means, but how many times in a row can a blackjack player hold 20 and watch the dealer draw out to 21, with a $25,000 bet on the table, before he can't stand it any longer? Five times. He counted. And then he said, "That's it. I'm never playing again."

He remained friends with Cyr. He knew what Steve's job was, what he had to do, how he earned his money. He knew that sometimes Cyr blew smoke up his ass—"Hey, Gus, I had to kick someone else out of a Villa for you." He was never disappointed that Cyr didn't mean everything he said. It was okay, because it was all a game. The friendship was there, despite the fact that Cyr worked it to his advantage.

Besides, on the business side, he was doing the same thing to his own customers.

❖ ❖ ❖

Not all of Cyr's players wind up in the grease, frying themselves alive. Ramon Desage, for example, is a fiftysomething Lebanese merchandiser who's gambled nearly every night for 26 years and doesn't have a burn mark on him.

Desage is a roundish guy who seems surrounded by a sort of Zen calm (along with an entourage that typically consists of five or six people) as he meanders through his casino nights. He looks a little like an Arab Buddha. He stays in Las Vegas roughly six months a year, to be near his largest warehouses, which contain $200 million worth of inventory. Desage handles 14,000 products, everything from cashews to plasma TVs. When asked to describe his business in a word—is he an importer, broker, reseller, distributor, wholesaler, middleman, merchandiser, or what?—Desage, with a dismissive flick of his wrist, says, "Everything."

He also has a nice little place in Lebanon, with 86 rooms and 90 attendants. In Beirut, he gambles at Casino de Liban, run by the London Club. He flies non-stop between Lebanon and Las Vegas in his own Boeing 727. He likes Las Vegas, where the casinos, topless clubs, and bars remain open all night. He stays out late, but he also makes it into the office every morning on time.

Somewhere along the way, someone told Desage that he should hook up with Steve Cyr. So he called Cyr and said, "This is Ramon Desage. You need to know me."

"What did you say?"

"You need to know me, I said." Then he hung up.

Cyr gets lots of phone calls like this. But after checking around, he heard from his moles that Desage had a suite at Caesars Palace reserved for him every night of the year, even when he wasn't within 10,000 miles of Las Vegas. After all, he could board his 727 and be there in 18 hours from anywhere on the planet—fast asleep half the way.

His Central Credit file is two inches thick. He has credit lines at 56 casinos around the world, generally $250,000 to $500,000. At Atlantis in the Bahamas, where he stays and plays for a few days at a time, his line is $1 million.

He gambles to come down from the day. He likes to spiral off the momentum of all his wheeling and dealing by playing a little blackjack. He's a slow hit-and-run player. He sits at the table for an hour each night, betting $5,000 to $15,000 per hand, two or three hands at a time. He'll lose $100,000 or $150,000, but when he gets ahead $10,000 or $15,000, he walks. Eats like a bird, shits like a moose.

Desage hates being bothered while he plays. His entourage stays 10 feet away, some munching on the canapés from the small buffets in the high-limit rooms. A cocktail waitress hovers nearby. He might call her over for a bottled water that she has at the ready. He might call her over just to lay a black check on her tray.

Along the way, Cyr hunted and harpooned him.

One routine evening, Desage plays for 45 minutes at a premium Strip casino. The night before, he was down $150,000, then scratched and clawed his way back to even and finally cashed out ahead $15,000. Tonight he's ahead, by $15,000. He goes up and down for a few more minutes, then quits with 10 yellow checks: $10,000. He dispatches Cyr, Cyr's girlfriend Tanya, a couple of his assistants, and a friend of a friend to the cage to cash in two $1,000 chips apiece, in order not to have to fill out a lot of federal cash-transaction paperwork. It's not like the bosses and cashiers don't know what's going on: Ramon Desage has just walked out of the high-limit room with 10 bananas and now they're showing up at the cage two at a time.

The cashier might also get a clue when the last gofer, the friend of a friend, approaches the cage and hands in the checks.

She asks, "Any markers you want to pay off?"

He responds, "Markers? What are markers? You talking about a *magic* marker? A Sharpie?"

The cashier shakes her head and frowns, but hands over twenty $100 bills nonetheless. Now Ramon has a hundred $100 bills in his pocket, and this is a man who lives to grease palms.

He distributes his fun money discreetly, but everyone lights up with the glow of anticipated greed fulfillment when he appears. The guy who holds the door to the elevator to the restaurant gets one of the hundred-dollar bills. The maitre d' at the restaurant pockets another. The cocktail waitress gets a third.

"Ass-kissing" is just another hyphenated term until you're sitting in a five-star restaurant and the sommelier fills your glass with $250-a-bottle Bordeaux, accompanied by a brief lecture on the varieties of this particular vintage. When you recite your dinner order, you're speaking to the chef himself, the guy who'll prepare the food. He asks if you'd like beef, veal, or fish; how you'd like it cooked; what kind of sauces you want on it; and your preference for vegetables and potatoes on the side. Next time you look up, at least six waitpeople are in motion around the table, changing china and replacing silver, refilling goblets and asking if you'd care for anything more. You glance around the room and notice that the other diners have one server. They're all staring at your table, wondering who it is that's getting all the ass-kissing.

With a little flick of his wrist, Ramon Desage signs the comp for this meal for eight and tucks a $500 toke under the slip.

❖ ❖ ❖

Of all of Steve Cyr's customers, a third have more money than they know what to do with. They're so rich that no matter how much they gamble away, it doesn't make a dent. Ramon Desage falls into this category; nothing Cyr could do can damage him.

Another third consists of wealthy company owners, dot-com and Wall Street winners, professional athletes, and others pumped full of currency by Alan Greenspan's monumental inflation of the money supply over the past 15 years. This group is trying on the sensation of betting $5,000,

$10,000, even $25,000 a hand—before mounting the final bru-tal bucking bummer and flaming out for good.

And a third shouldn't be doing what they're doing, pe-riod. Often, the second group winds up in the third. Out of any given 100 customers, Cyr burns out 30 of them. And other hosts burn out more, many many more.

Fast Eddie, for one, the retired Montana timberman and dice player, had more money than he knew what to do with—until he got in the grease and had to put up his $28 million Montana property to pay off his markers.

Gus Johnson, for another, thought he had the deal fig-ured out—until he lost $6 million and cooled it.

Denny Mason was a big player and a big loser.

Nowadays, casino "gaming" is housed in elaborately themed edifices and marketed as casual, recreational, good clean fun, an acceptable alternative to movies and ballgames and day trips. But though casinos are now dressed up in the fineries of gaming, the people who run them are still after what they've been after since the beginning of time: all the money that the losers are willing to part with. And oftentimes more.

The psychology of removing as much money as possible from a gambler's pocket is an artform that's been evolving over many millennia. For the most part, this psychology was perfected by modern-day gangsters who would've found it more expedient to stick a handgun in a guy's ribs and take his money in the parking lot. But that tends to have nasty repercussions. At the slots and tables, they can rob the suck-ers legally and in style, and have them begging to come back for more. What a racket!

And it doesn't stop with a gambler's cash on hand. In-deed, exploiting the pathology of a *compulsive* gambler to take *all* of his money is a down-and-dirty science. From bust-ing him out in one night to soaking him for a 30-year annu-ity, the only variable is timing.

12

Alone in the Casino,
Just Me and My Machine-o

Steve Cyr likes to be around high-powered people. He likes successful entrepeneurs. He likes risk-takers. He's especially partial to casino gamblers. And they like him. He's good at making his players feel good about themselves. He's good at giving them what they want. He gets them to want to do what he wants them to do. He's part Woody Harrelson in "Cheers" (the Midwest farm-town ingenue), part Kevin Spacey in *Swimming with Sharks* (the edgy mid-'90s Hollywood producer), part Tom Cruise in *Jerry Maguire* ("Show me the money!"), part Jon Voight in *Midnight Cowboy* (the raging sexuality), and part Alec Baldwin in *Glengarry Glenn Ross* ("What's my name? Fuck you; that's my name.").

Cyr's dream-come-true is for a guy to lose $100,000, shake his hand, and say, "Thanks a lot, Steve. I had a great time. See ya next month."

But there's a dark side to what he does.

❖ ❖ ❖

Some experts believe pathological gambling is a learned behavior disorder, often starting in childhood. Weaned on pitching pennies against the stickball wall, playing nickel-ante poker, shooting dice with classmates after school and on weekends, learning to read the racing sheet, participating in foot-

ball pools, and adding excitement to life by betting on its innumerable random events, some people forge a potentially
calamitous relationship to gambling early in their lives.

Other experts attribute it to a physiological cause—the
physical high of being in action comes from the release of
endorphins and similar biochemicals, which have narcotic-
type effects of pain relief and euphoria.

Many psychiatrists link gambling to the anal stage of development. They trace the joy of having money to the pleasur-
able anal sensations of infancy and consider gambling to be an
obsessive displacement of unresolved conflicts from toilet training as a toddler. Freudians are forever citing the anal references
in American dice: "Craps" is played in a "pit" with "chips";
bets include "pass" and "don't pass" and the "hard way."

The anal sensations turn into an anxiety originating in
the emotional responses to childhood events. These fester-
ing feelings are buried beneath masochistic and obsessive
behaviors—such as participating in gambling games. It all
gets tied up in the eroticization of gambling, you see, where
the many levels of neuroses laid down atop anal stimulation
converge in sexual arousal. The playing of the games, thus,
is likened to masturbation. In dice, again, the new "shooter"
is "coming out."

The games are also an invitation to chance (Freudians
refer to this as "father") to state whether "he" approves of
the playing (masturbating) by allowing you to win (have an
orgasm). In Oedipal terms, chance is allowing you to kill the
father and marry the mother. Of course, the opposite can
also occur: The father disapproves and the punishment is
castration or death at his hands (in other words, the gambler
taps out).

It takes years (at $150 an hour) for a compulsive gambler
to grasp the psychoanalysis of his pathology. It's been said
that psychiatry actually does cure gambling, but only by
transference—the rerouting of gambling money from the
tables to the couch.

Whatever causes it, a gambling disorder begins as an exhilaration derived from the excitement of the action, a more satisfying sensation than susceptible people—whether children, teens, over 21s, or seniors—have ever before experienced. The surging adrenaline of a crap game, the hypnotic trance of a video poker machine, the fast pace of a securities market—as long as the susceptible gamble, they're riding the high; stopping means coming down. They have to gamble to get back up again. A compulsive gambler is driven to bet in the same way an alcoholic needs a drink or a drug addict needs a fix.

The worst thing that can happen to someone vulnerable to this compulsion is an early win. An initial positive result can put a player on the path to ruin. The rules of the game, the house edge, the free booze, the leggy cocktail waitresses, the pumped-in aromas, the flashing lights, the clanging coins all add up to negative numbers. The player starts to lose, then loses more, then chases his losses. Once out of funds, desperation to be back in the game sets in, causing the gambler to consume all available resources: valuables, cars, houses, other people's cash. When all that's gone, 90% of pathologicals commit crimes to gamble—embezzlement, forgery, bad checks, insurance fraud, credit-card fraud, outright theft, burglary, sometimes even armed robbery.

And always, at the center of the compulsion, is the certainty that the gambler must lose. This increases the desperation, which feeds the compulsion, a vicious cycle that doesn't end until, in the terminal stages of ruin—hounded by creditors, terrorized by loan sharks, in trouble with the law, abandoned by family and friends—life is reduced to two choices: suicide or treatment. Attempted suicide wins out in 25% of the cases, making compulsive gambling the deadliest addictive disorder, by far.

Treatment options are limited at best. The public perception of gambling addiction is a good 20 to 30 years behind that of alcoholism. Every state (except one) with casino

gambling has some sort of agency that attempts to deal with
the problem (the only one without is Nevada, which typically eschews state-sponsored recovery programs), and
GamAnon has its successes. But serious treatment remains
hard to come by and is often a case of too little, too late.

❖ ❖ ❖

It's this, the darkest part of the consciousness business,
that engenders the darkest part of the casino business. The
psychology of the chronic loser might be complicated, but
exploiting it is child's play.

Take the case of Cyr's customer Dr. O. The good doctor
was an obstetrician who loved to play blackjack, but constantly got in over his head and cried on Steve's shoulder
when he lost. Finally, after the OB M.D. had just tanked to
the tune of $200,000, together they sat down and set a firm
credit limit—fifty grand.

On his next visit, the doc lost and lost until he was down
exactly 50 large, at which point he went right to Cyr and
begged him for more. Cyr refused, "No. We decided." And
the host went home. But the doctor didn't.

The next day Cyr came to work and learned that Dr. O
had lost $90,000. He immediately wanted to know who gave
him the extra 40 grand. He went around asking the other
hosts and bosses. Each one, in turn, denied knowing anything about it.

"I didn't give him credit."

"I didn't give him credit."

"I didn't give him credit."

Dr. O hadn't used casino credit. He'd emptied every casino cash machine in the house. And all of a sudden, he was
in for $90,000—$50,000 in casino markers and $40,000 in cash
advances on his credit cards. This, after losing $200,000 on
his previous visit.

Now the obstetrician—or any gambler in a situation like

this—is in a spot. He has 30 days, 60 maybe, 90 max to put together the cash to pay off his markers before the casino bean counters will be tempted to snap him (run his unpaid markers through his bank account). If the markers bounce, he can be brought up on felony charges.

So Dr. O might begin to schedule ultrasounds and amnioacenteses like there's no tomorrow. He might recommend the gruesome amnio, a standard procedure for pregnant women over 35, to younger and younger couples, feigning surprise when a few complain about how expensive it is. "You're *kidding*! I had no *idea* it cost twenty-one hundred dollars these days!"—after selling at least seven or eight of them day after day to try to retire his casino debt on time.

Until one couple, a savvy 32-year-old husband and a healthy 29-year-old having her third baby, refuses to agree to the procedure and the good doctor goes off his rocker, trying to scare them about *gambling* with the health of their baby and playing Russian *roulette* with genetics and working up such a righteous lather that the husband—and the office nurse—begin looking at him like he's gone stark-raving mad (or, perhaps, has a casino-marker problem). Dr. O decides then and there that he'd better straighten out, pay off his debt, and get help for his compulsion.

But at least he still has his practice and his family and his freedom. He could lose them all eventually.

And probably will.

For a while, he keeps his head above water by selling 16-year-old date-rape victims the deluxe pre-natal and delivery package, including videography of the blessed event, six months of soy formula, and a framed birth certificate. He's paid off the $200,000 from the casino visit before last, settled up the credit-card cash advances, and is down to his last $50,000 in markers. He's sworn off gambling for good, and day by day, he thinks he might just make it.

Until one morning he answers the phone and hears, "Hey, Doc! STEEEEVE CYYYYR from the Las Vegas Hilton. Listen, buddy, I know you still owe fifty. And I know it's been sixty—days, that is. Tell you what I'm gonna do for you. Why don't you come in this weekend? Bring ten or fifteen with you. Let me pick up your airfare, give you a limo and a suite, and buy you dinner. We'll retire an old marker and I'll give you a new one. I'll even split your winnings with you. Hell, you'll probably win out! Those blackjack tables are running hot hot hot! One of my players took down a hundred and fifty large last Saturday ..."

And, of course, the doctor's a goner. All his good intentions, and 60 days of abstention, go right down the drain.

Meanwhile, Cyr is buying some time for himself. He knows Dr. O is an established player. He's got credit at six other joints around town. He doesn't have any derogs on his Central (short for derogatories, meaning late payments or snapped markers or stiffed casinos). Still, he's over 60 days, so he's definitely a trouble gambler, and he's in danger of becoming a collection problem. With this deal, Cyr reduces the overdue debt from $50K to $35K and converts $15K to new debt, which Dr. O now has the full 60 days to repay. Cyr also gives him a shot at some winnings (from which the casino'll keep half), and gives himself a shot at the fifteen, which he'll probably win anyway.

Why will he probably win?

Simple. The old play-and-pay ploy. With only $15,000 in cash and no credit, the doctor'll have to stick to much lower limits than he's used to. He'll have to play scared. He won't be able to fire it up at $10,000 a hand and win back the $50K in five or six rounds of lucky blackjack. He'll have to start at $500 a hand. And the casino'll grind it out of him as sure as the good doctor stands on soft 17 and doesn't split 8s against a ten.

Inevitably, Dr. O loses his new $15,000 and still owes $50,000 and now he goes back to trying to sell amnios to 23-year-olds and Cyr gets another 30 days to hold off the tweezer butts ("Stick a lump of coal up a casino CFO's ass and it'll turn into a diamond," goes the joke among marketing executives) who are dying to run those unpaid markers. If they snap him, the good doctor's done. No more credit. No more gambling at the Hilton. No more nothin' in Las Vegas.

And Dr. O still doesn't really believe he has a problem, and still hasn't decided to seek help.

❖ ❖ ❖

A good host tries to establish and maintain ground rules. He tries to manage a situation wherein big-time gamblers are often on the edge of spiraling out of control.

A host can mouth all the marketing platitudes. "We want you to win, but the reality is, it's usually the casino that wins." It's the truth, but what gambler believes it?

Not Mr. P, who calls Steve Cyr and says, "I hear you're the guy with the juice. I just sold my business to Adelphia for three-point-two million. I also get twenty-thou a month and fifteen percent of sales for a year. I want a hundred-thousand-dollar credit line."

Cyr knows he could fry this guy on the spot. "Sure, sure. No problem, Mr. P. C'mon in for the weekend. Sign on the dotted line. Here's your limo, suite, room service. Go have a blast." Chances are good that the guy'll get broke by Sunday. His own damn fault.

Instead, a good host wants to milk a cash cow, not slaughter him then and there for all the meat on his bones. So he's up front. He runs the likely scenario by his eager-beaver bovine.

"All right, Mr. P. Let's say I give you the hundred. You sit down at the table. What's your first bet?"

"Two-fifty," the mark moos.

"Two hundred and fifty dollars?"

"That's right. I told ya I'm gonna play."

"Well, you don't need a hundred grand for a two-fifty average. That's four hundred units."

"I want it anyway. I hear the comps really top out at a hundred."

"Sure, but let me ask you this. Are you gonna be comfortable writing me a check for a hundred large on Monday morning, just before you catch the limo to the airport?"

"Why would I do that?"

"To cover your losses."

"No way! I'll never lose the whole thing in a weekend!"

"Famous last words, buddy. I've seen it happen a thousand times. Once you start losing and steaming, before you know it, it's all gone. Are you gonna write me that check for the full amount, then go up to the twenty-eighth floor and jump? Are you?"

"Well, I probably wouldn't go that far."

"How about fifty large? Can you write me a check for fifty-thousand dollars on Monday morning and go about your business without losing your mind?"

Silence.

"No? How about twenty-five?"

"I could go twenty-five."

"You sure? You could pull out your checkbook, cut me a check for twenty-five, and your wife wouldn't raise hell?"

"Yeah, I could handle twenty-five. And I'm not married."

"Good. We'll start you off with a fifteen-thousand line and a hundred-fifty minimum bet."

The host knows that by establishing the ground rules and holding the player to them, he can run this guy's string for years, possibly forever. A steadfast basic strategy blackjack player with a $10,000 to $25,000 credit line who stays within his limits has an average longevity of seven to ten years, sometimes more. He's the proverbial responsible gambler, who's in it for the weekend out, the entertainment value, the comps. Over his lifetime at $10K to $25K, he might lose four times the original $100K he wanted.

This is Old School 101. This is how it used to be, when hosts were loyal to players and players were loyal to casinos. But in today's racket, the hosts are up against it. There are 30 major casinos in Las Vegas (and 30 minor ones). If a host doesn't lock up a gambler good and fast, the guy goes next door.

In addition, all the while the host has to fight against his own greed. He'd love to beat Mr. P for $100K up front. He won't have to beg his bosses for comps. It'll add a quick thousand to his end-of-the-year performance bonus. Best of all, he won't have to deal with the cocky son-of-a-bitch every time he wants to come out.

In the final analysis, Cyr knows he can bury anyone at any time with a snap of his fingers. Mr. P might turn out to be a whiner—"The comps *suck* at fifteen K! I'm good for fifty at least! I want fifty! I want fifty! I want fifty!" Cyr can tell him, "Fine, I'll give you fifty grand and the better comps. But I'm gonna have to raise your minimum bet to two thousand." That'll kill him in no time. With a bankroll of $50,000 and only 25 units of $2,000 each, Mr. P's risk of ruin skyrockets. It's just a matter of ... timing.

❖ ❖ ❖

Not even casino employees are immune from the pathological pull of gambling. Casino people have always considered their fellow men suckers to be plucked. Which makes it the ultimate irony that casino workers fall into the same sucker traps themselves. In the old days, casinos usually restricted employees from playing at their own joint. But now it's different, as long as they're out of uniform. Bartenders, bellmen, cocktail waitresses, even dealers get off work and think, "Hey, I've got a couple hundred on me. Maybe I'll take a shot." When they watch it all the time and see the occasional big score, they begin to think that they can beat it too. They get the vicarious love and start to feel the greed. Before they know it, they're working to play. Talk about a busman's holiday: Some 21 dealers stand behind a table all day, then sit in front of one all night.

And it doesn't stop with the front-line personnel. When Steve Wynn owned a mansion up in Incline Village at Lake Tahoe, he had a $20,000 credit line at the Hyatt Regency at Incline, owned by the Pritzker family of Chicago. On occasion, Wynn would go and stand at a crap table, trying to beat the Pritzkers out of their joint.

❖ ❖ ❖

The casino is like the IRS. It has every nuance of every possible transaction in its vast universe wired in every direction. The only difference is this: The IRS has a gun to taxpayers' heads, while the casino taxes every gambler according to his or her own willingness to pay.

And pathological gamblers hold the gun to their own heads.

13

From Pathological to Professional

Professional gamblers, the rare players who make their entire living by winning at the games, scoff at the notion of treatment programs and conventional cures for compulsive gambling. From their point of view, one single factor separates the pathological from the professional: discipline. Give a problem gambler an *edge*, and get him to play only when he possesses that edge, and get him to play perfectly, and he can be transformed from a loser into a winner. It doesn't always work; random chance is involved, of course, and the cards have to fall his way. But the odds of his long-term survival are much better than they are with suicide.

Actually, there *is* a symbolic suicide involved—or, to be slightly more accurate, a symbolic murder.

Both the degenerate and the professional want action, because without action, nothing can happen. But the former will gladly take the worst of it just to be in the action. The latter wants the best of a bet and knows the difference. And it's not just discipline that ensures that the addict-turned-pro won't play without an edge. It's not even strong-minded iron-willed self-control. What's required is no less than the figurative murder of the pathological gambler by the professional gambler. One body is simply not large enough to contain the two of them.

An extremely fine line separates the sicko and the pro,

but it might as well be the Great Wall of China for the few times it's ever been crossed. To become a professional, the pathological gambler has to scale the wall with grappling hooks, rope, and brute strength, fight a veritable division of demons at the top, then jump down to the other side and lay up till his wounds heal, bones fuse, and heart mends. And if you think that after all that, wild horses couldn't drag him back to the other side, think again. It's exceedingly easy to cross that thin line and return to compulsive patterns.

❖ ❖ ❖

The classic example of the gambler with a sickness who cured it with an edge is Billy Walters.

Walters started gambling at his uncle's pool hall when he was five. At 10, he risked his life's savings, $30, on a bet that the New York Yankees would beat the Brooklyn Dodgers in the World Series (he lost). By the time he graduated high school, he was playing poker every night after working all day at a used car lot and betting on every college and professional sporting event; predictably, he spent most Mondays on the car lot paying off bookies. He bet $300 on the first golf game he ever played, at age 20.

He made the pilgrimage to Las Vegas several times a year, blowing all the money he'd brought—and some he hadn't.

In the early '80s, Walters quit the automobile business and spent a couple of years bookmaking in Kentucky. When he got arrested, he cut a deal and left for the promised land, Las Vegas. Like many degenerate gamblers, Billy was also a drinker and a sucker. Drunk, he'd flip a coin for all the money he had in the world. Or he'd bet huge sums at the golf course. Or he'd be the biggest player at the baccarat table at Caesars. Or he'd be in on the biggest poker game in town, going up against the likes of Johnny Moss, Doyle Brunson, Chip Reese, and Puggy Pearson. Like another notorious degenerate, Nick "the Greek" Dandolos, who could win and lose a million or two in a 36-hour marathon session of dice or poker, Billy Walters went through more money in a week than most of us see in a lifetime. At any given moment, he was either straddling the world or lying in the gutter. Finally, he had an epiphany.

For the previous couple of decades, Walters had believed that casinos cared equally about winners and losers. As long as a gambler stepped up and played, at the end of the day it didn't matter who came out ahead. But at the end of one particular day in the middle of a rare winning streak, he began to notice that the casinos did feel differently about winners than losers. As soon as he beat the casinos a few times in succession, he saw that he went from being their best friend to their worst enemy. This royally pissed him off and he promised himself that he would never again drop so much as a nickel in a machine if he didn't have a mathematical edge. Then he gave himself a crash course in advantage play.

From there, Walters never looked back. He was a founding member of the infamous Computer Group, the first sports bettors to employ computers to beat the bookies at football; he went on to become the biggest sports bettor in the country, known as the Line Mover for his ability to skew the odds on a game after making his whale-sized bet. He won Amarillo Slim's Super Bowl of Poker in Lake Tahoe, the second largest poker tournament in the country at the time (1986). He beat an Atlantic City roulette game for what has to be a world-record $3.8 million by analyzing and exploiting a bias in the wheel (it's said that the casino shipped the wheel to the Johnson Space Center in Houston to be tested and adjusted by the engineers there). And for the past 15 years, Walters has been a developer—subdivisions, industrial parks, and golf courses, including the Bali Hai, a stunning 18-hole course just south of the Las Vegas Strip, adjacent to Mandalay Bay.

Successful gamblers are rare enough, but Billy Walters is

a breed unto himself: a high-stakes gambler who overcame his compulsion and became a professional.

❖ ❖ ❖

Though whales are rarely professional gamblers, professional gamblers are *like* whales: Worldwide, only a few hundred people make all their money at gambling.

It's a very dicey gig.

To be a professional gambler, to win year in and year out, you have to be part mathematician, part banker, part actor, part geek, part martial artist. You have to be skilled, dedicated, and disciplined. You have to be willing to spend your life in casinos. You have to eat, sleep, and dream game theory. You have to carry a lot of cash and chase small edges with big bucks. You have to stay healthy as a racehorse in unholy environments, alert as a hoot owl under distracting conditions, and cool as a spring breeze under the blazing heat of scrutiny.

And you have to be able to get away with the money. The casinos are managed by the most suspicious people in the private sector, who breathe down your neck every minute of your working day. Casinos are also the most surveilled environments this side of the National Security Agency. So even if you're able to fool the dealers, floormen, pit bosses, shift bosses, and hosts, you still have to fly under the eye-in-the-sky radar, as well as avoid being picked off by roving private detectives, always on the lookout for players who already appear, or are destined for a spot, in the Griffin Book of persona-non-grata casino professionals, advantage players, and cheats.

You have to ride the financial and emotional roller coaster of gigantic bankroll swings. You have to take the big losses in stride. And you have to take the big wins without going on tilt and blowing the whole wad, which you'll undoubtedly need to see you through long losing streaks in the future.

Harder still, your family and friends wonder what kind of life you've chosen for yourself. And for them.

In blackjack, just learning and playing perfect basic strategy takes some effort, more than most players, even high-stakes gamblers, are willing to invest, and it alone is not enough to give you an advantage over the house. As for card counting (the ability to track the cards and calculate the corresponding advantage or disadvantage at a high rate of speed and degree of accuracy, then further calculate the proper bet for each circumstance), it takes months of study and practice even to attempt to keep the count under casino conditions. And once that skill is mastered, it takes years to perfect the comportment required to walk with the winnings and still be welcome to come back and play another day. After all, casinos have known that blackjack is beatable for as long as the players have—for the past 40-odd years, since Ed Thorp's *Beat the Dealer* was published in 1962. Known and even suspected card counters have been getting the bum's rush ever since, especially after advanced and powerful count systems began showing up in the early 1970s. To further combat them, highly sophisticated detection techniques and technologies have been added to the countermeasures employed by pit personnel and surveillance agents.

In an effort to escape the heightened scrutiny, some advantage players have turned to video poker. Here, too, the proper strategy—innumerable nuances worth fractions of a penny per hand—must be mastered. Those pennies add up fast when you're banging away at 700 hands an hour (or more) for 8 to 12 hours a day. Adding to the drudgery is the fact that you lose during the majority of playing sessions. The small losses accumulate to the point where you have to hit the royal flush—an event that happens, on average, every 70 hours of play—to secure your profit. The player's edge is tiny, percentage points of percentage points; strategy-card perfect play (yes, there are cards that show you how) at the loosest video poker machines yields an advantage of seven-

or eight-tenths of one percent. And it's boring. And via machine electronics, the casino can track the accuracy of video poker play to within thousandths of a point, thus identifying the experts with ease.

Despite the public's perception that *high-stakes* gambling somehow equates with *professional* gambling, there are only a handful of cases in which the ranks of winners and whales ever intersect. Sure, even the losers get lucky sometimes, and at their levels, high rollers can wind up tens or hundreds of thousands, even millions, of dollars ahead. But it's a fundamental fallacy that people who play for high stakes win the house's cash in the long run.

Rarely happens.

❖ ❖ ❖

The whale business in the late 1990s and early 2000s went through something of a recession. Since then, the economies of whale have recovered, to a certain extent, though they're still not quite what they were in the heady days of the mid-1990s before the Asian deflation. The implosion of the high-flying economies of Hong Kong, Japan, Korea, Indonesia, Malaysia, the Philippines, and Thailand cut deeply into Las Vegas' overseas whale market.

Then in the aftermath of September 11, the Blubber Express practically dried up completely. Japan Air Lines, which had a near monopoly on flights into Las Vegas from the Far East, cancelled all non-stops into McCarran. One of the main-stays of the Asian hosts was the junkets from Tokyo and Hong Kong, but al Qaeda took care of those. And not because JAL itself feared terrorists, but because no one wanted to get on the planes.

So, with the Asian Monstros clinging to their own shores, no longer could the first-tier casinos count on a single Japanese high roller, betting $150,000 per hand, to take the place of 30,000 punters firing up $5 per hand, or even 1,500 of them betting $100 a hand, or even 150 of them betting $1,000 a hand. Though the casino has to deal with the whale's comps and fade his idiosyncrasies, not to mention those of his family and entourage, give a joint like Bellagio or MGM a choice and it'll opt for one big player over 30,000 five-dollar bettors every time.

With the foreign big player suddenly scarce, there was nothing left for the casinos to do but turn to the domestic high roller—lower the credit-line minimums, lower the comp criteria, do what they had to do. Now, Steve Cyr didn't have to battle Asian hosts for the best suites, highest discounts, and biggest shopping sprees. Suddenly, Robert Coury's players, the ones with the $50,000 and $75,000 credit lines plunking down $500 bets at blackjack and baccarat, were experiencing a level of luxury and service known previously only to those with million-dollar credit lines and $25,000 average bets.

Among the legitimate suckers—true gamblers who tried their luck at the house games like baccarat and craps or hunch 21—lurked the professional blackjack players. The expected profit potential of this cadre of card counters remains stable day in and day out, year in and year out. A gambling pro, who factors every dollar of comp value into his per-hour earnings, is in the rare position to actually beat the hosts and their casinos at the card and comp games. Give this elite player the value of the amenities previously available only to the world's mightiest whales and they'll manufacture a profitable situation, if one exists. Given, all of a sudden, that the complimentary outlay had increased dramatically, could the bj pros avail themselves of the better comps without paying for them one way or another?

Butler service, for example. Whales typically enjoy the total attention of butlers in the best suites in the house, at absolutely no charge. Anything and everything a butler does for his guests is gratis. He can arrange for nine loads of drycleaning, oversee a cocktail party for 50, or serve a five-course dinner for six, and the player will never see a bill for butler charges. But when the lower-level players began staying in the butler-attended suites, the line between comped butler service and plain old room service blurred into oblivion.

A casino can tell a smaller fish occupying the bigger digs that he has butler service, and a butler can actually attend to him. But if breakfast in the suite comes with a bill, this is room service, no matter what uniform the server happens to be wearing.

An additional complication. The high-stakes pro walks a fine line between maintaining the image of an ordinary millionaire sucker and protecting his edge; thus, he has to seriously consider the difference in tokes extended to a room-service waiter and a bona fide butler. Gratuities for the occasional room-service bill (even at a generous 15% on the inflated prices) usually won't come near the size of a tip for a butler who's worked all weekend. And, for the utilitarian pro, there's zero monetary value in staying in a three-bedroom four-bath villa over a standard hotel suite. Thus, in the end, it's much more cost-effective for the pro to forego a penthouse and butler in favor of a standard mini-suite and occasional room service.

So much for big digs.

Another example: gifts and shopping trips. The typical casino profferings have little to no monetary value. Flowers, chocolates, champagne, bathrobes, shirts, jackets, even watches and jewelry tend to fill up storage rooms and garages and garbage cans. Even a $1,000 watch will fetch only $80 or so from a pawn shop or $200 on eBay.

And those vaunted shopping sprees at the local department stores? Surprise. The casino usually has an arrangement with the stores whereby 1) the player cannot return the merchandise for cash; 2) the casino charges the full amount of the spree against a player's comp account, whether he spends it all or not; and 3) the casino pays the wholesale price while the player is charged retail. Here, too, the resale value of overpriced designer merchandise ($80 silk ties, $500 logo windbreakers, $900 necklaces) is negligible, probably not even worth the time it takes to shop and purchase the stuff, with the tiny hope of unloading it.

So much for goodies.

What's left? As usual, the deal. Some pros can lose enough in one gambling session to qualify for a rebate on losses. If he can get a discount, he'll take it every time; it accrues directly to his bottom line.

Likewise show up-money. When a pro gets an appearance incentive, the casino is giving him a huge edge. Of course, a player accepts the bonus with the understanding that he'll live up to his end of the average-bet hours-played bargain. But because the pro plays a winning game, the incentive of free money can be converted directly into profit.

The casinos know this. That's why they have offices full of bookkeepers and accountants, more offices full of executive hosts, plus legions of managers and bosses and floormen and dealers to protect the games and guard against scams or even slight player advantages. The bigger the bets and the higher the comps, the more scrutiny a player is subjected to. A pro who intends to get away with the money *and* the amenities has to play to the toughest audience in the world—and win an Oscar.

14

The Fall of a Gambler, the Rise of a Host

The day before he started working at the Hilton, Steve Cyr went down to Phoenix and talked Al Franco into coming in for the weekend. That Friday night at the Hilton, Cyr and Franco had dinner together and hit it off. Then Franco proceeded to drop $164,000 at the blackjack tables. He wrote the Hilton a check to pay off his markers and went home.

Franco was hooked and he established a casino routine. Every Monday morning at 6 a.m., Cyr flew to Phoenix in the Hawker and fetched Franco. He started gambling at 9. He and Cyr had lunch together at noon. Then he gambled till 3:30 and Cyr had him home by 4:45. This went on, like clockwork, for two years.

Greed and fear. Al Franco had all the money he needed. Millions in the bank and a million in cash in the safe at his construction company. He wanted more. And like Gus Johnson, Al Franco had caught some luck in the beginning. It was the same old story: He didn't need the money, so he won. It was as if the money *knew*.

He always came alone. No one was aware of his habit—not his wife, his daughters, or his partners. Only once did he bring along a buddy, another high roller from the neighborhood. It turned out badly. At first it was fun, especially when he was ahead $100K. But then his buddy tanked and was in the toilet for $200,000. So he borrowed the whole $100K from

Franco, which he promptly lost. Then Franco began heading south himself and had to take a marker. He never again gambled with a buddy.

Once, however, he brought his family to the Hilton for a long weekend. Cyr had to run around for hours beforehand, warning everyone to act like they'd never seen him before. By then, he'd lost more than a million dollars in the casino.

Within the year, he'd lost another $3 million there and probably another $2 million at the Desert Inn and a million each at Caesars and the Mirage. Seven million down in less than three years.

Greed and fear. In his lucid moments, Franco knew that once he'd lost the money, it was gone and he should forget it. Tomorrow was another day. But always in the back of his mind was the little voice saying, "Hey! We're down two-point-five million! We need it back!" He started making rash decisions.

Another thing he noticed: When he was winning, he played for pleasure. When he was losing, he played for pain. All he had to do was get up from the table and walk away. But the pain wouldn't let him. For some reason, he had to descend to the point where the pain was literally unbearable, where his head was about to pop off his shoulders, before he could stop.

One Monday morning, Cyr picked up Mr. F as usual. The contractor had just landed a $200 million contract with a built-in $30 million profit. However, he had to come up with a large cash bond. He'd taken loans against his office buildings, his house, his daughters' houses, and his equipment. But he was still $350,000 short. He decided to try to win it at the Hilton blackjack tables. *Very* bad decision.

On this fateful Monday, Franco quadrupled his usual bet of $5,000. At $20K per, his first four-deck shoe was heaven-sent. He won every double down and the dealer busted hand after hand. By the end of the first shoe, he was ahead $300,000 and it was only 9:30. His good fortune continued and four shoes later, he was up $700,000. He had the casino write him a check for $400,000 to cover his nut and went to lunch, planning to gamble with the other $300,000 till it was time to go home.

Then, as luck (in the casino, sometimes you can't tell if it's good luck or bad) would have it, Mr. F won another $800,000. Now he was up $1.5 million. If he'd lost the $300,000, he would've gone home at 3:30 as scheduled. But he was on such a monster run he couldn't pry himself loose.

The problem was, now the big bosses had him in their sights. They plied him with Cristal, wined and dined him at dinner, and put him up in one of the Sky Villas. At 10 p.m., he called home and made up a story about having to spend the night somewhere. He was pretty tanked up by then, but he still had the presence of mind to take Cyr aside and hand him the $400,000 check. "Don't, under any circumstances, let me have this back."

At the tables, he continued betting $20,000, but this time, each hand was a nail in his coffin. As divine as his earlier run had been, the evening's play was a debacle engineered by the devil himself. He was dealt 16 after 16 after 16, busting every time. In the rare event he held a 20, the dealer drew to 21. It wasn't that he didn't know it was happening. The pain! It forced him to sit there, watching the whole train wreck in slow motion. The next hand was dealt and he held a 20 against the dealer's 6. She turned over a ten, then ... Franco smashed his chips on the table when she pulled the five. By midnight, he'd lost back a million and went looking for Cyr. Spotting his host walking into the men's bathroom, he followed him into the john, *then into the stall,* to get Cyr to hand over the $400,000.

Cyr was familiar with every detail of the situation. He knew that Franco was on tilt. He was acutely aware that without the $400,000, his player would be in deep trouble, both professionally and personally. He even, by more than one yardstick, might have had an obligation—as a host; as a friend; perhaps, even, as a man of character—not to give him back the $400,000 under *any* circumstances, as he'd agreed. He could claim that he'd already put the check in the mail. He could make up a story that he'd left it on his kitchen table. Anything at all to get Mr. F away from the tables and out of the casino long enough for him to cool off, calm down, and take a long hard look at the bottom of the abyss toward which he was hurtling, without a parachute.

But Cyr, in the final analysis, knew on which side his bread was buttered. And hosts are gamblers too. They get caught up in the action and the adrenaline. When the player is losing, the host is winning. It's fun when you're winning, and hard to stop.

Cyr also knew that if Franco didn't lose it all at the Hilton, he'd leave the rest of it scattered around town at the Mirage or DI or Caesars in a desperate attempt to get even. Steve Cyr would've bet any amount of money at that point that Mr. F was going out broke, so he might as well lose it to Steve Cyr.

Did he hesitate in handing over the check? Did he pause to ponder the implications of doing so? So what if he did? This was the end of the line, the moment of truth, when the casino, via its errand boy, decided to snap Al Franco. To break him. To bust him and burn him and bury him. To beach him.

When the sun came up, he'd not only lost the whole $1.5 million, but also another $500,000 in markers. The bosses beat him out of another half-mil, then cut off his credit. Franco was forced to go to the other casinos where he could sign for money, but the ugliness continued. By the end of the week he'd lost another $2 million around town and six months later he declared bankruptcy. He was sued by everyone under the sun. His daughters wouldn't talk to him; they lost their homes. He went from $3 million liquid to having 25¢ in his pocket. In the end, he had to go work for people who had worked for him.

An irony, especially from a host's point of view, was that

Mr. F never benefited from any comps, except the Hawker. He always came up only for the day; he stayed overnight twice. He went to a few big fights, and one time Cyr talked him into going to Alaska on a fishing trip. But for him, unlike Gus Johnson, it wasn't about the comps. Al Franco was a gambler. It was about greed and fear. He went up against the casino. And the casino laid him low.

❖ ❖ ❖

The owner of a chemical company that serviced the automotive industry, Bill Nilsen first visited Las Vegas in 1973, gambling at the Sands, the Sahara, and the Stardust. Over the next 25 years, as his bankroll grew, so did his bets. By the mid-'90s, he liked to come to the Las Vegas Hilton twice a month for a few days, sleeping in a Villa, winning or losing $75,000 to $100,000 a whack at blackjack.

Cyr cut into Nilsen one day and they struck up a relationship. Nilsen was a partier and he appreciated Cyr's tremendous capacity for staying up all hours. But for a high roller, Nilsen was unusually down to earth. He liked to carry a cooler and battery-operated blender on the back of his golf cart to make margaritas. When the butlers were in his Villa, they weren't allowed to wear tuxes; he wanted them to wait on him in their street clothes and eat with him; it was often dinner for four—himself, his wife, the butler, and Cyr. He enjoyed grilling steaks on the barbecue out on the Villa lawn. He'd also bring his own chicory coffee, grind it in the blender, and serve it with dessert. He liked his Cohiba cigars and top-shelf cognac. And he especially appreciated the trips in the Hilton's jet to Alaska, Pebble Beach, and a week-long getaway with Cyr to Belize.

All at once, two messy divorces—one with his wife, the other with his business partner—left his finances in a shambles at a time when he had outstanding markers totaling $650,000 at the Hilton and a couple other casinos. The

Hilton was cool. Nilsen sent Cyr and Guy Hudson $15,000, $10,000, $5,000 a month, anything to show he was trying to pay up. Same with the second casino. But the third casino, where he owed $250,000, dumped the markers through his bank account where they bounced, so the casino had the Clark County District Attorney (the official collection agency for the Las Vegas gambling business) charge him with fraud. The D.A. had a judge issue a warrant.

Nilsen was coming into Los Angeles from a trip to Latin America when Immigration scanned his passport and saw the arrest order. He could've made bail, but first he had to be extradited to Nevada. So he sat in the L.A. County Jail for three weeks before being put on a prison bus to Las Vegas. A few days later, Cyr heard that his player was in Clark County lockup. He and Doug Bean visited Nilsen every Tuesday and Thursday, bringing him toiletries and cash.

The prosecutors tried to get him to plead out, but he wanted his day in court, where he explained that he'd had an impeccable reputation in Las Vegas for more than 20 years. He'd paid and played millions during the last 10 of them. If he'd been a brand new player, taken a marker for $100,000, blown 10 at the tables and put 90 in the stock market, that would've been fraud. If he hadn't had the money in the bank when he signed those markers, he would've been guilty as charged. But he did have the money. It was the bitter divorce and business break-up that had left him temporarily strapped. Still, he'd been paying down his markers and had every intention of continuing to do so. He'd stopped gambling. He wasn't playing anywhere else. If he hadn't been pulled up, everyone would've gotten paid. But this way, no one ever would.

In the end, the judge ruled, "Right. No fraud." So Bill Nilsen beat the felony rap. But he lost everything else. After a couple of months in stir, he was ruined.

❖   ❖   ❖

The stories are legion. Steamers and screamers. Chasers and disgracers. Whiners and breadliners. Pigeons and fish. Losers and more losers. The insatiable casino eats them for breakfast.

The epidemiology of problem gambling is in its infancy. The American Psychiatric Association didn't define pathological gambling as a mental-health disorder until 1980. And as late as 1990, the Americans with Disabilities Act, aimed at prohibiting discrimination against people with disabling illnesses, excluded gamblers. Compulsive gambling became a bona fide public-health issue only in the late '90s; the fourth annual conference on problem gambling was held in Las Vegas in late 2003.

In 1998, the Nevada Gaming Control Board mandated that casinos had to prominently post problem-gambling hotline phone numbers, along with brochures about getting help for the disease. "When the Fun Stops" is the headline on one of the small flyers that sit in racks near the cage. One of Cyr's gamblers picked it up once when he was cashing out $80,000 in winnings. During dinner, he regaled some friends with his responses to the questions posed in the brochure, designed to identify a gambling problem.

Have you ever lied to your loved ones about going to Las Vegas? "Only every second or third time I come here."

Do you sometimes neglect your family because of gambling? "Yup. I take excellent care of my family ninety-five percent of the time. The other five percent, when I'm in Las Vegas, I completely, totally, and without guilt neglect them."

Have you ever borrowed money to gamble? "Of course! Isn't that the definition of a casino credit line?"

Have you ever lied about the amount you've lost? "Every time. What gambler in his right mind would tell his wife, banker, boss, customers, or even close friends how much he really loses?"

Have you ever gambled more money in an attempt to win back losses? "Only every time I sign a marker."

And the best one: Do you gamble to escape worry? "I run a huge corporation. I have a thousand employees. Every one of them fucks up somehow every day. Half of the fuck-ups wind up on my desk. The big half. When I get home, my wife's pissed off over something and my kids are out of control. I'm always being hit up for loans. I've got the insider-trading police shining flashlights up my asshole. Of course, they can't *see* anything, because I'm always so fuckin' *constipated.* I drink ten cups of coffee a day to keep me going. I take sleeping pills to crash.

"I come to Vegas every three months. I fly here in the casino's jet. I have dinner with my friends. I get to see Bruce Springsteen on the house. Once in a while I cash out eighty thousand. When the fun *stops*? Are you shittin' me? If it wasn't for gambling and Las Vegas, I'd blow my fuckin' head off."

❖ ❖ ❖

A drug dealer had $50,000 in cash on him (this was before cash-tracking regulations). He kept pulling out hundreds, betting, and losing. Finally, he reached into his pocket and there was no more cash. So he pulled out a gram of coke and asked, "Can I bet this?"

Compulsive gambling is, in fact, a lot like an addiction to cocaine. Getting lucky and winning big early can be compared to doing blow for the first time. It's never better than that. For the rest of your life, you try to recreate that buzz, but each time it takes more coke and you get less high. Sure, every line makes you a new man, but then *he* needs a line. Ultimately, you wind up out of coke, out of money, and sometimes out of your mind.

❖ ❖ ❖

Mr. Q, a high-stakes blackjack pigeon, plays so poorly that the bosses always give him a private game. They make a big deal out of how special it is to play heads-up against the dealer, but the truth is, they're afraid that if he gets on a real game, he'll see how blackjack is supposed to be played. They beat him for $600,000 a year—and he lives in Las Vegas! Mr. Q also happens to be a George, so no one says a word. The bosses don't say anything. The dealers don't say anything. And Mr. Q is none the wiser.

❖ ❖ ❖

Mr. R owed $300,000. He was a good guy and he wanted to pay, but the $300K would've bankrupted him. Mr. R owned rental property in Portland, Oregon. Cyr cut a deal with him for the house. The player signed it over to the Hilton and they put it on the market. It sold for $350,000. The Hilton wound up making $50,000 over and above the debt. Mr. R was cool with it. What choice did he have?

❖ ❖ ❖

Mr. S, a stockbroker from San Francisco and by all accounts a stand-up guy, came down every couple of months with five grand cash to shoot craps. He put the money in the cage and drew markers off of it. One night, as usual, he took a marker for $500 and began making his typical $50 pass and come bets. When it was his turn to roll the dice, he held them for a half-hour and won exactly $20,500. Mr. S paid off the marker, then went to the cage and deposited the other twenty.

Now he had $25,000 in reserve. He took a break, went to the bar, and had a drink. Then he headed over to another table, took a $1,000 marker, grabbed the dice, and boom, went up another $50,000. The rest of the night was the same routine: Mr. S wound up ahead $225,000.

Great, right? Wrong. Worst thing that ever happened to him. He chased his big score all the way to ruin and damnation.

Mr. S came back a week later and started betting $1,000 a whack. He lost. He came back the next week, and every week, betting big and losing losing losing. Finally, one weekend, he didn't show up. But the FBI did. Turned out Mr. S had embezzled $1.5 million from his firm and blew it in Las Vegas. Busted. Divorce. Prison. Thirty days after he got out, he was back at the Hilton, betting red chips at the crap tables.

❖ ❖ ❖

A high mucky-muck in the Kuwaiti oil ministry was, to everyone who interacted with him, the biggest prick who'd ever walked the Earth. He might be rolling the dice, then all of a sudden set them down and say, "I'll be right back." He'd go have his shoes shined, get something to eat, even take a nap. Meanwhile, the rest of the players at the table stood there, waiting and hating. The game couldn't continue until he returned, not only because he was still holding the dice, but because he had a half-million dollars in chips holding his place.

Everyone in the joint—players, dealers, bosses, and hosts—rejoiced when he finally beached himself. First, his family fell from power. Then, he lost at crap tables all over town and wound up stiffing half the casinos on the Strip.

He's been back since. Now he bets green chips, cash only. Play and pay. And he's very humble.

❖ ❖ ❖

The town president of Cicero, Illinois (headquarters for Al Capone's bootlegging empire in the 1920s), was convicted of looting $12 million from one of Cicero's insurance funds to support a serious gambling habit. Investigators estimated that she logged 1,600 hours over a three-year period in Las Vegas casinos and on Illinois and Indiana riverboats. She was found guilty of racketeering, fined $100,000, ordered to forfeit $3.2 million and repay $8.3 million, and sentenced to eight years in prison.

She continued to gamble during her trial and after her conviction, feeding her beloved machines with the restitution money. In an interview with Fox News, she claimed she wasn't proud of her gambling expenses, but denied being a compulsive gambler.

❖ ❖ ❖

A player who'd registered for one of the new "self-banning" programs instituted in some states' casinos wasn't allowed to collect $64,000 from Bally's Atlantic City. The gambler had put his name on New Jersey's self-exclusion list, acknowledging a gambling addiction and agreeing that he "shall not collect any winnings or recover any losses." When he won the $64K, the casino checked the list—and didn't have to pay.

❖ ❖ ❖

Fast Eddie D, the Montana timberman, always wanted to win $5 million; it would be his biggest hit ever. One weekend he started out by taking a half-million-dollar marker and proceeded to run it up on a dice game: $10,000 on the line, $20,000 odds, buy the 6 and 8 for $24K each, $5,000 on the hardways—he had $100,000 on every roll.

Over the course of the next couple days, Mr. D topped out at $5.3 million.

Unfortunately, in the heat of the early winnings, he'd paid off his $500,000 marker, but then forgot that he had. Later, thinking he still needed to buy back the marker, he figured he was up only $4.8 million and continued playing.

He began to tank and lost back $4.1 million before walking with $1.2 million. When he went to pay off the original marker, the casino gave him the bad news: He'd already paid it! Only then did Fast Eddie realize that he'd achieved his ultimate goal of winning $5 million. Only he didn't realize it at the time. And then it evaporated into thin air.

❖ ❖ ❖

The grandson of a well-known multi-billionaire Texan had just turned 21. The kid had been wild for years, mainly on money his grandfather had put into a checking account for him, unbeknownst to his mother. He'd won $89,000 playing high-stakes blackjack at the Rio when he was 19. But when he went to cash out, he was asked for ID. The Rio found out he was underage and called Gaming Control. Busted. His mother had to bail him out. And goodbye $89,000.

Cyr got the kid's name a couple of months before his 21st birthday from a mutual friend. The kid'd wanted to come back and play for two years. They exchanged paperwork. Cyr, of course, found no information about him in Central Credit, but his bank account held just under a half-mil, so the host set him up with a $400,000 credit line.

If Cyr thought that the kid was naive, he had another thing coming. A week after turning 21, the newly legal gambler flew in on a G2, put up $50,000 cash, negotiated an up-front discount if he lost more than $100,000, asked for a double-deck blackjack game where he could resplit aces, and played perfect basic strategy.

That first trip he won $28,000. Three weeks later he lost $150,000. The check for the full amount, minus the discount, arrived in two weeks. Next trip, boom, he lost. Next trip, boom, he lost again. After two more trips he'd lost a total of $400,000. He paid off $260,000 of it.

Now the kid owed the other $140,000, but it turned out he also had a substance-abuse problem. He went into rehab and, all of a sudden, Cyr stopped hearing from him. He did hear, however, from a well-known actor who was the kid's sobriety coach. The actor tried to soft-sell Cyr, asking him to be reasonable and fair and to give a kid a break. Cyr told him he'd like to, but the bosses were watching this one and on day 30 he'd have to run the $140,000 through the checking account. If it bounced, the kid would go to jail.

The coach kept promising to send a check, but never did. At 45 days, Cyr left a message: "Either pay something or I'll take it to the D.A."

This time the mother called. "He's just a screwed-up kid," she said. "I'm not coming to his rescue. He has to clean up his own mess this time. If he goes to jail, that's fine with me."

Next the family rabbi called with an offer to retire the debt at 15¢ on the dollar.

And then the lawyers started calling. Cyr went to L.A. to be deposed. He showed them that he'd done everything by the book. He had the credit application, the bank-account numbers, a surveillance print-out of the kid's perfect basic-strategy play, even a history of play and pay. He told the lawyers they were lucky the kid wound up with him. He'd kept him down to what he had in the bank, while a host somewhere else might've taken him up to a million. He yelled at them, "If he'd *won* a hundred and forty K, would you be coming to me saying, 'Hey, this kid's in trouble. We want to give you the money *back*'?" He told them they had 10 days to send him $10,000, and he expected to receive $10,000 every 10 days until the debt was retired, or he'd dump (deposit) the markers, all 14 of them (for $10,000 apiece). Every unpaid marker's a felony. As he left, Cyr added, "I'll visit him in prison."

Finally, the stepdad called. Cyr laughed out loud. "*Now* you're involved? After the celebrity coach, the mother, the rabbi, the lawyers? What a joke."

Eventually, the kid's mother started paying up. She sold his car and pawned his possessions and sent Cyr checks for $7,000, $13,000, $17,000, and so on, until it all added up to the $140,000.

❖ ❖ ❖

Think the innocent casino, the good-time volcano-erupting pirate-battling entertainment venue, doesn't know *exactly* what's going on with these players? Take the story of Brian Moloney, a 25-year-old Toronto bank manager who figured out a way to embezzle eight figures from the bank's loan accounts. Over the course of several months in 1982, he lost it all to Caesars Atlantic City. By circumventing international money-transfer procedures, Caesars management was actually able to draw Moloney's money directly out of the bank he was stealing it from. In the end, Moloney lost $10 million.

The whole affair came to light only because of a fluke: A routine audit caught wind of the scam. The regulators closed Caesars for 24 hours in 1985 as punishment; the casino also reportedly settled up with the bank. Moloney got six years in prison.

The saddest part was that like Al Franco, Moloney barely got a comp in the course of his losing. He was so young and ingenuous that round-trip rides in Caesars' jet, along with barbecued ribs and Coca-Cola, were the extent of it.

❖ ❖ ❖

The pathology of extreme greed punctuates nearly every move the casino makes with an exclamation point, to where the employees often think of the house's money as their own. Among the most common throwaway lines in the pit when a player walks away a winner are, "Aw, he's just holding it for us. He'll give it back shortly." And, "He went to dinner with a rack of checks; he'll bring it back after he eats." And, "It's temporarily on loan. He'll pay up next time."

After watching a player make $150 bets, the casino manager asks a floorman why he's rating the player at a $50 average: "Can't you see he's flat-betting a hundred fifty a hand?"

"Sure," the floorman responds, "but he's playing with winnings. When he's betting his own money, he only bets fifty."

Some casinos even have guidelines on how to treat players who happen to be ahead, temporarily in possession of the "house's money." One had a policy by which a guy who put up $5,000 in front money and bet a minimum of $50 per hand would get a comped room. But if he started winning and pressed his bets to $500 a hand, then asked for a comp for two to the gourmet restaurant, they told him he "didn't qualify." The rationale was that he started with only $5,000 of his own money and the rest of it—the winnings—wasn't his, but the house's.

Well, now that casino is in the mind-reading business. When the player gets up and walks next door, no one knows his bankroll consists of winnings from another joint. So the new casino will treat it as the player's own money! And they'll give him dinner for two, or four or eight if he asks for it, because they're focused on the money itself. Not on what casino happens to consider the money theirs.

❖ ❖ ❖

People gamble in response to a primal itch, imprinted into human consciousness a couple thousand generations or so ago. It's an impulse akin to the urge to have sex and take drugs. Forget morality. Forget politics, religion, culture, ethics, the law. Forget, even, crime and punishment. Attempting to regulate gambling behavior, which exists at the deepest level, where psychology meets genetics, where nurture meets nature, is no less irrational and futile than attempting to control sexual relations or consciousness alterations.

History is lousy with stories about people gambling more than they could afford to lose, then paying the price. Gamblers through the ages have lost all their possessions and assets, or had them confiscated. They've been ridiculed, pilloried, jailed, banished, and sentenced to life at hard labor. Their hands have been chopped off, their tongues cut out. Nothing has stopped them—not even the punishments that they've inflicted on themselves, which are often the worst of all. That's how profound the urge to gamble is.

A Vedic hymn tells of an ancient Indian king who staked 100,000 slaves on one roll of dice made of sheep anklebones, and lost (the anklebones were loaded). On subsequent rolls, he wagered away his kingdom, his children, and his kingship. He finally bet his wife the queen, but she objected, rightfully claiming that since he'd lost himself first, he was hardly entitled to gamble her.

The Scythians—mounted warriors from the eastern Crimea who in the seventh century B.C.E. ruled from the Balkans to the Middle East—were known to gamble on their very lives. The losers actually submitted to being tortured and murdered, often in public. Did that stop the next Scythian sucker from gambling on his existence? Fat chance.

Ancient history? Fat chance.

The economic boom resounding in the People's Republic of China is prompting an interesting (in the Chinese sense) unintended consequence. Gambling, of course, has been a part of the Chinese character since the beginning of recorded history. It's believed that as far back as 2300 B.C.E., a Chinese emperor developed an early form of chess to simulate war games for young military students; presumably, enterprising cadets booked side bets on the outcomes. It's known that the Chinese played dice games in 300 B.C.E. and when they invented paper a hundred years later, one of the first applications was in the making of playing cards. Chinese railroad and mine workers introduced the game of keno to the western U.S. in the mid-1800s. Shanghai in the 1920s and '30s hosted the hottest and most degenerate gambling fever the world has ever seen, making modern Las Vegas look like a casino night in the basement of a church in Altoona.

Though the Chinese were among the world's most rabid

gamblers, the Communists prohibited all forms of gambling when they rose to power in 1949. They might as well have outlawed eating rice with chopsticks. While wide-open gambling in the PRC was brutally quashed, the racetracks in Hong Kong and the casinos in Macau continued to pull in billions every year. And since the 1980s, when capitalism opened the trade floodgates into the People's Republic, burgeoning personal fortunes, the easing of international travel restrictions, and the Chinese political system's vast capacity for corruption have thrust the genetic itch of gambling directly to the surface. Chinese government officials, private businessmen, underground gambling operators, and out-and-out gangsters have been cutting a new migration route straight for the shores of Las Vegas, where they're welcomed with open arms in their capacity as the new whales.

These Chinese high rollers, however, embody the whole gamut of the compulsive-gambling galaxy. The many hoops these poor saps have to jump through attest, like nothing else in this world, to how irresistible the desire to dance with the casino dragon can be.

First, they have to come up with the millions they play with. This involves, from start to finish, a gauntlet of illicit activities in one of the most repressive environments on Earth. How do they make money? The same way whale-sized gamblers all over the world do. Underground bookies fade local action. Mobsters run the gray and black markets. Businessmen smuggle. Bureaucrats and officials rake in payola from all of the above. A few of them even earn legal fortunes.

Second, they have to qualify for U.S. visas, which often means lying on applications and forging documents. Also, China prohibits travelers from carrying more than $2,000 out of the country. This means sneaking out the millions, which entails a panoply of iniquity, such as bribing customs officials, laundering the money via private Hong Kong money handlers, or setting up shell companies in the U.S. None of these procedures is easily managed from deep within a communist country—especially these days, when governments are on the lookout for terrorists' financial schemes.

Third, like all compulsive gamblers, they have to be able to fade the losses. This is a bit more problematic, presumably, when the stakes are stolen or illegally obtained in the first place. That's why many Chinese whales want to go to Las Vegas to play, rather than Macau, where secret police post surveillance crews to videotape big players for reasons of "national security." The *Washington Post* reported in March 2002 that one such whale, a deputy mayor of the northeastern China city of Shenyang, was taped in Macau losing $4 million in "public funds" (the loot from the looted)—and was executed for the capital crime of corruption.

The *Washington Post* also cited the official New China News Agency, which reported that an executive with a Guangdong food company made average bets of $100,000 in a stretch at the Macau gambling tables. Guilty of corruption. Executed. The boss of a telephone-equipment company in Xian made average bets of $130,000. Guilty. Executed. And the government manager of a company in Hubei province lost $20 million in Macau over a two-year period. Guilty. Dispatched with alacrity to the Great Baccarat Game in the Sky.

Over Chinese New Year 2002, according to the *Washington Post*, several Chinese gamblers blew $20 million in one night at the baccarat tables at one of MGM Mirage's properties.

Casino sources, of course, strongly deny that their companies are aggressively wooing Chinese bureaucrats and businessmen and buccaneers. (Caesars long denied any wrongdoing in the Brian Moloney case, too.) Follow-ups to the *Washington Post* article appeared in both Las Vegas daily newspapers, which dutifully printed the casino-industry response. One public-relations executive claimed that 99% of such big-loss stories are exaggerations—proving, inadvert-

ently, that he knows what he's talking about when it comes
to exaggeration. Another spokesman explained that his company contracts with a Chinese private investigator to do background checks on potential customers, to ascertain whether
the money comes from sources legitimate or otherwise. More
exaggeration. And the chairman of the Nevada Gaming Control Board stated that the regulations do not address the suit-
ability of gamblers and that that part of the business is up to
the licensees. In plain English, the state leaves the details of
where gamblers get their money up to the casinos.

The fact is, it's not hard to believe that some of the biggest whales among the upwards of 50,000 mainland Chinese
who visit Las Vegas every year have been swimming in pol-
luted waters. And as long as the casinos can maintain plau-
sible deniability, they'll happily divest them of their money,
even if these doomed sons of Scythians get executed for it
later.

And do such executions—16 for corruption in December
2001, by one report—deter the Chinese from public gambling
with embezzled or laundered or illicit gains?

Fat chance.

15

It's a Small World After All

For the first three decades of legalized gambling in Nevada, there was no such thing as an international high roller.
All gamblers were domestic and they played craps, blackjack,
poker, even a little faro, but they'd never heard of baccarat.
Casinos didn't offer the game. Accounts vary, but most place
the advent of baccarat in Las Vegas somewhere around the
late-1950s, at the Sands, having found its way from Europe,
where it was called chemin de fer, via the casinos in pre-Castro
Havana, where it was called Cuban baccarat. To retain the
European mystique of baccarat, the original tables at the Sands,
and later at the Desert Inn, the Dunes, and Caesars Palace,
dealt paper (bets were placed and paid off in cash). The betting limit was $2,000—an astronomical sum in the late '50s
and early '60s, when nickels and quarters ruled the slot floor
and the max bet at the other table games was $250—and the
dealers had stacks and stacks of cash on the table, twenty $100
bills bundled in each, so they wouldn't have to count down
the bills after every hand. It was very exciting at the time and
low rollers loved to watch the action.

In those days, especially, baccarat was imbued with an
aura of glamour and exclusivity. The baccarat tables, even
more than today, were segregated in a secluded pit off the
main casino, complete with dealers in tuxedoes, showgirl
shills in thousand-dollar gowns, casino managers talking in

hushed tones behind the dealers, a ladderman (boss) sitting
on a high chair overlooking the pit, private buffets, beefy
security guards, and million-dollar artwork on the walls—
in short, James Bond in Monte Carlo circa 1958.

In addition to the thrill of the cash, baccarat was—and
is—simple to play. It's merely a guessing game as to which
hand, player or banker, will come closest to nine. The only
decision a player has to make is on which hand to place his
bet. Even today, baccarat is the preferred game of international high rollers, especially Asians, who don't need to speak
English to play, can sit 10 to a table, and are allowed to bend,
corkscrew, fold, and peek at the cards, using all their *chi* to
try to affect the outcome.

A number of the earliest international marketing executives came out of the baccarat pits, where they started as
dealers and rose through the ranks, working the floor, then
managing the room. From the pit to the jet was a natural
transition, since the dealers and bosses knew the game and
its players, and thus knew how to handle all the different
situations—cultural, financial, and personal.

Still, the learning curve was often steep. The earliest
globe-trotting hosts had never even traveled domestically,
let alone abroad. They grew up in Brooklyn or Cleveland or
St. Louis or even Las Vegas. They went to UNLV or Washington State. They'd never been to the exotic American cities
like New Orleans, Miami, Albuquerque, or San Francisco.
They might've heard of Houston.

But they were sponsored by a new breed of gambling
executive, who began showing up during the Howard
Hughes whirlwind of the late '60s, corporate guys rather than
casino guys. These businessmen took the international guys
on shakedown cruises and gave them enough exposure to
people and customs and cultures that they could subsequently get around the world on their own.

This new derivation of casino executive was educated,
sophisticated, more at home in a boardroom than a bingo

room. They got their training in business, rather than gambling. They had one eye on the top line and the other on the bottom. They could see that the world was shrinking, wealth was expanding, and gambling was no longer disreputable. They looked around and, like so many other corporate executives of the late '60s and early '70s, set their sights on emerging markets south of the border.

❖ ❖ ❖

The first incursion by Las Vegas marketing executives into the international arena landed in Mexico. Suddenly, generals, police chiefs, and high-end businessmen were populating the Strip baccarat rooms. Normally hushed and subdued, the high-limit pits turned riotous when the boisterous Latinos occupied them. They loved to drink and get loud. They loved the Americans fawning all over them. They loved the attractive *gringa* shills sucking up to them for tips and more. They loved to flash their cash. And they loved watching the stacks of 20 American hundred-dollar bills change hands.

They also loved to take shots at the dealers and the house. They'd run out of cash and have to sign markers. That whole transaction was usually a monumental hassle: *"No comprende! No comprende!"* But then, if a brash dealer grabbed a betting stack and put it up next to the bet, to demonstrate how to toke, these Mexican megarollers would respond, in perfect English, "What the fuck is *that*?"

What the high-limit dealers and floormen loved about the Mexicans was their machismo. At blackjack, for instance, they liked to hit hard 18. Why? Anyone can hit a 9 or 10 or 11, but it takes a *real man* to hit hard 18.

The high-flying Mesoamericanos kept bumping up against the $2,000 bet ceiling and wanted to wager more. So, over the course of a few years, the upper limit at baccarat doubled to $4,000, then doubled again to $8,000, and finally

topped out at a whopping $10,000 per hand. The first inter-
national whales were Mexicans with credit lines of $100,000,
$250,000, even $500,000 and could fade those $10K wagers.
Back then, you could buy an apartment in Manhattan for
$50,000. Cadillacs cost $13,000. The Mexicans played and
played—until the peso bottomed out, erasing most of the
original whales.

Next, the international hosts went trawling for new high
rollers overseas. They knew that Europe, where casino gambling has been readily available, on and off, for centuries, held
little potential. London, Monte Carlo, and Campione d'Italia,
among others, have long catered to the old money on the Continent and beyond. The Sultan of Brunei, for example, has always preferred the casinos in understated England, where the
whole casino culture is much more reserved, private, stiff
upper-lipped. He and his entire entourage can come in and
gamble millions while remaining almost entirely invisible.
They pull up in blacked-out limousines, walk in through secret entrances, disappear into private gaming rooms, then
leave the same way, and no one—not the British tabloids, not
the world of Islam—is ever the wiser.

Still, in the '70s, Las Vegas went into competition with
Europe for whales from the Middle East—Saudi Arabia, Ku-
wait, even Lebanon and Syria. Oil money. Black gold. Yemen
tea. Because of the type of behind-closed-doors society that
prevails in these countries, representatives from Las Vegas
found fairly easy pickings when they first arrived in the '70s.
Sure, the women were veiled and everyone purported to be
righteous and religious and to follow the puritanical strictures
of Islamic law, but there was plenty of lasciviousness and de-
pravity and urge-scratching in private, as there always is everywhere. Las Vegas was a mecca for the kind of mischief that
nouveau mega-riche oil sheiks had in mind.

This was predominantly first-generation money, which
the overseas hosts considered as hitting the jackpot. First,
they were dealing with people who'd created phenomenal

wealth, but didn't know quite what to do with it yet. They were typically unsophisticated in the ways of the wealthy. They hadn't figured out how to acquire art or houses in foreign countries, or to give it away. Casinos were a convenient way for them to buy an adrenaline rush.

Second, these players usually weren't particularly sensitive, Islam notwithstanding, about others knowing what they were doing.

And third, gambling was consistent with their lifestyles, similar to their entrepreneurial mode of making money: action-driven, risk-oriented, clawing and scratching for the slightest edge. They didn't graduate from business schools as accountants and work their way up to vice president of Shell or Texaco. They borrowed money and dug a well. In addition, they were often so addicted to adrenaline that their recreation had to be just as heart-pumping and blood-boiling as their normal lives. (It's often impossible for someone who's a heavy player in life to lie on the beach and read Tom Clancy for a week. Where's my cell phone, where's my laptop, where're my assistants? The pager's not beeping; what's wrong?)

If first-generation money tends to be hot and flighty, second-generation money tends to be cool and stable. The sons of successful entrepreneurs are often graduates of business schools and become bankers, lawyers, investors, CEOs. They grow up surrounded by the shield of privacy, which becomes second nature to them. They also see their responsibility as protecting the money and tend not to fritter it away at the idle pursuit of cards and dice.

This isn't always the case. Sometimes it's just the opposite. A $5 million Indonesian player who frequents Las Vegas is the essence of dispassion, moderation, even restraint. He didn't grow up with money. He learned his place in the overall scheme of things. He's conservative, subdued. His sons, however, are as flamboyant as it gets. They wear $2,500 Versace shirts, $5,000 Italian shoes, $50,000 watches.

When asked, "How can your sons be so flashy when you're so down to earth?" he answers, with obvious pride, "It's very simple. My sons have an extremely wealthy father."

First-generation money moves around the planet, stopping for a while in locales where new wealth is generated at a furious pace. From the Middle East, the focus shifted to the Far East—specifically, in the 1980s, to Japan. A dramatic portrait of Japanese high rollers appears in the novel *Fools Die* by the late Mario Puzo. Puzo describes 10 Japanese men filing into a casino, in frumpy black suits, white shirts, and black ties, looking like "undertakers come to collect the corpse of the casino bankroll." These 10 men, the board of directors of Japan's most powerful conglomerate, "terrorized the casinos of Vegas," all playing at the same baccarat table and betting the limit when Fumiro-san, the chairman of the board, held the shoe. Despite being worth $500 million, Fumiro-san pounded the table and shrieked when he won a bet for $2,000 (something akin to a guy with $250,000 in his pocket winning a bet for a buck).

The Japanese economy, of course, collapsed in the late '80s and the hot first-generation money moved again, this time circulating south along the Pacific Rim. Although a mere 3% or so of all Las Vegas visitors hail from Asia, most of the whales swim over from Hong Kong, Taipei, Bangkok, Jakarta, Singapore, Kuala Lumpur, Manila, and lately, Beijing, Shanghai, and Guangdo. Today, Las Vegas does between $400 million and $600 million a year in Asian business, almost entirely at the baccarat tables. Most of those customers come for one or more of three events: New Year's Eve, Chinese New Year, and a heavyweight-championship boxing match.

International whale hunting is a highly competitive business, and not just among the premium Las Vegas casinos. Though casino business comes from all over the world, there are now casinos all over the world, too: South Africa, Europe, Australia, New Zealand, Asia, South America. High-roller casinos in Las Vegas are in direct competition with Macau and Manila and Melbourne and Monte Carlo. Six-star Australian casinos can fly in their customers from Tokyo, Taipei, Singapore, and the like in their Gulfstreams in 12 hours less time than those customers can fly to Las Vegas. And they only cross a few time zones in the process. It's much more convenient.

However, over the course of one week in February, Chinese New Year, pods of Asian whales migrate to Las Vegas, which sees the year's largest concentration of big players. The bosses bank on this holiday to generate strong first-quarter results.

Perhaps the most visible whale, media mogul Kerry Packer, is Australian. But in terms of pure blubber, a handful of Far Eastern leviathans are heavier.

❖ ❖ ❖

At the uppermost echelons of the casino-management hierarchy, you won't hear the word "whale." It's too crude, too cetaceous. You probably won't even hear "high roller." Too gambling-associated, too atavistic. Today's euphemistic monikers of choice are "preferred guest," "special guest," "esteemed guest," or "VIP." These terms have an Asian connotation. They imply, by understatement, the colossal éclat and cynosure of the few hundred richest men and women who like to play casino games—a critical distinction separate from just being rich—in the world.

The Asian implication is no coincidence. In today's distribution of gambling wealth, Asians make up 80% to 85% of the world's Monstros. And it's not limited to high rollers either: More than half of *all* gamblers in England and Australia are Asians, as are 75% of the players in New Zealand.

To compete for this handful of esteemed guests from Asia, big casinos maintain international marketing departments. Gambling companies such as Caesars Entertainment (Caesars Palace, Paris, Bally's, Flamingo), MGM Mirage (MGM Grand, Bellagio, Mirage, Treasure Island, New York-New York), the Venetian, and Mandalay Resort Group (Mandalay Bay, Luxor, Monte Carlo) maintain far-flung offices in the VIPs' home countries, where high-powered casino hosts—the Steve Cyrs of the Pacific Rim—speak the languages, understand the cultures, and harpoon and harvest the big sea-going mammals.

The international hosts are supervised by international casino-marketing bosses from the corporate office in Las Vegas. These are the most peripatetic executives in the industry, taking two- to three-week trips every couple of months or so. The executive emissaries touch base with their casinos' biggest fish and sign off on deals. Nine out of ten of their meetings in Europe, Latin America, the Pacific Rim, and the Middle East are with repeat customers. It's a matter of giving them face.

The players, whether they're first-timers or so inveterate that they remember when the international marketing guy was a baccarat dealer, always want to talk about the deal. The numbers. It's swell to have big properties and lots of amenities to help satisfy all the whale whims, but the deal is the important thing. It's the same all over the world. Deals transcend cultures. It always comes down to business.

What changes are the logistics of the approach. In Japan, for example, the marketing executive has to visit one customer at a time. Though from the outside Japan might appear to be a somewhat homogeneous culture, each person remains an individual. No matter if it's a $100,000 high roller or a $20 million whale, each is treated with the same respect. The traditional bow. The strict rules of etiquette. A marketing emissary who wants to see 20 customers in one week is in for a continuous round of offices and more offices, lunch, maybe dinner, maybe a nightclub. Especially in the cities—Tokyo, Nagoya, Osaka, Kyoto—going two miles can take two hours. The day is long and tedious. And the next day's the same.

Still, at least Tokyo is good for 20 customers. In Europe, you have to travel all day and half the night to see a single $100,000 player; in a week, you can probably call on three or four.

In Taiwan and, to a certain extent still, in Hong Kong, you can have group dinner parties and entertain three tables of 30 people each, six or seven of whom, sitting there politely, will be million-dollar customers. In Taipei or Hong Kong, you can talk freely. Not so in mainland China. Here, the casino representative has to be careful. He can't talk about gambling. He doesn't even want to *think* about gambling. It's illegal. So he lays down a soft sell. He talks about the weather, the villas, the entertainment. He shows a video of the spectacular Shadow Creek golf course—these days, translated into Mandarin, Cantonese, and French.

Mainland China's the promised land, with upwards, some estimates have it, of 200 to 300 new bona fide whales ready for harvesting. All up and down the coast, these new customers have shown up in the past five years or less. The big-time international hosts are drooling over this new frontier. Yet they have to be circumspect. They have to bide their time. These players have to come in on their own.

Once a year, between Thanksgiving and Christmas, the overseas executives take a diplomatic tour of the key ports of call. On this trip, they're accompanied by the company chairman, president, or highest vice presidents, who also need to travel, pump flesh, carry the casino torch, give face. The functionaries—from local hosts to international bosses—might be great guys, but they're still just employees. The biggest players want to party with the owner. Steve Wynn is his own best advertisement. Sheldon Adelson, chairman of the Venetian, likes to talk. Asians like to listen. He loves to sell his city, his casino, his convention center, and himself. He's got a new audience every night at different cocktail and dinner parties. Sheldon Adelson—worth billions, boss of thousands—is one of the world's greatest hosts.

❖ ❖ ❖

No travel schedule is set in stone. The international marketing boss might return home from a 20-day trip abroad,
only to find that he has to go right back out again. He might,
for example, have to fly directly to Jakarta. From Las Vegas
by air, it's 90 minutes to San Francisco. From there it's 14
hours to Hong Kong, not including a three-hour layover, then
another five hours to Singapore, with an hour layover there,
and finally an hour down to Indonesia. Thirty hours or so
altogether, from his garage door in Vegas to his hotel-room
door in Jakarta.

Why does he have to do it? Maybe a new big fish has
been hooked.

The universe of potential super-high-limit players is
small. The whales are all known; this kind of player doesn't
exactly fall out of the sky. And an international marketing
executive who's been in the business for a few decades, especially in Las Vegas, has turned out peers who populate
casinos around the world. He's done plenty of favors for players and hosts and bosses, thus he has contacts in all the right
places. Any Las Vegas overseas marketing executive worth
his mid-six-figure salary talks every day to his colleagues in
Sydney, Genting Highlands, Macau, Monaco.

So the boss knows all about the established players, and
when the blowhole spray of a new Moby does appear in casino binoculars, he wants to know everything there is to know
about him, and then he wants to sit down with him as soon
as possible.

The minute he hears about the prospect from his local
hosts or from his network in the business, his staff goes right
to work. They research everything about him—his business,
his net worth, his likes and dislikes, where and how much
he gambles. Then, after all the background is accumulated
and assimilated, it's the boss' job to visit him and get to know
him personally. His goal is to get into the player's head a bit,

then try to talk him into giving his property a shot.

More likely, though, the boss has to get back on a plane, right after he got off one, to go visit a customer who owes the casino money. This type of meeting, predictably, is uncomfortable for both the executive and the player. International casino-marketing bosses employ every trick in the book not to have to take a player's face away, especially in person. His staff exhausts every opportunity to collect through letters and e-mails and phone calls—and the player representative.

The reps are independent contractors, usually from the whale's home country, liaisons between the gambler and the casino. They bring in the whale and they get paid only when the casino collects on losses. The arrangement is similar to the old-time junkets, where a junketmaster vouched for his players. It's much more intense, of course, because face and high stakes are involved. The embarrassment if a rep can't bring back the money that his gambler loses is so great that he often can no longer do business in Las Vegas.

If neither the marketing department nor the player rep is successful over a certain period, the executive emissary has to pay the visit. He's responsible for all international collections—a million, a half-million, even as little as $50,000.

Even then, it's a mellow exchange. The boss knows the gambler. The gambler knows the boss has just flown 30 hours to collect. He also knows he's months overdue. He knows that he can't hide, not anywhere in the world. Most of the time, the boss just has to show up for the player to broach the subject of the debt himself. He, too, is embarrassed. He wants to work it out. But sometimes, the executive has to clasp his hands and say, "Well, you owe us some money. Let's get down to it."

The boss explains, "The worst thing that can happen now is that it's taken out of my hands. If your debt goes to legal, then I have no more say in the matter. You owe us a half-million. Can you pay fifty-thousand today? And another fifty-thousand in a month? I'll let you pay fifty-thousand a month for six months, but then you have to pay off the other two hundred in a lump sum. Deal? Fine. Let's shake hands. Your word's good with me. After all, we've known each other a long time. I was your floorman at Caesars twenty-five years ago."

Collections is so important that when the first month is up, the host will be on the phone to Jakarta, inquiring about the next $50,000 installment. "Hi. You promised us, remember?" And he'll go back to Jakarta, a 60-hour round-trip door to door, to see the guy as often as he has to.

As a last resort, overseas collections sometimes go through collection agents. The casino executive invites a recalcitrant player who's owed millions for months to dinner. He says, "I've got good news and bad news. The good news is: You don't owe us any money. The bad news is"—and a guy missing a pinky and both front teeth slides into the booth—"now you owe *him*."

Business gets done one way or another.

❖ ❖ ❖

The casino representative, whether a local host or the chairman of the board, always wants the same thing from the player: a visit to the casino from him and his checkbook.

The player, meanwhile, could and usually does want anything and everything from the casino representative. Many like to socialize and become friendly with their counterparts in the gambling industry; where the highest-echelon casino executive and the top-shelf businessman meet is a rarefied realm. Others want to talk business—investments, joint ventures, and the facilitation of offshore-haven benefits (the U.S. is the biggest and best tax haven in the world—for non-Americans). Some don't want to see anyone from the casino at all and only do so out of obligation or face. Most love to talk about casino comps and gifts. Every one of them, to a man, likes to talk about gambling. The itch transcends all tribal, national, and racial boundaries.

Las Vegas, for all its crass single-mindedness and provincial lack of depth, does a surprisingly good job at crossing cultures. Beyond the obvious theming of megaresorts like Monte Carlo, Paris, Bellagio, Mandalay Bay, Venetian, and Aladdin, Las Vegas' sensitivities span the globe in the quest for suckers. The international executives are like diplomats, hyperaware of protocols and rituals and agendas.

But it goes deeper than that, all the way down to the level of superstition and mysticism. Gambling, obviously, is a superstitious business and Las Vegas is a superstitious city that attracts superstitious people on both sides of the tables. Asians seem to have more superstitions, numerical imperatives, and subtle idiosyncrasies going on in their minds than Westerners. Numerology is a big part of the Eastern paradigm. Numbers have magical powers. When your number comes up, it tells you something about your place in the cosmic scheme of things. Through play, the gods show you your standing in the universe and you accept it.

Asians, of course, also love the action, the excitement, and the group experience. That's another reason for their proclivity for baccarat. You'll rarely see high-rolling Asians sitting solitary in front of a slot or video poker screen.

In addition, gambling is so ingrained in their worldview that putting some—or most, or all—of their wealth at risk is almost a cultural dictate. To an Asian, if you make money, you have to put it back onto the wheel of life. On the wheel, the money goes around and all kinds of forces act upon it. Players pray for the money to gather momentum and multiply, then come around again to them. So if they gamble away a million dollars in a casino, all they've done is put money onto the wheel. And since that money and more will come back (though perhaps not in this lifetime), they didn't really lose it. It's just karma.

Casinos occasionally, and inadvertently, cross the line into a player's superstitious universe. You don't, for example, put bookshelves in your baccarat room, because a library is a sign of death in some Asian cultures (the Mirage reconfigured its baccarat room to get rid of the bookshelves). You don't build a six-story lion's head, with his open muzzle doubling as the casino entrance, a sure sign of submission to a predator (the MGM Grand reconfigured its lion). You never book an Asian player into a room with the number four. The same word for it can also mean "death" in some Asian languages. (Eight is the magic number. Casinos in Australia, such as the Crowne in Melbourne, have the last four digits of their phone numbers lucky 8888.)

Las Vegas' Rio took the avoidance of the number four to new heights, so to speak, when it put up a 42-story tower, but decided to skip the 40s; the rooftop restaurant, bar, and observation deck, along with the Presidential penthouse, are on the "51st" and "52nd" floors. They did so, they claimed, in deference to Asian beliefs, but it's not too hard to picture the Rio designers chuckling when writers and others interested in truth in numbers have to explain that at the Rio, 51 and 52 really mean 41 and 42.

Naturally, since the Rio saw fit to pretend that its tower is 50-odd stories, the subsequent Palms, situated catty-corner from the Rio across West Flamingo Avenue, couldn't very well erect a 46-story tower that was *shorter* than the Rio's at 42 stories. Accordingly, when you press the button for the Ghost Bar on the "55th" floor of the Palms, you're actually whisked only to the 45th.

❖ ❖ ❖

As Einstein proved, everything is relative. The high roller of years past is but a shadow of the standard premium player of today, let alone the gigarolling whale. Similarly, nowadays only the casinos that can swim in the deepest waters hunt the great Mobys.

Though worldwide there are only a handful of true whales, regular high rollers are plentiful. For every quarter-million-pound blue, there are thousands of 500-pound halibut frequenting the second-tier casinos, and tens of thousands of 150-pound porpoises cavorting in the older smaller joints.

The Stardust is a good example of a casino where players packing middle-class bankrolls tend to feel more comfortable than at the flashy, posh, and nouveau megaresorts opened since the late 1990s.

As late as the early '70s, the limit for blackjack, even at Caesars, the Desert Inn, and the Hilton, was $500 a hand. Big players from back then recall large crowds gathering to watch them fire up two hands of $250 each (the limit was cumulative). In the mid-'70s, around the time it began pursuing international bankrolls, Caesars raised the maximum to $1,000, but it stayed there for nearly 10 years. To be sure, high rollers could bargain higher. But little more than 15 years ago, the posted limit on the BJ tables was a mere $1,000, 1%-2% of today's maximums.

The Stardust was never an upper-crust hotel, not even when it opened in 1958. Today, nearly 50 years later, though it's been extensively upgraded, it's still an aging dowager owned by Boyd Gaming, which merged with Coast Casinos in spring 2004 to create yet another mega-casino corporation. Other than the tiny Barbary Coast, the Stardust is Boyd's only Strip hotel.

The relativity of rollers is immediately evident at the Stardust, where the maximum bets are $3,000 a hand at blackjack and $5,000 per at baccarat. Even these are steep for Boyd properties. Anyone playing $500 to $1,000 a hand at the Stardust is a big hitter and can have just about anything he wants. When the same guy goes into the MGM or Bellagio and bets $1,000 a whack, he's surrounded by 25 or 30 guys, all betting five or ten times that amount. He'd be lucky to get a comped suite. At the opening of Bellagio, Ian Andersen, of the Ebony and Ivory caper, was moving his bets from $500 on one hand to $5,000 on each of two hands and was never the biggest bettor at his table.

Like most of the other pre-megaresort casinos on the Las Vegas Strip (the Sahara, the Riviera, Circus Circus, Westward Ho, New Frontier), the Stardust is in the volume business. It's going for the 150 players betting $150,000 in aggregate baccarat action ($1,000 per hand each). The house edge is exactly the same, but the volume smooths out the variance and lets the vigorish (house advantage) perform its custodial-side magic.

It's just not worth it to the Boyds to cater to megarollers or to take big gambles. A casino can't decide to court the big action simply by hanging out an open-for-whale-business shingle and raising its baccarat limits from $5,000 to $150,000. First, it needs all the hooks, lines, and sinkers—the fleet of jets, the big suites, the top chefs, the wine cellars, and the international marketing network that provides the connection to players. Plus, it needs the bankroll and the balls to ride the high-roller roller coaster.

There's a story about a big player at Boyd's Sam's Town, where the posted limit for blackjack at the time was $500. This guy was betting the whole $500 a hand and attracting attention from top to bottom—operations, marketing, security, and surveillance. He wound up losing $25,000, all the money he'd brought, and wanted another $25,000. He told the casino manager that he had the money at Binion's. The casino manager informed the president. The president called the Horseshoe to confirm that the money was there. He then sent a security guard downtown to get the money and transfer it into Sam's cage, so the gambler could play it off.

Chasing his losses, the player asked the casino manager to up the limit to $1,000. The casino manager asked the president, who thought, *We're in the gambling business, aren't we? Let's take a shot.*

But the house had to sweat it for a while; at $1,000 a hand, the guy could go on a $25,000 or $50,000 tear, which would dramatically impact the casino's cash flow. One of the Boyd partners had to go into the bar and pound highballs, because he couldn't stand the tension. Ultimately, the player went broke. But it was a whale of an episode at Sam's Town. And it would've been at all but the biggest casinos in town.

In fact, a single whale can cripple a casino like the Stardust. To succeed in the high-end business, for the percentages to work in its favor, a casino needs 30 or 40 humpbacks. Even if 10 or 12 of them win, 25 still lose. That's why the more whales the better on the risk side, but it also means a much larger marketing infrastructure and much higher comp expenses. And even after all that, what if only four or five show up one year? Then it's Russian roulette—if two or three win, the casino gets crushed.

A casino has to be in or out of the whale grease. It's either in the high-roller business or not. It's either Bellagio or Slots A Fun. If it tries to sit on the fence, it gets impaled every time.

❖ ❖ ❖

Whales are coveted and feared, loved and hated, all at the same time by the Las Vegas casinos that cater to them. A half-dozen do; more than five dozen, like the Stardust, don't. Few casinos have the fortitude and fortune to fade the gut-wrenching sphincter-squeezing high-wire action of the world's heaviest hitters.

On the one hand, the top casinos will do anything to get them, spending millions on high-roller mansions and villas, plus a quarter-million in show-up money, plus 10% to 20% in discounts on losses, plus tens of thousands more for transportation and gifts and comps and amenities and personal attention and and and—to hunt the great creatures who can afford to lose $5 million, $10 million, $20 million in one visit.

On the other hand, with a single hot streak a single whale

can decimate a huge publicly traded corporation's entire quarterly earnings.

In the briny deep of whale hunting, the casino is actually gambling, one on one, *mano a mano*, eyeball to eyeball, with the gigantiroller, whereas the rest of the casino is a gargantuan numbers game, relying on low stakes, high volume, and the long run to grind its percentage out of every bet. The MGM Grand, for example, the largest hotel in the world, is a $2 billion resort with 5,034 rooms, 8,000 employees, endless rows of slot machines, hundreds of table games, and thousands of players (it has a higher "population" at any given time than all but a few towns in Nevada). Yet here you'll find the bosses staking the quarter on one whale.

This is where the greed and the fear, finally, manifest in management. The number-crunching honchos should know better—that it's the customers who should do the gambling, not the casino. They're supposed to be methodical, analytical, mathematical. And now they're gambling like grifters. It's the tail wagging the dog.

Consider a publicly traded casino company with 100 million shares of outstanding stock. The vice president of international marketing succeeds in luring a Japanese banker through the doors for a weekend of $200,000 bets at the baccarat table. If the gambler runs lucky and gets ahead for any extended period, the casino's losses will be in the millions, and in some cases, tens of millions of dollars.

Now the dealer is sweating as the pit boss tries to explain the bad run of cards to the shift boss who's worried that the casino manager will have to break the news to the chief executive officer who knows that the board of directors will be furious if the stockholders are forced to swallow a $4-a-share hit to the company's projected earnings for the quarter due to a single hit from, say, a Japanese banker. (And this is the same board of directors that, when presented with this very proposition two weeks earlier, gave it its wholehearted blessing.)

And though the Japanese banker abhors publicity, word quickly gets around. The local press picks up on the staggering loss sustained by the casino corporation. For sound bites, business reporters speed-dial the Wall Street financial analysts and CNBC talking heads who might now have to downgrade those 100 million shares, a move that could lead to a sell-off and subsequent nose-dive of the market price. This could conceivably render the casino company a takeover target for an acquisitive competitor, a value investor, or a corporate raider.

And here's how deeply such a seemingly obscure run of luck at a Las Vegas casino can impact the domestic economy: Some of the largest U.S. mutual funds and public-employee retirement groups are invested in the megacasino corporations. Because these corporations collectively constitute a percentage of the major stock indexes, a large loss at a single Las Vegas baccarat table can actually mean a slight downtick in a fund tied to the Standard & Poor's 500. And the high-school teacher in Milwaukee, the Fish and Game warden in Anchorage, the firefighter in Newark, even the Protestant minister in Indianapolis all actually believe that they don't have a thing to do with casino gambling.

On the other hand, the whole thing works in reverse when the whale runs aground. Then the floorman basks in the positive glow from the pit boss who winks knowingly at the shift boss who gets a pat on the back from the casino manager and the whole complex machine is oiled with whale blubber all the way up to S&P 500 index funds. (Only the dealer's still sweating. It takes a lot of confidence to deal a game where the players are betting six figures a hand.)

Some stock investors, tied in to casino employees who are aware of the huge financial tides created by the ebb and flow of whale wins and losses, regularly profit from this information. It's not considered insider trading to buy or sell casino stock should the investor happen to hear gossip from a butler, dealer, or shift boss about a loss too large to be offset by normal daily activity, especially late in a quarter. Casino companies may "guide" the market about significant earnings fluctuations by way of forecasts forged by a whale-generated tidal wave. But this often takes days or weeks while the accountants sort out the impact and decide what kind of spin to put on it. Buying or shorting casino shares can be good business and whales (and whale watchers) have a ringside view into the action.

And who knows? It's been rumored that the biggest whales hedge their bets at the tables by shorting the casino company's stock (as soon as they win big) or going long (as soon as they lose). At those dizzying heights, it doesn't take much imagination to win when you lose, and win even more when you win.

High-Rolling Tycoons,
Superstars, and Women

Most whales are used to running everything and every-one in their lives. They generally get whatever they want whenever they want it. An international marketing execu-tive has to see to it that they only get what they have coming to them in return for their play. He knows that because of the habit of running their own businesses, whales'll run his business too if he lets them. He tries not to let them, but it doesn't always work out that way.

The high roller with the most ferocious reputation for trying to run the business of the casinos where he plays is Kerry Packer. In the casino world, Packer is the Prince of Whales. He isn't Asian. He's Australian. And he's the wealthi-est man in the country. Estimates of his fortune range, de-pending on the day, from $4.5 billion to more than $8 bil-lion. He owns Australia's largest television station, 60% of all magazines sold Down Under (including the venerable *Women's Weekly*, inaugurated in 1933 by Kerry's father, Sir Frank Packer), pieces of Casino Sydney and Melbourne's Crown Casino, and a host of other media, entertainment, gambling, and mutual-fund interests. His holdings have put him into nearly perpetual conflict with the Australian gov-ernment and other media moguls (his arch-nemesis is Rupert Murdoch).

It's probably apocryphal, but the story of the Packer

family's road to riches starts with Kerry's grandfather, who found 10 shillings on the street in Tasmania and parlayed it into a passage to mainland Australia and a big win on a longshot bet on a horse race. From those humble gambling roots, Packer, a tall heavyset man born in 1938—who's had a series of heart attacks and a kidney transplant (the kidney was donated by one of his employees, who is now report- edly set up for life)—has become one of the few true blue whales in the gambling world. He's easily the biggest known player.

Ironically, the chairmen, CEOs, and presidents of Ameri- can casinos who deal with Packer don't consider him a whale in the fully developed sense of the term. He's a quintessen- tial hit-and-run high roller. A U.S. casino rarely gets enough play from him to dig too deeply into his pockets. Unlike most gamblers, low roller and high, for whom love and fever are the great motivators, Packer is aroused by pure sport. Just the thrill of it. Nothing can happen in the casino that will significantly impact his standard of living. If he makes or loses ten or twenty million in a session, it's inconsequential. But he loves to see the impact his gambling has on the casino bosses. A cutthroat-style businessman, Packer reportedly derives greater satisfaction in victory if he can see his oppo- nent bleeding at the side of the road as he walks off.

He likes to *put* the fear into their hearts. If a boss acts like nothing's a big deal and Packer can do whatever he wants, he doesn't get as much of a charge out of it. He starts perk- ing up when he's told, "No, we can't really let you go *that* far." That's when he knows he's reached the level where the casino is starting to feel uncomfortable. He keeps pushing until he hears, "No, sorry, we can't do it." And then he pushes some more.

He's so big, he can get away with being difficult to exe- cutives. He's exorbitantly generous to widows and orphans and front-line casino workers, but he seems to take a per- verse pleasure in undressing the bosses.

And always in the back of his mind must be the knowledge that he could actually, single-handedly, bankrupt one of these joints.

The story goes that Packer was flying somewhere—Singapore, Bangkok, London—from Sydney and he called the cage at the Darwin Casino at the northern tip of Australia, which was on his flight path. He asked the cage supervisor how much cash was on hand. When he was given a number, he said no thanks. When the supervisor asked him how much cash he needed to stop off and play, he quoted three times the number.

The next time Packer called, Darwin had enough cash in the cage and he landed. He played, won, and emptied the cage. He tipped everyone well and took off again, with a little extra walking-around money for his trip. He doesn't go out and buy jewelry with the win. He doesn't celebrate. He just likes the feeling of having free cash on him (who doesn't?) to spend on whatever strikes his fancy.

The stories of his gargantuan wins, losses, and tokes are the stuff of legend.

Packer is rumored to have taken the biggest dump ever in a U.K. casino, losing 11 million pounds (US$16 million) in 1999, playing blackjack over a three-week span at Crockfords Casino in Mayfair. (He's less hit-and-run in England, where he lives part time.)

On March 31, 1992, Packer waltzed into Caesars Palace and began firing it up. At midnight as the books for the fiscal quarter closed, he was up $9 million. It was a loss of 37 cents per share for Caesars World and cut into the company's earnings for the first quarter by a full 50%. Between midnight and dawn, Packer lost back the $9 million and then some, and Caesars second-quarter earnings rose with the tide.

In 1995, he showed up at the MGM Grand in the wee hours one morning, asking that an entire blackjack pit be cleared of players. He went from table to table, betting six hands at $75,000 a hand. (A $75,000 bet for someone worth

$5 billion might equate with a 75¢ bet for someone who earns $50,000 a year. Several "PackerWatch" Web sites have a meter that calculates how long it takes him to earn your yearly salary. The $50,000 guy? Twenty-two minutes.) In a couple of hours at MGM, he won a reported $26 million, then cashed in his checks and went his merry way. It's rumored that MGM eventually let him bet $500,000 a hand, so he had to be up more than 50 bets—a phenomenal hot streak.

According to rumor and myth, Packer's winning streak at the MGM lasted several visits until he was barred for life. Apparently, Kirk Kerkorian, the majority shareholder in MGM Grand, wasn't happy. At the time, he was wheeling and dealing in Chrysler stock and he needed the price of his MGM shares to stay high. The Packer debacle hurt him. Heads rolled; the old management team was termed and a new one came in.

Terry Lanni, the incoming CEO, dispatched Larry Woolf, one of the outgoing executives and Packer's handler, to London to personally tell him that the MGM was no longer interested in his action. Woolf was staying at the Savoy, where Packer sent a chopper to pick him up and bring him to his polo ranch outside London. After Woolf watched Packer play polo for a while, they got back into his BMW and returned to the ranch house, where Woolf broke the news that he'd been 86ed from the Grand.

Packer was hurt. He'd been to dinner with Kerkorian several times. "How much can I play?" he asked.

"Nothing," Woolf told him. "You can't play at all."

"For how long?"

"Forever."

"I'm gonna make you walk back to London!" Packer roared.

"It's not my decision," Woolf said. "Don't kill the messenger. When I was there, you were more than welcome. We gave you good limits. But now there's a new management team. They want to reduce their exposure."

Then Woolf eased the blow. "You're just too tough. You know that the only way the casino has a chance to win someone's money is if he plays long enough. In London, during polo season, you go to the casinos every night. They've got a bull's-eye on you. But in Vegas, you play an hour and win a million or two and you're gone. You're not giving them a fair shot."

Though Packer ranted and raved a while longer, Woolf believes he was also secretly pleased to hear that he was too tough for the MGM.

Packer is, in fact, a pretty good blackjack player. He's had some tutoring from experts along the way. So he has a hard time finding a joint that'll fade his blackjack action. Casinos will book his big baccarat bets, but they don't want his 21 play. Also, he doesn't go off on temper tantrums as much at baccarat as he does at blackjack. At baccarat, you don't have to do anything but choose player or banker. Because decision-making comes into play at the blackjack table, he's a lot more volatile when playing 21. Occasionally, he'll even have a problem finding places that will fade the maximum baccarat bets he likes to make.

When Cyr was at the Hilton, Packer liked playing there. The bosses not only booked his blackjack action, but they dealt to him at $75,000 a hand and he could spread to multiple hands. One time he had $825,000 out on one round and the dealer busted; it was a $1.65 million swing.

A story has long gone around Las Vegas that in the late '80s, Packer had a $5 million credit line at Caesars. It was as large a line as anyone could get at the time, but he still wanted to increase his credit. He got on the phone with the president of Caesars and said, "Look, I can buy this company with petty cash."

The president said, "Great. When you buy the company, you can give yourself any credit line you want. But while we still own it, you'll have to abide by our limits."

Packer is also justly famous for being George. By most

accounts, he's the biggest tipper who ever lived. His tokes to dealers and cocktail waitresses typically run in the tens of thousands of dollars and stories abound about his dropping a few thousand here and a few thousand there into the hands of needy employees.

While playing baccarat at the Mirage shortly after it opened in 1989, Packer made a $100,000 bet for the dealers (and won). After winning the $26 million at the MGM Grand, he went around and tipped each dealer on duty $2,500, which added up to $105,000. And once, after bumping a cocktail waitress and causing her to dump a tray of drinks, he asked for her name and address. The next thing she knew, her $130,000 mortgage had been paid off.

He doesn't like his generosity publicized, however. He hates to read about the size of his tokes in the newspaper and has been known to tell his dealers, "If the word gets out about how much I tipped tonight, I'll never leave another dime." In July 2001, Packer was said to have lost $20 million playing baccarat at Bellagio. Still, he toked big. But then he read about it in the *Las Vegas Review-Journal*. The next time he went in, no one got a thing. He stiffed them all—while he was winning $9 million. He's obviously a man of his word. Someone talked. He walked.

In 1991, Steve Cyr saw Jimmy Newman, the senior vice president of Hilton Corporation, and Guy Hudson, the senior vice president of Hilton credit, *running* across the casino. These guys were casino *gods*; they were *never* in a hurry. And here they were at a full sprint all the way from the front to the back of the joint, looking like they were being chased by demons.

It turned out that early the night before, Kerry Packer had shown up unexpectedly at the Hilton's high-limit pit, but it was closed and wouldn't open for an hour. Packer walked right back out the door and heads rolled. The next night, Packer pulled up again unannounced; warned by the valet manager, Newman and Hudson were in a rush to make sure the room was ready for him. He lost $10 million that night. It was a record at the time—the first time anyone had lost eight figures in one session. Hilton bean counters couldn't get the size of the loss into the computer, which only accepted up to seven digits.

Engelbert Humperdinck was in the showroom that night. Waiting to see the show was a little girl, in a wheelchair. When Packer walked by, he looked at her. Stopping in his tracks, he left the side of Newman and Hudson, reached into his pocket, and stuck something in her hand.

After getting Packer settled in at a gambling table, Hudson walked by the showroom again. The little girl called him over and asked who that man was.

"He's a good customer of the Hilton's," Hudson replied.

"Do you know what he gave me?"

"No, and it's none of my business anyway."

"He gave me three thousand dollars and I'd like to thank him."

"Honey, he gave it to you because he's a nice guy and he wants you to have it. You thanked him just by accepting it. Now go and enjoy the show and when I see him, I'll tell him that you expressed your deepest appreciation."

She said, "No, I'm going to skip the show and wait for him."

"Please don't," Hudson said. "That would only disappoint him."

So the girl sat through Engelbert and when she came out, Hudson made sure Packer came around so she could thank him.

Later, playing at the Hilton, Packer took a liking to Kristine W of the Sting. Kristine and the Sting did a stint as the house band in the Hilton Nightclub and Packer thought she was great. One night he was playing blackjack between sets and Kristine came out to hang with him. He was betting $50,000 a hand on five or six spots on the layout. He pointed to one spot and told the dealer, "This one's yours." Then he pointed to another spot, looked at Kristine, and said, "And this one's yours." The dealer played out the hands and the dealer's bet lost, but Kristine's won. All of a sudden she was $100K richer.

Finally, Packer's known for not wanting to gamble around other gamblers. A story circulated after one of Packer's trips to Las Vegas that while he was playing in the high-limit pit at Bellagio, a gambler at another table was being particularly obnoxious. Packer suffered the boorish player in silence for a while. Finally, he got up, walked over, and asked the man to pipe down.

The man looked at Packer, incredulous that anyone would dare address someone of his caliber and standing in such a manner. "Do you know who I am?" he demanded.

"No," Packer replied.

"I'm [so and so] from Texas and I'm worth fifty million dollars!"

Packer cocked an eyebrow, shrugged, and said, "I'll flip you for it."

❖ ❖ ❖

Speaking of tokes, praises have been sung about the generosity of other mondo gamblers. One guy goes around buying tables. He'll breeze up to a blackjack layout where the players are betting $5 and $10 a hand and hand each one $500 to leave. Then he takes over the game.

A grizzled old floorman tells another tale of magnanimity. His big player, an Asian, was betting $15,000 a hand with yellow $1,000 bananas. Naturally, he drew a little crowd, among them a pregnant woman standing there with her husband. The pregnant woman asked out loud to no one in particular, "How much is that bet?"

The player looked over and said, "Thousand-dollar chips." He picked one up, handed it to her, and said, "Hold this for me, for luck."

Asians believe that pregnant women are lucky. Many won't play if the dealer is pregnant. Baccarat tables in high-limit pits clear out post haste when a pregnant dealer sits down.

The gambler kept playing and every time he won a bet, he handed the pregnant lady another banana. Over the course of 15 or 20 minutes, he gave her 25 or 30 of them, till finally the husband tried to give them back. But the player insisted they keep them. "No. Those are for you—and the baby."

The pregnant woman started crying. And everyone else at the table started crying. Even the seen-it-all floorman admits to getting choked up himself.

❖ ❖ ❖

Perhaps the most visible American whale is also a media mogul. Larry Flynt's life has taken him from an isolated upbringing in Appalachian Kentucky and stints on a General Motors assembly line, in the military, and in federal prison to an assassination attempt and an appearance in front of the U.S. Supreme Court. The result is a media empire that includes an I.M. Pei-designed Los Angeles skyscraper and upwards of 30 periodicals, including everything from the seminal *Hustler,* along with *Barely Legal, Busty, Legworld,* and *Hometown Girls,* to *PC Portables* and *Sci Fi Universe.* He's also a huge blackjack player who was losing millions at Caesars and the Rio when, in early 1996, Cyr noticed his jet-black G2 at McCarran Airport's private-aircraft terminal. He figured out who it belonged to and immediately went to work.

Cyr cold-called Larry at Flynt Publications. He was connected to his personal secretary and got by her with the line, "I'm supposed to talk to him in the meeting." Flynt hung up on him and scolded the secretary, but Cyr'd made the connection, and he began sending Flynt a weekly fruit basket. Every Monday like clockwork for six months, that $125 basket, filled with exotic fruits and chocolates, made its way to

Flynt's desk on the eighth floor of his Wilshire Boulevard office building. One Monday, the basket didn't show up and Flynt's secretary called Cyr: "Hey, where's the fruit? It's late."

Twice, Cyr flew down to L.A. in an attempt to see Flynt. The first time he made it as far as the secretary's desk on the seventh floor. Finally, the second time, Flynt's bodyguard came down to usher him up to Larry's office on the eighth floor, where he sits behind a 200-year-old five-foot-deep desk.

In his gravely voice flecked with a residual Kentucky accent, Flynt said to Cyr, "You're one persistent host. I feel like I owe you money."

"On the contrary, Mr. F, *I'm* trying to give *you* money— a hundred grand to come in and take a shot at the Hilton."

"Well, I'm gonna do it, this Saturday night. And I'll do the right thing, too. I'll match your hundred with a hundred of my own. Cash."

That Saturday night, Flynt's bodyguard phoned Cyr to confirm that they were coming over, then asked, "Is it all right if we bring a camera crew from '48 Hours'?"

Cyr knew all about the casino business' traditional aversion to media coverage, which more often than not has a negative slant. At the time, a number of network news magazines had recently aired uncomplimentary Las Vegas features. He didn't have the authority to give permission to a TV production crew to enter the casino and start shooting, Larry Flynt or no Larry Flynt.

He said, "Let me get back to you on that."

He reached the Hilton's director of publicity, who determined that it would be a great coup to get the casino some prime-time TV coverage. CBS was airing a Flynt segment in anticipation of the release of *The People Vs. Larry Flynt*, a movie starring Woody Harrelson and Courtney Love, and he gave Cyr the go-ahead.

Cyr and Jim Bradshaw met Flynt and his fiancée Liz Berrios at the front door. Flynt told Bradshaw, "Your boy Cyr's the best. He never gave up on me, and here I am."

In a quick whispered conference, Cyr asked Flynt not to talk about three things on camera: his 20% discount on losses, his $100,000 show-up money, and the $30,000 diamond earrings Liz selected on her shopping spree at the Hilton jewelry store.

Also, before letting him gamble, Cyr whisked Flynt up to the Sky Villas, figuring he'd hook Larry and get some footage for the "48 Hours" cameras at the same time.

Finally, Flynt sat down in the baccarat room at a blackjack table specially lowered to wheelchair height. Cyr presented him with four $25,000 promotional chips, then Flynt opened his briefcase and pulled out $100K in cash. With the "48 Hours" cameras rolling, he looked directly into the lens and said, "If I lose a million, I only have to pay eight hundred thousand."

Cut to Liz. "And they gave me these beautiful diamond earrings!"

Flynt won a million that night on camera at the Hilton (then went over to the Rio and lost it all there). Subsequently, Cyr's phone rang for a week non-stop, with big and small players alike demanding, "What the fuck is this business about rebates on losses? Why don't you give *me* one?"

(Still, the Hilton didn't do too badly. There was no negative publicity. In fact, the piece made a big deal out of Flynt winning a million dollars there, which is always good for stimulating the gambling itch in viewers. It showed the Sky Villas. It showed the baccarat room. It showed someone famous having a good time. There was, however, a little fallout, stemming from the fact that Flynt walked the million right over to the Rio, and promptly lost it. The Hilton bosses thought they looked like marks. A head had to roll. The Hilton's PR director was immediately termed—casino PR people are almost as vulnerable to the whims of the pink-slip gods as dealers.)

Cyr hosted Flynt for a few years at the Hilton. Larry always wanted a Sky Villa. He always wanted to be told that he was the biggest player in the joint—and he almost always was, playing three hands of $10,000 to $15,000 each, hour after hour, sometimes 24 hours in a row. He was a tough, disciplined, basic-strategy player (though the pros noted that he made a strategy mistake on camera). And he never got bombed at the table. He drank coffee. If he had wine during dinner, Cyr knew he was going to bed.

He was Cyr's only player, in nine years at the Hilton, whom Barron Hilton himself deigned to meet. Hilton liked to dine on occasion with Flynt and it was a huge harpoon for Cyr: "Larry? Barron Hilton wants to have dinner with you this weekend."

On one occasion, Flynt had been on a phenomenal winning streak. He'd beaten the Hilton up for more than $10 million over the course of a dozen visits. As always, Jimmy Newman was solid granite; he knew Flynt was just borrowing the money. Jim Bradshaw, too, successfully fended off the CFO and the Hilton kept dealing to Flynt. Finally, the casino ordered a three-foot-tall trophy with the inscription, "From Barron Hilton to Larry Flynt, the World's Greatest Blackjack Player." Barron Hilton presented it to him personally. But it was all a set-up, a little superstitious play: They were giving Flynt the broom (a hex). That night, he lost $3 million. And he continued to lose, to the tune of many millions more.

At one point, Flynt stopped paying. He owed $3.2 million and was 90 days overdue. The Hilton had yet to make a penny off him. They'd paid out millions in winnings. They'd given him show-up money, the Villas, gifts, and discounts. Cyr had no choice. He had to snap him and dump the markers. He went to Flynt's bank, on the bottom floor of his own office building, and asked for the money. The bank called upstairs. A small scene ensued, but the Hilton got its money, though Larry and Steve's relationship soured for a while.

Finally, Flynt asked Cyr for a favor. He was marrying Liz and he wanted to have his bachelor party at the Beverly

Hills Hilton. Cyr called the sister property and asked; it took approximately two seconds for them to turn him down. Then Cyr came up with a better idea and called Jeff Armstrong, the blackjack high roller who'd performed at the Hard Rock's Joint. Thanks to Armstrong's palatial L.A. home and Steve Cyr's party planning, Flynt's bachelor party was a smash and Cyr was back in Flynt's good graces.

❖ ❖ ❖

Plenty of famous businessmen, athletes, actors, entertainers, and politicians like to gamble in casinos. They play a little, tip appropriately, and don't make a big deal out of themselves. Bill Gates, for example, enjoys low-stakes blackjack and poker (though he's stingy with tokes). John McCain, U.S. Senator from Arizona, likes to shoot craps. Once, shortly after making a rousing speech on the evils of legal betting on college sporting events, he showed up in Las Vegas that same night and fired it up at a dice tables at Caesars. Actor Chuck Norris and former tennis champ Jimmy Connors are low-limit crap players. Golf pros Greg Norman and Phil Mickelson like to gamble.

Only a few famous people, however, fall within the ranks of high rollers. One is Ben Affleck, who has a $500,000 credit line at the Hard Rock. He plays in the Peacock Lounge, the Hard Rock's high-limit room (in which Jimi Hendrix's famed peacock vest is on display), and he's been known to make bets as high as $10,000 a hand.

Affleck's a well-known George who's been known to toke the dealers and waitresses thousands of dollars at a time. However, after hooking up with Jennifer Lopez, a.k.a. J.Lo, he seemed to change his ways. It wasn't surprising, perhaps, given that players are always a little more conservative when they're with their significant others. Still, the dealers blamed Affleck's change in attitude on Lopez—whom they dubbed "Pay Lo."

Affleck reportedly won $700,000 playing blackjack in the

Peacock Lounge in May 2003, then slipped a $500 tip to a poolside cocktail waitress. A lot of good it did him to sneak the toke: Jenny from the Block might have read about it in one of several hundred newspapers that ran the wire-service item. When Ben and Jen broke up, the tabloids reported that his gambling was partly to blame. Ironically, a short time later, Jennifer Lopez' mother hit a Wheel of Fortune jackpot for $2.4 million at the Borgata in Atlantic City and Affleck won a big poker championship in California.

Affleck's friend Matt Damon, who starred in the poker movie *Rounders* and is occasionally seen at Las Vegas poker tables, reportedly has a $100,000 credit line at the Hard Rock.

❖ ❖ ❖

For a time, Steve Cyr hosted Michael Jordan, whom he met through a clothing-industry contact. Cyr likes to attend Jordan's Senior Flight School basketball clinic, which costs $15,000 a pop.

Jordan is a gambler in the Denny Mason and Kerry Packer mold. To him it's not gambling; it's competition. He's driven to win. He's looking for every edge. And if the money on the line makes his opponent choke, raise the stakes! It's not like he doesn't have enough; Hanes alone could cover his high-roller action for several lifetimes. He likes to gamble on golf. And there's a lot of betting at his clinics. He'll bet $100 that you miss your next free throw. He'll bet $1,000 that he can beat you 10-zip in a game of one-on-one. And the stakes aren't limited to money. He'll bet cigars. He'll bet push-ups (you have to do a certain number if you lose)—then he'll bet again that you can't do them.

His Airness likes to play blackjack at $500 to $10,000 a hand. He'll lose $200,000, $300,000 at a session. He plays basic strategy and he's a fairly dangerous player. Why? Bankroll. He's not afraid to press his bets or chase his losses, and he's got so much money, he can go on a tear and rip up a joint. Jordan is said to have won $1.7 million playing black-jack at the MGM Grand in February 2003. But it didn't get him even; it's believed that he was into the Grand for $2 million at the time.

By all accounts Jordan's a regular guy. He likes to smoke a cigar while he plays. He adores women, who respond in kind. He's friendly with guys. One time he agreed to make an appearance at a Cyr-hosted party in a Sky Villa; Cyr's top players were thrilled to meet the superstar.

There's the love. There's the fever. And then there's Michael Jordan, the rare soul who transcends gambling for the sport of it.

❖ ❖ ❖

Of all the Las Vegas high-roller events Steve Cyr has planned, hosted, or attended, two have surprised him.

One was during the World Wrestling Federation road show. He never, in a million years, expected any of his players to want to attend a WWF (now WWE) performance. He didn't even buy tickets. But all of a sudden, customers were calling and clamoring to get in. He managed to handle most of them, but Tina Jones had to run down to the arena with cash to buy the rest from scalpers.

The other was Howard Stern.

Stern has made four public appearances at Las Vegas' Hard Rock: over Super Bowl weekends 2001 and 2002, in April 2003, and in May 2004. It's rumored that he received more than a million dollars from the Hard Rock for each appearance.

Cyr couldn't believe his eyes on the shock jock's first visit. He wasn't able to park within a half-mile of the casino. People began lining up 24 hours before Stern's arrival so they could get in. At one point, security guards had to lock the Hard Rock doors when the size of the crowd exceeded the fire-code limit. That only happens on New Year's Eve. Forget the Rolling Stones. Forget Barbra Streisand. Forget New Year's Eve! Howard Stern could be the current biggest draw in Las Vegas. Especially for the Hard Rock crowd.

During his first three appearances, Stern sponsored a $100,000 hand of blackjack. The proceeds of the bet, if it won, were promised to the winner of a contest to find the sorriest sob story among listeners. The Hard Rock agreed to book the bet—Hard Rock versus Hard Luck.

The first year, a dealt 19 stood up against the dealer's draw to 18 and Hard Luck won the cash. The second year, Hard Rock got its revenge when Hard Luck hit and busted a 15 against a dealer 10. The third year, Hard Luck was dealt a 16. The dealer turned up a 10. Hard Luck, predictably, was a big dog. According to basic strategy, the better play is to hit. It's not better by much—the difference between hitting and standing in this situation is among the closest decisions in all of gambling—but hitting is still better.

An on-air debate ensued. Almost everyone within microphone range endorsed standing on the 16. Stern, to his credit, argued for a hit. In the end Hard Luck stood and Hard Rock flipped over a 10 in the hole for a pat 20 and its second $100K win in as many years. Would the correct play have saved the day? Not this time—the next card was a 6. Hard Luck, true to its name, was doomed from the deal.

All four years, predictably, sex was the prevalent theme of the event, but gambling was a close second. Every radio segment broadcast from Las Vegas seemed to touch on blackjack in one way or another. The on-air personalities played. Special guests played. And the audience played … for all kinds of things. They played for dates with porn stars, for boob jobs, and, of course, for the cash.

Stern played, too. Not on the air, but in between shows. Each morning, he discussed his forays to the tables, during which the listening audience got significant insight into his gambling modus operandi. Is Howard Stern a skilled gambler? Not even close. In fact, he could be the poster boy for gambling misinformation. He talked about streaks and luck and a progressive system he'd bought into. None has any bearing on gambling results, but it's not uncommon for otherwise intelligent people to believe that they do. Why? Because they're easy, and no one wants gambling to be hard.

Though he doesn't appear to be much of a casino gambler, Stern and his morning radio crew continually bet on different propositions. In one bit from early 2003 known as "Stump the Stripper," they wagered on whether a girl would know the answers to simple questions. "What's the temperature at which water freezes?" "How many people are in a quartet?" "What's twenty percent of two hundred?" "What's income-tax deadline day?" Stern, who gave one particular stripper some credit for intelligence, bet that she'd know most of the answers—and cleaned up against sidekick Robin Quivers, who went on tilt and wound up losing more than $2,000.

During his second appearance at the Hard Rock in 2002, Stern reportedly had a party in his room with all the girls from Club Paradise (the jiggle joint across the street); they all said he was mellow. He was also cool about hosting a meet-and-greet event for invited guests. Cyr was blown away by how many of his top players wanted to get into that party. Whatever Stern's charging the Hard Rock to appear, even if it's a million, he should double it—for all the big play that follows in his wake.

❖ ❖ ❖

When Cyr first got into the gambling business, 100% of his good customers were men. Their wives or girlfriends, if they gambled, played roulette or slot machines. At roulette, they plunked down red and green chips on the numbers. At the machines, they fed in quarters and dollars; here and there a woman loaded up $5, $25, even $100 slots. Then as now, any woman (or man, for that matter), playing $100 slot machines with abandon is a whale. Today, almost all female whales are million-dollar slot players.

Ten years ago, Cyr hosted one $100,000 female dice player. She was more than just a rare exception; she was one of a kind. Not only did she play craps, she was a crap high roller. She was also the loudest player at the table. Of course, as a trader on the floor of a stock exchange, she was accustomed to loud, and she could well afford her $1,000 bets.

This state of distaff affairs remained in place up until the mid-'90s, when Cyr began noticing more and more women playing the table games. By then, casino gambling had spread around the country. All of a sudden, it was cool for women to gamble at the tables. They got to fire it up alongside the guys, proving that they knew the rules, strategies, etiquette, and lingo. They got to show off their *own* money.

Today, a lot of women have $10,000, $20,000, even $50,000 credit lines. Some are in business, especially real estate. Others are flush with divorce settlements or alimony. They mostly like blackjack; the biggest 21 bet Cyr's seen a woman make was $5,000.

Another gender trend of the past few years has been premium male players burning out on tables and turning to video poker. At the machines, they don't have to toke hundreds or thousands of dollars, or not toke and run the risk of earning a reputation as a stiff. They don't have to be sociable when they're losing. They don't have to bet as high. They think they can beat the game, because it requires skill. And the comps are just as good.

Also, the jackpot is always hovering. If a crap or blackjack player with a $25,000 limit loses $20,000, he's in the grease. He has to put out the rest of his chips and hope to luck into the run of his life just to get even. That same player on a video poker game, loading up a $5 single-play machine with $25 a hand, knows that all he needs is one royal flush to make it up. And it's been known to happen.

The differences between male and female high-stakes

gamblers, and what they want for their play, are pronounced. Men and women want limos and suites and shows, but that's where the similarities end.

For example, women want the spa. Men could care less about manicures and pedicures and getting the same hairdresser every time. Women like their shopping sprees. But except for the shopping, they prefer to stay on property.

Most women don't want to play golf. They don't want to go to prizefights (they'll come in for fight weekends and hosts often hold out tickets for them, but it's just for show; the tickets almost always go to men players at the last minute). They don't bet sports. They don't want hosts to accompany them to topless clubs. They don't want paid sex; Host X, in his long experience, has never, not once, been asked for a male hooker by a female gambler, though they are available, especially on the Web. They don't pound alcohol at the tables and they don't get falling-down drunk.

The deal's not as important to women. They rarely bargain at all, let alone hard, for show-up money, discounts on losses, or airfare reimbursement. For all intents and purposes, women gamblers are still the "new virgins of the casino." Hosts don't have to go through a big rigmarole to say no to a woman. In fact, women players often prefer to deal with the VIP Services hostesses for their comp arrangements and reservations. Surprisingly, they're much lower maintenance for hosts than men.

Some women are whiners, of course, though others are less immediately vocal about everything. If a host angers a woman gambler, she might not tell him. She simply won't come back. Piss off a guy and he'll be in your face. It's a simple fact of nature: Women are harder for male hosts to read. Even so, they prefer male hosts and VIP services hostesses to women hosts. They like the guys fawning over them.

One thing they seem to share with most men gamblers is that streak of exhibitionism. Women players like to be seen. They get spiffed up in fancy clothes and jewelry to play. They want to be recognized for having money. Ironically, when a man sees a woman betting big, he automatically thinks, *Oh, she's with the guy over there at the baccarat table; he threw her ten grand to go have a good time while he plays twenty-five K a hand.*

The young female high rollers are often mistaken for hookers. They're dressed to kill, they're alone, and they're firing it up at the high-minimum tables. It's a bit strange, since hookers, in casinos anyway, no longer look like hookers. But women gamblers, especially the young, attractive, well-dressed ones betting $250 or $500 or $1,000 a hand, are still unusual enough to draw attention, which suggests to many uninformed observers a certain stereotype.

This isn't to imply that some women gamblers aren't workin' it. They're playing in the big leagues and trying to attract attention from the moneyed males.

Deep down, in the final analysis, women gamblers are no different than men. They too have the gambling itch, and in today's world they can scratch it with relative impunity and anonymity. If they have a big bankroll and the gambling gene, they can play to win with the best of 'em. They want more.

17

Where Are They Now?

The job of the high-level casino marketing executive is to get the premium player into the casino. Once he sits down and starts to gamble, the host can relax. Now it's up to operations—the dealer, floorman, cocktail waitress, credit manager, and cage cashier, along with the house advantage and all the bells and whistles—to get the money. The host is simply a game *starter*. The game never stops. Love and fever, greed and fear, make sure the game goes on and on and on. It's going on right now.

Only the players change.

❖ ❖ ❖

Jeff Armstrong, the high-stakes blackjack player whose dream was to perform on the stage of the Joint at the Hard Rock, died of a heroin overdose in 2002 at the age of 44. At the time of his death, he owed casinos seven figures. (Before gambling debts became legally collectible, when a gambler died, his outstanding markers were mostly buried with him. The casinos wrote them off after they received a copy of the death certificate. That didn't mean they were happy about it. In fact, a story is told about a credit manager who heard that a player passed away and his first words weren't, "How did he die?" or "Sorry to hear that," or "How's his wife taking it?" Instead, this credit manager's first words were, "Does he owe?" To-day, gambling debts are paid off by the estate of the deceased.)

Gus Johnson, the L.A. dot-commer who flew to Las Vegas every weekend for two years, got over his $6 million in losses—and his broken heart. Eventually, he went back to playing blackjack, but only for thousands, rather than millions. He realized somewhere along the way that he doesn't enjoy gambling all that much. It bores him. But he still does it—for the comps. And to impress the girls. And to get his ass kissed. But now he bargains hard over his required minimum bet and hours. If he's told he has to gamble only an hour a day, that's all he plays. The three words he hates to hear the most are, "You haven't qualified."

Fast Eddie D, the crap whale, now lives in Costa Rica and owns part of a casino there. He finally got fed up with the long cold winters in Montana. His 25,000-square-foot house is still for sale.

Carroll and Jean Cyr are retired. They sold the Howard Johnson's motel and now travel around the country, visiting their kids and grandkids and attending University of Kansas Jayhawks basketball games.

Guy Hudson is retired. He misses the action and would love to work a day or two a week. He reads Nelson DeMille, John Grisham, and Tom Clancy. He plays golf. He gets together with Cyr on occasion to talk about high rollers.

Johnny Oakes is retired and living in Nebraska.

Denny Mason got fed up with table games and slots and swore them off for five full years. But that doesn't mean he wasn't in the action. He scratches the itch by betting on lots of different things, especially athletic propositions in which he participates. The appeal to Mason is getting good enough at something—ping-pong, pool, golf, tennis, darts, foosball—that he can make money on it. That's what the sporting life is all about.

Tina Jones went to work for the Rio as a floor host. She

was extremely aggressive, telemarketing constantly, but she still got termed. She now works as a host at the Palms.

Speaking of secretaries, the day Charlie Myerson, the superhost from the Mirage, retired, his $45,000-a-year secretary was the most popular girl in town. She'd been with him for more than a decade and knew everything and everyone. The Rio tried to get her. The Hilton tried to get her. She and her Rolodex finally wound up at MGM Grand, making three times her secretary's salary.

Al Franco, the Phoenix contractor, didn't blame Cyr for giving him back the check for $400,000. He claims he would've killed Cyr for the money at the time. He started a small construction company that specializes in home repairs and remodels. He and his wife live in an apartment. He comes around once in a while and tries his luck at a blackjack table with a hundred-dollar bankroll playing $5 chips. He knows now that there's nothing like a monster loss to get your greed under control. He takes it one day at a time. Every day is a better day than his worst days. Even the bad days.

Bill Nilsen, the high roller who wound up in jail in L.A., never recovered financially from those travails. After settling the legal matter, he moved in with a relative, where he still, at last report, lives.

The 21-year-old kid who lost $400,000 in a few months got out of rehab. The last time Cyr heard about him, he owed a bookie $100,000.

Kerry Packer hasn't been back to the MGM Grand since being barred.

Larry Flynt was loyal to the Hilton till Steve Cyr left. After that, he never went back. He now plays at the Venetian and the Golden Nugget.

Robert Coury, the MGM floorman who wound up as one of Cyr's orangutans, went back to being a floorman, at Green Valley Ranch Station in Henderson.

Doug Bean is a financial planner.

Dan London sells Cadillacs at a big San Francisco car dealership.

Ray McIntosh is the head host at Palace Station.

Nick Ippolito for a time was the lead host at Paris. He's now in charge of all the branch offices at Caesars, where he and Cyr first met more than 15 years ago.

Ian Andersen wrote a second book about beating black-jack, in which he divulged a number of ploys in his casino-busting repertoire. He's still out there, flying first-class around the world, plying his trade as a professional player, pretending to be a high-rolling sucker, employing ever more sophisticated gambits to get away with the money.

Caesars and the other premium casinos that sent bill-backs to their competitors finally got smart and started dispatching security guards to pick up show tickets for customers, which means they no longer have to go to the competitor's VIP Services, just the showroom. Every measure has a countermeasure, but it took millions of dollars of lost play before Caesars, the Mirage, et al. wised up.

A mere five years after investing nearly $60 million in six villas, the Hilton's high-roller days were mostly over. Now, you can get a Sky Villa with a $100,000 credit line and there are no butlers on the 30th floor. In fact, Hilton no longer owns the Hilton; it was bought for $280 million in early 2004 by Colony Capital, one of the largest real estate investment trusts in the world.

Steve Wynn sold Mirage Resorts to MGM Grand in 2000, bought the 180-acre Desert Inn property, imploded most of the buildings, and is developing the $2.4 billion Wynn Las Vegas. He has a huge harpoon for high rollers in the completely refurbished 18-hole golf course on the property. He's also building 18 stand-alone villas that line the links for his premium players. Five minutes before tee time, a player will be able to walk out his villa door and right onto the course. Five minutes after his round, he'll be able to have a drink on his own patio. No 25-minute limo rides necessary. In addition, WLV will boast a high-roller hotel-within-a-hotel, with 300 premium suites strategically positioned to feed directly into the baccarat pit.

Blue whales are still as long as 10-story buildings are tall. Humpbacks still do back flips. Kids still ride orcas around aquarium pools.

❖ ❖ ❖

At the end of nearly a decade in its employ, Cyr finally wore out his welcome at the Las Vegas Hilton. But they had to live with him for a while longer, for two reasons: First, he was their superhost; second, he had an airtight contract. They'd investigated him for years. A few of the casino bosses, but mostly security, wanted to catch him at something—with a hooker, taking kickbacks, drunk on duty—that would allow them to term him. They eventually came up with questionable cause and set him loose. Cyr sued for wrongful termination and lost. The judge barred him from soliciting customers for casinos in Clark County for the remainder of his contract, almost a year.

So he went independent and began working as a contract player representative for Barona, a big Native American casino near San Diego, as well as Atlantis and the Crystal Palace in the Bahamas. After waiting out his year, he picked up the Hard Rock and Binion's Horseshoe. His host company is called HSix, his host code at the Las Vegas Hilton. It's symbolic: The Hilton might've termed him, but it's still full speed ahead for HSix.

Cyr always thought he had to be a suit. He had to work for a large corporation and navigate through the corporate culture to make a lot of money. Now he knows how wrong he was. But he didn't come to that realization on his own. He had to be forced out to see it. In the end, the Hilton did him a favor.

As an independent player rep, Cyr doesn't earn a salary

or year-end bonus. No casino corporation pays for vacation time or health insurance or matches his Social Security taxes. He's remunerated strictly on the play of his gamblers.

At Barona, he has a straightforward deal based on the amount of money he brings in. Being one of only three casinos in the San Diego metropolitan area, Barona can get away with deals that wouldn't fly in Las Vegas. It doesn't offer show-up chips. It doesn't offer discounts on losses. It ponies up with plenty of other perks, of course; in 2003, for example, Barona executives spent millions on tickets to the Super Bowl played in San Diego—40-yard-line, seventh row, $5,000 apiece.

Also, being in California and on a reservation, Barona does other things a little differently than Nevada casinos. It has private entrances to its high-roller facilities: parking, suites, gambling parlors. It also offers some of the best blackjack rules in the country, along with some of the highest limits: up to $50,000 a hand. It's got the San Diego area wired and comps players everything from Coronado and Catalina to Sea World and the zoo. Cyr sells the sizzle of forsaking Vegas for a change and taking advantage of southern California.

His sales pitch for Atlantis on Paradise Island in the Bahamas is similar, though his deal with the casino is based on each player's theoretical loss. The Hard Rock and Binion's Horseshoe paid on theoretical as well, while Cyr repped for them. With his theo-based deals, he gets to root *for* his players. His commission isn't dependent on their losses, so it doesn't matter if they win or lose, and they're much more fun to be around when they win. With theoretical, he gets to be real, instead of pretend, friends with all his players. It's a new sensation for him, after nearly 20 years of secretly rooting against.

❖ ❖ ❖

In early 2004, Cyr joined forces with Tim Poster and Tom Breitling, two thirtysomething whiz kids who, in their early twenties, started a Web-based travel-reservations service, Travelscape.com, and later sold it to Expedia for nearly $100 million. In January 2004, they took over the Golden Nugget in downtown Las Vegas, after buying it for $215 million from MGM Mirage, and proceeded to turn it into the kind of mecca for hard-core big-time gamblers that Binion's Horseshoe used to be.

One of "Tim and Tom's" first moves was to lock up Las Vegas' premier superhost, who signed a contract making the Golden Nugget his exclusive casino in Nevada. Cyr can still host for Barona and Atlantis and Crystal Palace, but it was goodbye Hard Rock and the Horseshoe.

Cyr's back in the saddle at the Golden Nugget. He likes that Tim and Tom are ambitious, entrepreneurial, and have a bankroll—they don't mind spending money to make money. He likes that they're independent—they don't have to go to any board of directors and ask if it's okay to make a move. (They own a majority share. Tennis superstar André Agassi holds a minority share. A few of the bondholders own shares as well.) If Tim and Tom want to do something, they do it.

He likes having young bosses. They're not as set in their ways as the old-timers. They're open to new ideas. Actually, since they've never been in the casino business, all the ideas are new to them. They say to Cyr, "You tell us what it's going to take to bring your players in. You tell us what you want to make the Golden Nugget your new casino home." Cyr can't remember Jimmy Newman or Peter Morton or Barron Hilton ever saying such a thing.

So Cyr told them. He wanted to train their hosts on how to be aggressive and attract new business. He wanted to be involved with marketing. He suggested sponsoring celebrity poker tournaments and establishing a Sharper Image suite—filling one of GN's 1,500-square-foot high-roller digs with a couple hundred Sharper Image products, from plasma TVs and massage chairs to pinball machines and electronic toothbrushes. The idea is to shop for the stuff by using it; via the on-site touch-screen catalog, you can buy something you've tried and liked—the Bose wave radio, the electric tie rack, the shoeshiner, the shaving mirror.

His players like the Golden Nugget for its high limits. Tim and Tom have plunged into whale waters so deep that the Nugget now joins MGM Grand, Bellagio, Mirage, and the Venetian in taking Las Vegas' current biggest bets: $100,000 at blackjack and baccarat and $110,000 at craps (10X odds on a $10,000 pass-line bet when 6 or 8 is the point). Larry Flynt comes to the Golden Nugget now. Flynt's first trip to the GN was the first time in four years Cyr hosted him, thanks to the limits. Several other million-dollar players now frequent GN.

At the Golden Nugget, his deal is a closely guarded secret; Cyr is uncharacteristically tight-lipped about it. All he'll say is that for Tim and Tom to woo him away from the Hard Rock, they had to make him happy. And he's *very* happy. He claims it's the deal of the century and the only one of its kind in Nevada.

❖ ❖ ❖

Though he's still basically independent—no suits, no timeclocks, not much office politics—Cyr also likes being part of a team again. He missed the intense pressure of working on property, though he didn't miss working for limp dicks. He's also a bit wistful, interestingly, for the old days, when business was conducted a lot less formally and more autonomously. It's another reason he loves working at the Golden Nugget. He can call up, talk to one of the owners, and get something done. He doesn't have to yell at four bosses to sign off on a comp. No one tells him to fill out a form with a name and player tracking number that goes to accounting for approval. Hell, no one asks him if it's a player at all. A friend of a big gambler is coming in and needs a room? One phone call and it's all set up. It keeps the big gambler happy, and no one screams because the player isn't there himself, losing. In Las Vegas, comps make the world go round.

He's still friendly with plenty of holdover hosts and now likes to tag-team players with the older guys. If he makes a connection with Mr. S, a 70-year-old, and determines that he'd rather be hosted by someone his own age, Cyr'll lay him off on an old-school guy. It works in reverse too. "Don't deal with that old fart!" he might tell a younger player. "You're thirty-five years old. He'll take you to a fox-trot dance. I'll take you to the topless clubs. ..." All the while, Cyr's splitting the commission with the "old fart."

He's still down on greeter and maintenance hosts. He claims that of the 520 hosts in Las Vegas, only 20 are hustlers from the Steve Cyr School of Player Representation. These top hosts aren't afraid of getting termed from their cushy six-figure jobs. They're aggressive and creative. They know how to telemarket and hook new fish.

The other 500? According to Cyr, they're afraid of their shadows. They still stand around the cage trying to meet gamblers who're already in the joint. They cling for dear life— by overcomping them—to the few big kahunarollers they somehow bumble onto. They make $100,000 a year and haven't brought in any fresh business for half a decade.

What's more, Cyr insists that the service levels are down. The casinos simply aren't taking care of their premium players—like they would if he were in charge. If Cyr were running the joint, every host would make $52,000 a year. A grand a week in salary. That's plenty. But every three months, they'd get a bonus based on the losses of *new business*. That's how he'd create hungry stop-at-nothing root-for-losers salespeople, hosts who constantly push the edge of the envelope, tapping ever deeper into the love and the fever.

❖ ❖ ❖

It's not, however, the hosts' fault entirely. Part of the problem faced by Las Vegas' 500 or so casino marketing suits is caused by a lack of proper tools. The casino industry is still bringing up the rear of the parade of information technology. It's been said that you could put a dollar bill into a Coke machine decades before you could put a dollar bill into a slot machine. Casinos are getting up to speed in security and surveillance tech, operations electronics, accounting software, and the like, but they're still quite backwards in database marketing.

For example, at most casinos today, telemarketing systems often consist of hosts receiving players' names listed on a stack of green-bar graph paper that comes off dot-matrix printers. The host phones the players to invite them to the casino's New Year's Eve party, say, crossing them off the list with a magic marker. He needs to be computer savvy, strictly organized, and highly motivated to track even just the basics of his calls—if he left a message on a machine or got a busy signal or no one answered, or, if he spoke to someone, who it was and what was said.

To address casino marketing inefficiencies, a new software suite called Mariposa was recently launched, which combines player-contact, casino-mapping, and data-warehousing functions.

With Mariposa's player-contact program, all of a host's customers have dedicated file space in the marketing database, accessible with the click of a mouse. A host can call dozens of players a day, record exactly what transpires over the phone with a few keystrokes, schedule follow-up calls, build customer profiles, and track and analyze results.

In addition, when a player arrives at the casino, Mariposa uses mapping technology to locate him, via the existing player-tracking system, on the casino floor. A table-game player hands his rating card to a floorman who types the name into the system. A slot player inserts his club card into a machine, which relays the information to the marketing database at light speed. When the host pulls up a real-time map of the casino, he sees exactly where his two players are sitting. A host's every customer is displayed on the map whenever he cares to look.

Now that he knows he has two players on property, the host simply has to open their files to access accrued details about them. Even if the host has met a player only once and can't remember a single thing about him, Mariposa lets him know his play history, the games he prefers, the days of the week he comes in, whether he stays at the hotel, if he's checked into the hotel, what kind of room he likes, whether he eats at the buffet or the steakhouse—all the information a rep needs to have a meaningful conversation with the player.

After a customer stays in a non-smoking room with a king bed once or twice, a host should never again have to ask what kind of room that player wants. Instead, he merely has to verify. "Still staying in that non-smoking king?"

The host can also use Mariposa's filters to get a big-picture view of his players. He can instruct the system to give him a list of the customers with the highest value who are currently in the casino, or the players who haven't shown up for six months, or everyone with $500 or more in available comps, or even everyone eating in the buffet. The end game is to make the player feel like he's special, that someone at his favorite casino remembers him.

What Cyr sneeringly refers to as greeter hosts still work in an essentially reactive capacity—customers are taken care of when they get to the casino, but only if someone happens to know they're there. Mariposa (and other new marketing software) is proactive, allowing hosts to identify and locate customers as soon as they participate in a trackable activity, or to phone customers when they're not in the casino and invite them in.

Using the new tools, hosts can manage more players, which, in turn, allows casinos to lower the criteria that determine whether a player qualifies for hosting. Then host managers can hire more hosts and extend hosting services to more players.

It's as predictable as it is ironic: The young Turks of the new school eventually turn into the relics of the old school. Hosting is poised to become a giant video game and the practitioners most proficient with the game controllers will render Steve Cyr's once-revolutionary tactics quaint and antiquated.

❖ ❖ ❖

That'll be just fine with Cyr, though, who no longer wants to work as hard as he used to. At the ripe old age of 40, he'd like to slow down a little. In another ironic twist of fate, Cyr is in a position to sit back a bit and rely on his established heavy hitters.

That's not to say he turns down cush jobs when they're offered to him. He recently added Marriott St. Kitts to his Caribbean casino roster. He also signed on with Norwegian Cruise Lines as an independent rep for the *Norwegian Star* high-roller cruise ship. The *Star* has high limits, discounts on losses, villas, and a captive audience—nowhere to go and nothing to do but play high-stakes craps, blackjack, or baccarat for a week off the coast of the Mexican Riviera. Anytime his players' credit lines add up to $200,000 or more, he and Tanya get a comped suite on the ship.

Speaking of Tanya, who has the dramatic beauty of a Latin movie star, a sweet disposition, and a strong work ethic, she's never far from Steve's side—now that they're married. Her two kids, Nick and Chelcee, live with them. In addition, every week without fail, Cyr visits his eight-year-old daughter Savanna, who lives in southern California.

These days, Cyr's often in the media spotlight. He's been profiled in nearly every Las Vegas periodical and he was declared Casino Host of the Year by *Las Vegas Life* magazine. His story's also been told by *Details, Cigar Aficionado* (twice),

FHM, and *Maxim.* He's made a couple of cameos in *USA Today.* He's appeared on broadcast news magazines like "20/20 Downtown" with Barbara Walters, as well as on numerous Las Vegas specials on the Travel, Discovery, and History channels. And he has a small role as a host in the CBS "Doctor Vegas" TV series with Rob Lowe, premiering in fall 2004.

Lately, he's apt to be squiring TV producers and camera crews and stray writers around town in the Disco Bus, a distinctive 33-foot-long party on wheels. It's a customized rental-car shuttle—sort of a limo with enough head room to be popular with professional basketball players. The interior is pimped out with darkly tinted windows, Venetian blinds, a motorized privacy partition, fiber-optic lighting strips bordering the painted ceiling, and a plush leather couch that runs almost completely around the perimeter of the interior. A big-screen TV occupies the whole back wall (often playing some seriously nasty pornography), and the audio system fills the van with concert-quality sound. Three wet bars with open coolers are kept stocked with beer, booze, and mixers on ice. Prices vary, but roughly $1,000 a day provides on-call service from one of three buses running around town; they pick you up wherever you are and drop you off wherever you want to go. They're owned and operated by the aptly named Johnny Fever, who's been around long enough to have an A-list of clients—entertainers, athletes, executives, and, of course, hosts and their high rollers.

When last seen, in fact, Steve and Tanya were riding into the sunset in the Disco Bus, with a film crew taping the pilot for an eight-episode reality-TV series, tentatively titled "The Whale Hunter," based on their lives as a husband-and-wife Las Vegas superhost team. The show was scheduled to air on Showtime sometime in the summer of 2004.

Epilogue
Greed and Fear Redux

Why do people gamble? From where does the gambling impulse spring? Is it a different urge for a nickel slot jockey, an $11 sports bettor, a $1,000 blackjack high roller, or a $150,000 baccarat whale?

To arrive at the answers, it's necessary to examine the strata of skin that screen the genetic itch.

The surface layer consists of the slogans of casino marketing. Gaming is casual, recreational, social, a night out, over-21 fun. At the resort-casino, you can drink, eat, see a show or movie, bowl, ice skate, even drop your kids in the child-care facilities—and incidentally, you did realize you can also try your luck at our adult midway, didn't you? And if you do, your beverage, food, room, and entertainment will all be *free*. And the more money you play with, the bigger the kewpie doll you'll win. This is the love. And like the outermost peel of an onion, once this top layer is removed and tossed in the compost, the bitter fruit is exposed.

The next layer is a little more pungent. It's the one based on greed. Most mere mortals playing for nickel, quarter, dollar, even five-dollar stakes gamble because they want to be rich. They want to be struck by the lightning of instant unearned wealth, the life-changing jackpot that takes away their anxieties about survival, the drudgery of earning a living, the sacrificing to make ends meet, and replaces them with freedom from financial insecurity, limitless possessions, endless leisure, infinite pleasures, even control over lesser mortals.

Of course, instant riches typically happen to someone else. Still, greed remains the core of the calculus, that fond function of the mind that enumerates what you'd do if you ever *did* hit the elusive jackpot. Low rollers gamble simply to dream of being rich—the next best thing to having a fortune is having a shot at one.

Okay, but high rollers are already rich. Anyone who can lay down $1,000 to $250,000 per hand, 60 or so an hour, all weekend long, is free and secure and can well afford all the hedonistic pampering the mind can imagine and the body can withstand. Why do *they* gamble?

For that matter, plenty of players aren't materially wealthy, but are rich in optimism and creativity and fulfillment. Why do *they* gamble?

Why does anyone gamble?

After the whole skin has been peeled away, you're left with the seed of an answer: the ontogeny of risk-taking.

❖ ❖ ❖

Risk-taking is one of the great conditioning factors of life itself. Gambling was an integral force—indeed, often the guiding principle—in a majority of the most primitive cultures. Which means that the gambling impulse has been with us—in us—since we've been human.

The human race evolved in an environment of risk and danger and chance—in a word, uncertainty. The physiological attitude of readiness, the ability to assume risk, to challenge chance, to plunge into uncertainty, these are survival traits favored by natural selection. Senses, strength, coordination, reflex, judgment, metabolism are all heightened during an encounter with a challenge; they all increase the likelihood of not only the success, but also the efficiency, of the human response to risk.

The impulse to plunge into uncertainty is usually acquisitive in nature. A risk-taker wants to gain something—property, knowledge, experience, power—from the risk-taking. In this sense, greed is an evolutionary force for change.

This drive, in the most successful players of life's games, has to be stronger than its countervailing evolutionary force: fear. The only manner in which early man and woman could overcome fear in order to confront risk was a conviction of safety, a deep-seated self-confidence—in a word, certainty. Having a sense of certainty about the uncertain might seem paradoxical. But the conviction of certainty had to emerge from a real physical and psychic basis for self-confidence—a visceral experience of faith, the belief in a guiding power or some such determining will, whether inside or outside of one's self, that decides whether the individual is favored by triumph or condemned by failure.

Take Spear Man. The gut feeling of the certainty of survival allowed early *Homo sapiens* to confront the unknown. Success prompted greater confidence, which motivated further risk-taking, which contained a high selective value for the species. Hunting, for example, was a chance-filled activity that Spear Man risked out of faith in his own predatory superiority.

(In this model, modern gambling is a manifestation of a residual hunting instinct, repressed by urban society. And megarollers are the kind of predators who, had they been around, might have gone after the large carnivorous dinosaurs—T. Rex being the house, of course.)

Plowshare Man, in all likelihood, sensed that no degree of experience or self-confidence (internal) and no guiding star or guardian angel (external) could sway the outcome of a chance event, such as a good rain when the corn needed watering. An outcome based on chance is one that has no apparent cause or design—what farmers call nature and gamblers call luck. To them, nature or luck is the ultimate authority, the deciding will. Luck, good or bad, can disrupt the influence of all other powers over an event.

All actions are a gamble, a questioning of chance, and all results are an indication of how an individual, or even a society, fares in chance's eyes. That's why the deities of the earliest religions were nothing more than manifestations of chance. It can be argued that all religion, and in fact all philosophy and science, evolved out of gambling.

Think about it. The cornerstone of religion, philosophy, and science is certainty: the explaining, if not the conquering, of the terrible unknown. Certainty is the profound striving to remove chance from the game of life. After all, chance is too unpredictable, unfathomable, unreliable. Chance will never make the trains run on time or cook the *E. coli* out of chopped meat. Chance is too hard to bear, too tough to do business with. That's why we have religion and science.

(In this model, modern gambling is a means by which we strip away all our religious and scientific certainty in order to summon up the deep human instinct to appeal to chance as the deciding will.)

So certainty (or religion and science) gives chance (gambling) some competition—which is why most orthodox belief systems consider gambling immoral and why most sciences consider it a waste of time and money. However, because gambling predates religion, the most ambitious religions incorporated it into their mythos. Egyptian, Indian, Chinese, Greek, and Roman gods and goddesses all gambled. The Roman Catholic Church, in particular, understood that religious practices, both outward in form and inward in attitude, are a kind of deistic emulation of gambling practices.

Churches and casinos, for example, have so much in common it's spooky. Both are far removed from ordinary activity. Both involve highly arcane social rituals, vernacular styles, parochial properties, and belief systems. Both invite prayer and supplication to symbols and embodiments of a higher power, whether it be God or chance, the Virgin Mary or Lady Luck. Both are lavishly appointed and offer rewards, in the form of miracles and jackpots, to those of strong and unquestioning faith.

(In this model, it's no accident that the Church regularly employs raffles, bingo, lotteries, even casino nights as fundraisers.)

Gamblers Anonymous could be said to follow the lead of the Church, which believes its power is greater than gambling; GA also tries to instill the belief in a power higher than chance. The reverse, however, is also true: In this model, the prevalence of gambling is an indication—some say a symptom—of the decline in the power of religion.

The Reformation religions, on the other hand, never adopted gambling in an attempt to co-opt it. Rather, Righteous Man believed that gambling is a cardinal sin imprinted in players by Satan himself.

In roughly the same time frame and mind frame as the Reformation, the Industrial Revolution got going, and Lutherans and Protestants, in particular, reinforced it with the Puritan work ethic. Labor is productive. Poverty is righteous. Charity is pious. All upright, honest, impoverished factory workers go to Heaven as a reward for toil and virtue.

Gambling, Righteous Man argues, eradicates devotion to the Puritan ideal, the Christian God's capitalist order. It promotes idleness. It encourages avarice, degeneracy, profligacy. It furthers the faith in blind chance over the certainty in an omnipresent omniscient omnipotent God. Where the power of Christianity prevails, gambling is weak.

And vice versa. The power of gambling is continually expanding and contracting; it's one of the great heartbeats of civilization. Right now, gambling around the world is engorged with blood, at the possible peak of an expansion cycle in which the most expensive and exclusive resort destinations on Earth are being built by the greatest transfer of wealth over gaming tables ever witnessed in history. Righteous Man is in retreat. Casino Man is in ascendance.

But in the *final* analysis, it's all vanity and vexation of the spirit. Death, of course, has the last word. Death is the ultimate house advantage. It's always near in the short term where the luck factor holds more sway: Get terminally unlucky and you're busted out before your time. Over the long haul, the inexorable edge collects its inevitable toll, wearing you down day by day, cell by cell, breath by breath, heartbeat by heartbeat. And in the end, by the immutable law of the ultimate edge, death finally takes it all.

Life, as one gambler put it, is six to five against. If life were offered to you as a bet, you'd be a sucker to take it.

But you still have to. Because life boils down to an impulse to gamble against death. And while you're here, it's good to be in the action.

Index

About Huntington Press

Huntington Press is a specialty publisher of Las Vegas- and gambling-related books and periodicals. Contact:

Huntington Press
3687 South Procyon Avenue
Las Vegas, Nevada 89103
702-252-0655
www.huntingtonpress.com